D1450122

Tina Thoburn
Virginia Arnold
Rita Schlatterbeck
Ann Terry

Macmillan English

SERIES E ®

Macmillan Publishing Co., Inc.
New York

Collier Macmillan Publishers
London

ACKNOWLEDGMENTS

The publisher gratefully acknowledges permission to reprint the following copyrighted material:

"How to Care for Goldfish" excerpt from *A Zoo For You: Some Indoor Pets and How to Keep Them* by Winifred and Cecil Lubell. Copyright © 1970 by Winifred and Cecil Lubell. Reprinted by Permission of Parents Magazine Press.

"Night" from *The Apple Vendor's Fair* by Patricia Hubell. Copyright © 1963 by Patricia Hubell. Reprinted by permission of Atheneum Publishers.

"Silver" from *Collected Poems* by Walter de la Mare courtesy of The Literary Trustees of Walter de la Mare and The Society of Authors as their representative.

"Fog" from *Chicago Poems* by Carl Sandburg, copyright 1916 by Holt, Rinehart and Winston, Inc.; copyright © by Carl Sandburg. Reprinted by permission of Harcourt Brace Jovanovich, Inc.

"Destination Mars" from *Miss Pickerell Goes To Mars* by Ellen MacGregor. Copyright © 1951 by Ellen MacGregor. Used with permission of McGraw-Hill Book Company.

"Paul Bunyan and His Boyhood" from *Paul Bunyan Swings His Axe* by Dell J. McCormick. Copyright © 1936 by the Caxton Printers, Ltd., Caldwell, Idaho 83605. Reprinted by permission of the publisher.

"The Computer Game" by Steven Otfinoski copyright © 1982 by Macmillan Publishing Co., Inc.

"Dragons and Giants" and illustrations for "Dragons and Giants" from *Frog and Toad Together,* written and illustrated by Arnold Lobel. Copyright © 1971, 1972 by Arnold Lobel. By permission of Harper & Row, Publishers, Inc.

"School Meals Get Priority Over Junk" adapted with permission of The Associated Press.

"The Seven Sticks," "The Crow and the Pitcher," and "The Rooster and the Pearl," fables by Aesop.

Cover design: Nadja Furlan

Illustration Credits:
Frank Bozzo, Fuh-Lin-Hsin, Yvonne Fuka, Michael Garland, Jeremy Guitar, Meryl Henderson, Tom Herbert, Tom Ickert, Laurie Jordan, Tom Leonard, John McIntosh, Keith Neely, Hima Pamoedjo, Lynn Udhe, Yasemin Tomakan, Pat Traub, Jean Tuttle, Walter Velez

Photography Credits:
Clara Aich; Black Star, © Dennis Black, © Hiroyuki Matsumoto; Bruce Coleman, © Hans Reinhart, © Jane Burton; Leo de Wys, © Ernst Bordis; © Lawrence Frank; Focus on Sports, © Russell Kelly; International Stock Photo, © Mark Bolster; © Ken Lax; © Milton and Joan Mann; Monkmeyer Press Photo, © Paul Conklin, © Mimi Forsyth, © Freda Leinwand; © NASA; © Tom Pantages; Photo Researchers, Inc., © Bill Bachman, © Guy Gillette, © Roy W. Hankey, © Vance Henry, © Russ Kinne, © Tom McHugh, © Larry Mulvehill, © Charlie Ott, © Earl Roberge, © Leonard Lee Rue, © John Henry Sullivan, Jr., © Mary M. Thatcher; Shostal Associates, © D.C. Lowe; © Elliot Varner Smith; The Stockmarket, © Schneider Studio; © United Press International; © Wide World Photos; Woodfin Camp and Associates, © George Hall

Parts of this work were published in earlier editions of SERIES E: Macmillan English.

Macmillan Publishing Co., Inc.
866 Third Avenue, New York, New York 10022
Collier Macmillan Canada, Inc.

Printed in the United States of America
ISBN 0-02-247120-0
9 8 7 6 5 4 3 2 1

TABLE OF CONTENTS

Unit 1

Unit 2

Unit 3

Unit 4

Unit 5

Unit 6

Unit 7

Unit 8

NEIL ARMSTRONG ON THE MOON

Grammar and Related Language Skills

Sentences
Four Kinds of Sentences
Punctuation in Sentences
Subject Parts and Predicate Parts
Building Sentences

Practical Communication

STUDY AND REFERENCE SKILLS
Using the Parts of a Book

COMPOSITION
Writing a Direction Paragraph

Creative Expression

An Article

What would it be like to walk on the moon? Neil Armstrong walked on the moon in July, 1969. He told the world about the experience. How do you think astronauts prepare for flight? How might you react to the unusual sights and sounds of outer space? Astronauts must report their experiences clearly. What speaking and writing skills do astronauts need?

Learning About Sentences

You use groups of words to tell your thoughts or ideas many times every day. Some groups of words state a complete idea. Other groups of words may state part of an idea. But they do not give you a complete idea.

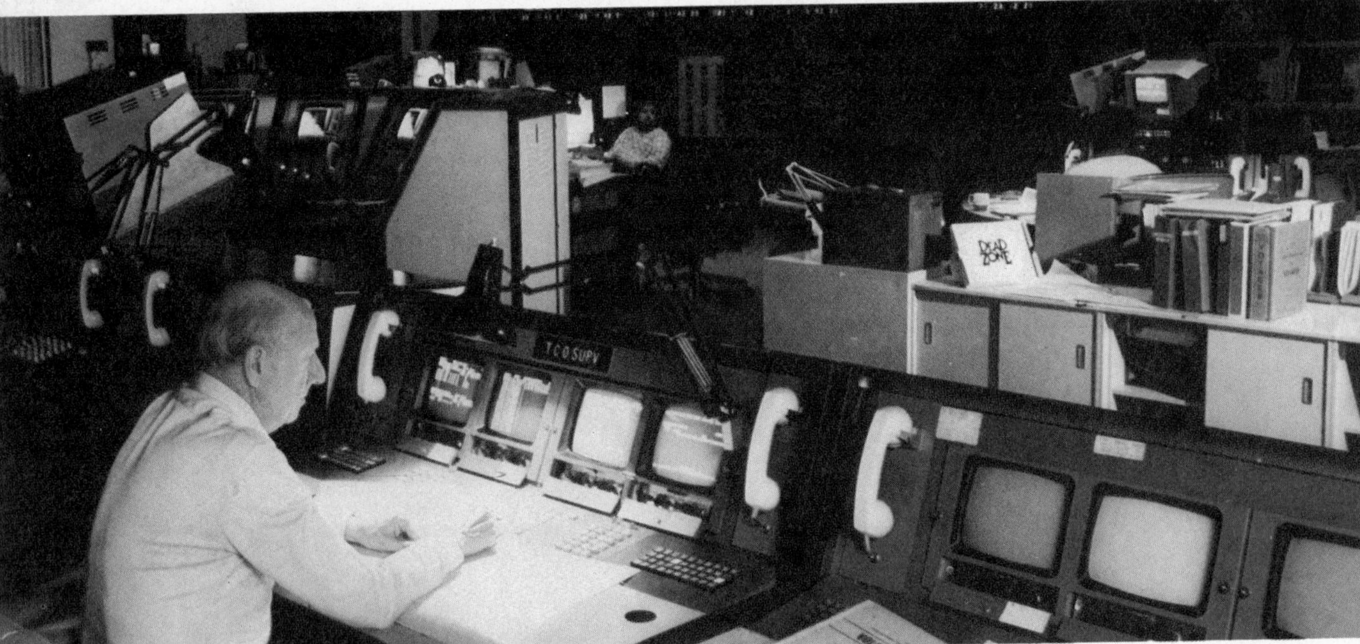

- Read these groups of words.

The scientists.	The scientists watch the screen.
A rocket.	A rocket leaves Earth.

The words at the left name a person or thing. But they do not say what action the person or thing does. The groups of words at the left are not complete ideas.

The groups of words at the right name a person or thing. These words also tell you what action the person or thing does. The groups of words at the right are sentences.

> A **sentence** is a group of words that state a complete idea.

Talk About It

Read each group of words. The words at the left name a person or thing. The words at the right name what action a person or thing does. Match the groups of words to make sentences.

1. Many young people	floats in space.
2. A trip to the moon	send pictures back to Earth.
3. A space explorer	carries people.
4. A large rocket	takes two or three days.
5. Television cameras	wonder about space travel.

Skills Practice

Read each group of words. Write **sentence** if the group of words is a sentence. Write **not a sentence** if the group of words is not a sentence.

1. The space station spins toward Mars.
2. Some space engineers.
3. The Chinese invented the first rockets.
4. The nose of a moon rocket.
5. A tower near the rocket.
6. Space suits with helmets.
7. Astronauts went to the spaceship in an elevator.
8. A little monkey traveled safely in space.
9. Packs of space food.
10. Explorers collect moon rocks.

Sample Answer 1. sentence

Four Kinds of Sentences

The scientist will talk to the animal.
Does the animal speak English?
What a strange animal that is!
Call the scientist.

You use many kinds of sentences to share your ideas with others. You use sentences to tell something. You also use sentences to ask a question.

> A **declarative sentence** is a sentence that makes a statement or tells something.
> An **interrogative sentence** is a sentence that asks something.

Sometimes you use sentences to show excitement or strong feeling. Other times you use sentences to tell someone to do something.

> An **exclamatory sentence** is a sentence that shows strong feelings.
> An **imperative sentence** is a sentence that tells or asks someone to do something.

- Look at the picture at the top of the page. Find a declarative sentence. Find an interrogative sentence. Find an exclamatory sentence. Find an imperative sentence.

- Read the sentences below. Find two exclamatory sentences. Find two imperative sentences.

Watch the animal.	Talk to the animal.
How slowly the animal moves!	How strangely the animal talks!

Talk About It

Read each sentence. Is it a declarative sentence, an interrogative sentence, an exclamatory sentence, or an imperative sentence?

1. Can explorers play games in a spaceship?
2. Baseballs float away in space.
3. What a hard time a ball catcher would have!
4. Word puzzles are the best games for a spaceship.
5. Invent a new word game for space.

Skills Practice

Read each sentence. Decide which kind of sentence each one is. Write **declarative, interrogative, exclamatory,** or **imperative.**

1. What do explorers do in a space school?
2. Explorers study space science and weather.
3. Visit a space center.
4. Watch the explorers train for space.
5. How well explorers fly airplanes and helicopters!
6. Can explorers go under the water in space suits?
7. Sometimes explorers train in jungles or deserts.
8. How hard the explorers work!
9. Explorers train for a long time before a space journey.
10. What wonderful things the explorers discover!

Sample Answer 1. interrogative

Capitalizing and Punctuating Sentences

When you talk, you use signals to make your meaning clear. You open your eyes wide to show surprise. You may wink your eye to show that you understand a joke. How do you change your voice to show surprise? How does your voice change when you ask a question?

When you write sentences, you also use signals to make your meaning clear. You use signals to show where sentences begin. You use signals to show where sentences end.

- Look at the sentences below. With what kind of letter does the first word in each sentence begin?

The Earth moves around the sun.
When did the sun first appear?
Look at the setting sun.
How red the setting sun looks!

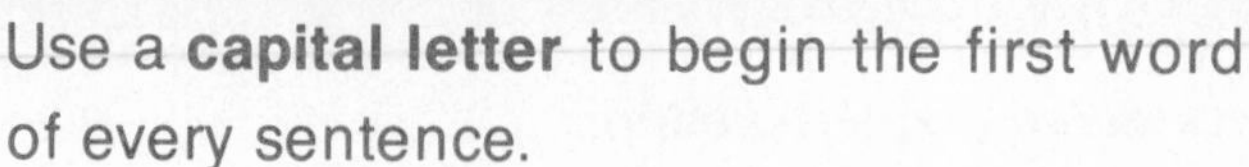

Use a **capital letter** to begin the first word of every sentence.

- Look at the sentences above again. What mark is used at the end of each sentence?

Use a **period** (.) at the end of a declarative or an imperative sentence.

Use a **question mark** (?) at the end of an interrogative sentence.

Use an **exclamation mark** (!) at the end of an exclamatory sentence.

Talk About It

Read each sentence. What signals are missing?

1. what a strange dream Anne had
2. when did the family move to Venus
3. the neighbors stayed on Earth
4. ask Anne about Venus

Skills Practice

Some signals are missing in each sentence. Write each sentence so that it begins and ends in the right way.

1. the land looked orange
2. did any animals live there
3. tell about the animals
4. a big green animal ran on many legs
5. the animal made funny noises
6. did Rex wear a special hat
7. the family lived in a space bubble
8. how does a space bubble look
9. ask Anne about the space bubble
10. what an exciting dream Anne dreamed

Writing Sentences

Imagine that your spaceship has stopped for repairs on another planet. When you get out of the spaceship, you meet ten talking robots.

1. Write a declarative sentence describing your meeting.
2. Write an interrogative sentence about your meeting.
3. Write an exclamatory sentence about your meeting.
4. Write an imperative sentence about your meeting.

Sample Answer 1. The land looked orange.

Skills Review

Read each group of words. Write **sentence** if the group of words is a sentence. Write **not a sentence** if the group of words is not a sentence.

1. A bright yellow light.
2. The Earth's bumpy surface.
3. The strange spaceship landed on Earth.
4. The noise of the motor suddenly stopped.
5. The spaceship door.
6. The strange visitors walked out of the spaceship.
7. The travelers looked at the new sights.
8. Some friendly Earth people.
9. The visitors brought strange food.
10. Earth people tasted the food.
11. Purple lettuce with blue spots.
12. People welcomed the travelers.
13. Many bright flags.
14. The visitors watched Earth people work.
15. The visitors took Earth rocks home.

Read each sentence. Decide which kind of sentence each one is. Write **declarative, interrogative, exclamatory**, or **imperative.**

16. How brightly that star shines!
17. Is that star really the planet Venus?
18. Venus is the brightest planet.
19. Rita brought the telescope outside.
20. Look at the star through the telescope.
21. Phil spotted a shooting star nearby.
22. How quickly the shooting star disappeared!
23. Did Lili see the falling star through the telescope?
24. Point out the Milky Way overhead.

25. Look at the full moon through the telescope.
26. How excited Phil felt!
27. Did Rita see the Big Dipper?
28. The Little Dipper is near the Big Dipper.
29. Can they see the sun at night?
30. The sun shines only during the day.

Some signals are missing in each sentence. Write each sentence so that it begins and ends in the right way.

31. people have no weight in a spaceship
32. space explorers can float around
33. how strange a floating explorer looks
34. must everything be fastened down in space
35. how hard the explorers work to keep the spaceship neat
36. can people walk up the walls of a spaceship
37. explorers can walk upside down on the ceiling
38. how funny upside down explorers must look
39. do explorers float around in their sleep
40. seat belts keep explorers in place

Before the printing press was invented, people did not have special rules for beginning and ending sentences in writing. This made some writing hard to read. Look at the group of words below. How many different sentences can you make? Do not change the order of the words.

Many goats ran happily they ran up the hill they ran

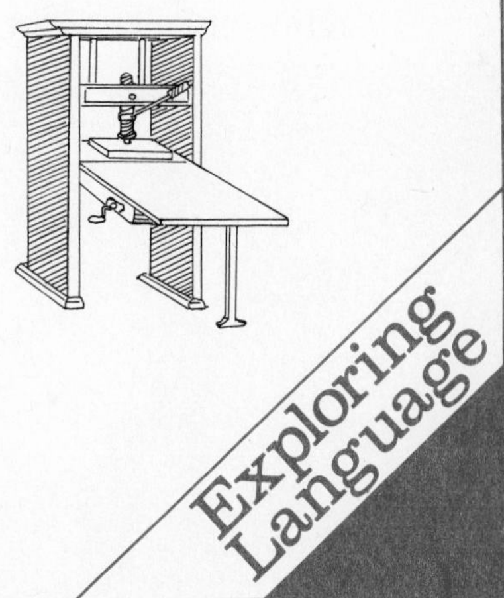

Subject and Predicate Parts

Did you know that a declarative sentence has two parts? One part names whom or what the sentence is about. The other part tells what action the person or thing in the first part does. You must use both parts to make a sentence.

> The **subject part** of a sentence names whom or what the sentence is about.

> The **predicate part** of a sentence tells what action the subject part does.

- Read each sentence.

The class | went to the museum.

A woman | showed a movie.

Bright stars | fell toward Earth.

The children | cheered.

Which is the subject part of each sentence? Which is the predicate part? The subject part of each sentence is in a blue box. The predicate part of each sentence is in a red box. In the first sentence, *The class* names whom the sentence is about. *Went to the museum* tells what action the class did.

Talk About It

Read each sentence. Is the part in the box the subject part or the predicate part? Explain your answer.

1. Scientists | plan trips.
2. Explorers | visited the moon.
3. The class | saw some films
4. Children | asked questions.

Skills Practice

Read each sentence part in the box. Write whether each one is a **subject part** or **predicate part.**

1. Spaceships | visit planets.
2. Cameras | film pictures.
3. Scientists | study films.
4. Planets | move slowly.

Write each sentence. Draw a line between the subject part and the predicate part.

5. Explorers landed on the moon.
6. Scientists found rocks.
7. The sun lights the moon.
8. One side receives no light.
9. People viewed the dark side.
10. The men returned to Earth.

Writing Sentences

Imagine that you just returned from a space trip. Write four sentences to tell about your trip. Use one of these subject parts in each sentence.

1. The surface of the moon
2. Strange animals
3. The planet Mars
4. Bright stars

Sample Answers 1. predicate part 5. Explorers|landed on the moon.

Building Sentences

A complete sentence must have a subject part and a predicate part. However some complete sentences give only a little information.

- Read these sentences.

The planet | appeared. Scientists | observed.

Both sentences are complete. They both have a subject part and a predicate part. However both sentences give only a limited amount of information. You can make a sentence give more information. You can add words to the subject part.

A new planet | appeared.

A red planet | appeared.

The words *new* and *red* give more information about *planet*.

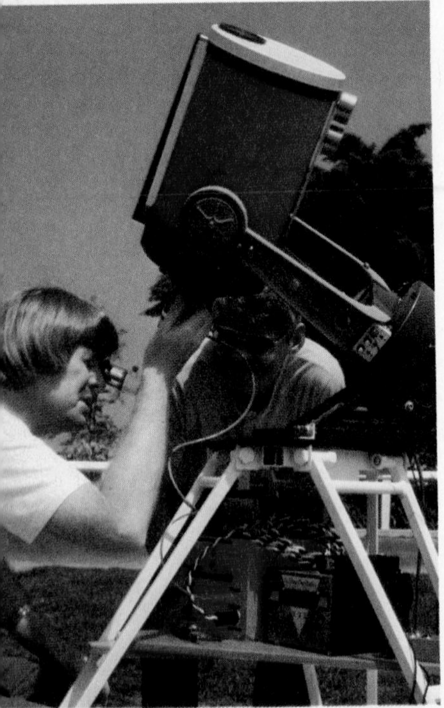

Sometimes you may want to add words to the predicate part to help a sentence give more information.

- Read these sentences. What is added to each predicate part? How does each new predicate part help the sentence give more information?

Scientists | observed the planet.

Scientists | observed with special telescopes.

Scientists | observed excitedly.

Talk About It

Read each sentence. Add words to the subject part to give more information.

1. Moons orbit.
2. Comets pass.
3. A scientist writes.
4. The sky sparkles.

Read each sentence. Add words to the predicate part to give more information.

5. The telescope moves.
6. A meteor whirls.
7. Stars flash.
8. Satellites travel.

Skills Practice

Add words to the subject part of each sentence. Then write the sentence.

1. Astronauts awake.
2. The ship waits.
3. Crews hurry.
4. The sun rises.
5. A breeze blows.
6. Engineers finish.
7. The spaceship opens.
8. The pilots arrive.

Add words to the predicate part of each sentence. Then write the sentence.

9. A worker signals.
10. Visitors leave.
11. A door closes.
12. Engines roar.
13. The crowd watches.
14. The rocket soars.
15. People cheer.
16. The mission begins.

Commas

When you speak, you often pause to separate one word from other words. In writing, commas take the place of pauses. Commas help you to make the meaning of your written sentence clear.

Some words interrupt the message of a sentence. Commas are used to set these words apart from the rest of the sentence. Some sentences may begin with *well, no,* or *yes*. Other sentences may begin or end with the name of a person who is spoken to directly.

> Use a **comma** (,) to set off words such as *yes, no,* and *well* when they begin a sentence.

Yes, the space shuttle completed its mission.

> Use a **comma** (,) to set off the name of a person who is spoken to directly in a sentence.

Did you watch the take-off, Todd?
Kim, here is the information you wanted.

Commas separate the name of the day from the date, and the date from the year.

> Use a **comma** (,) to separate the name of the day from the date, and the date from the year.

A satellite passed Saturn on Tuesday, August 25, 1981.

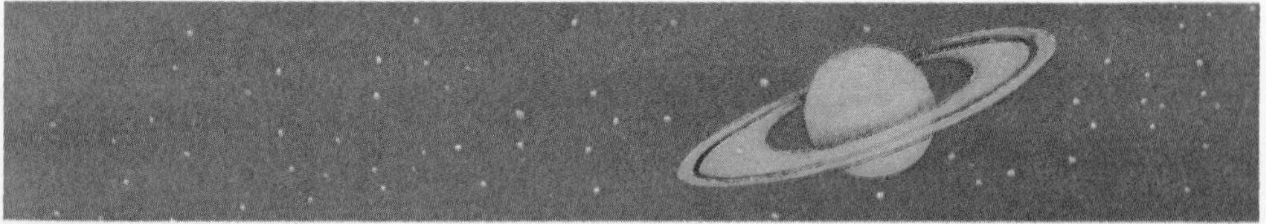

Talk About It

Read each sentence. Tell how you would use commas.

1. The space shuttle made its first trip on Sunday April 12 1981.
2. Why is the space shuttle important Meg?
3. Well we can use this spaceship again.
4. Yes it lands like an airplane.
5. Matt did you see the landing?

Skills Practice

Write each sentence. Use commas where they are necessary.

1. That first trip ended on Tuesday April 14 1981.
2. Did John Young command that mission Lori?
3. Yes he had a lot of experience in space.
4. The shuttle completed another trip on Saturday November 14 1981.
5. The third trip ended on Sunday July 4 1982.
6. Tim do you want to travel in space?
7. No I will stay on earth.
8. Well I want to live in space.
9. Do you really want to travel into space Tina?
10. Yes I will build a space station.

Writing Sentences

Imagine you are the captain of a space shuttle mission. Write three sentences using commas.

1. Write one sentence that names your co-pilot and asks him or her to check the radio.
2. Write one sentence that tells the day of the week, the month, day, and year you will return to earth.
3. Write one sentence that begins with *yes*.

Sample Answer 1. That first trip ended on April 14, 1981.

Skills Review

Read each sentence part in the box. Write whether each one is a subject part or predicate part.

1. The friends | started a model club.
2. The neighborhood | joined.
3. Aaron | makes airplanes.
4. Maria | makes spaceships.
5. Michelle | built a space station.
6. The parents | work in the space program.
7. Joy | studies space in school.
8. The Smith family | plans many models.
9. The teacher | explained one spaceship to me.
10. The class | went to the space museum.
11. An engineer | talked about a rocket.
12. Pedro | climbed into the rocket.

Write each sentence. Draw a line between the subject part and the predicate part.

13. The club went to a space fair this year.
14. Children brought models and space experiments.
15. Sandy made space explorer boots.
16. Tami built a small rocket.
17. Many parents came to the space show at the fair.
18. A scientist showed slides of moon rocks.
19. Judges gave prizes for the best models.
20. The people enjoyed the space fair very much.

Add words to the subject part of each sentence. Then write the sentence.

21. The explorer searches.
22. A camera films.
23. The rocks glow.
24. The robots stop.
25. The ship rises.
26. The trip begins.
27. The engineers watch.
28. The crew answers.

Add words to the predicate part of each sentence. Then write the sentence.

29. The ship travels.
30. The rocket crashes.
31. Each planet spins.
32. Space travelers eat.
33. The Milky Way shines.
34. Astronauts float.
35. Earth moves.
36. The stars twinkle.

Write each sentence. Use commas where they are necessary.

37. The Apollo II landed on the moon on Sunday July 20 1969.
38. It was exciting to see it Jack.
39. Tom are you interested in space travel.
40. Yes I want to become an astronaut.
41. Well it takes years of study and training.

Exploring Language

Try this activity. Start with one letter. Then make new words by adding one letter at a time. You can change the letters in any way to make the next word. Here is an example.

a **at** **tag** **gate** **great**

Now try this activity with the letter *o* or *i*.

Parts of a Book

Many books are divided into parts. You can use the parts to find out if a book has information you need for a report. You can also use the parts to find out if a book has the kind of stories you like to read.

The *title page* is the first important page in a book. It tells the title of the book. It also gives the name of the author and the name of the publisher.

Space Science

Allen Cohen, *Author*

Silver Publishing Co., Inc.
New York London

The *table of contents* comes after the title page. It lists the number and the name of each unit or chapter. It also tells on what page each unit or chapter begins. You can read the table of contents to see what a book is about.

Contents	**Page**
1 *The Night Sky*	*1*
2 *Planets*	*17*
3 *Moons*	*32*
4 *The Milky Way*	*40*
5 *The Sun*	*49*
6 *New Stars*	*56*
7 *Shooting Stars*	*64*
Index	*72*

The *body* of a book is the main part of a book. It contains all the units or chapters that are listed in the table of contents

The *index* is at the back of a book. It lists the things a book tells about. It is in alphabetical order. It also shows on what page you can find each thing that is listed.

Index

S
Saturn, 28
sky map, 2–3
space, 10–15
starlight, 41
sunlight, 50

T
telescope
how to make, 4
how to use, 5–7

U

V

Some books have special parts before the index. A special part in this book is called the Handbook. The *handbook* lists important rules from the body of the book. You will find a handbook on page 312. It lists important rules about your language.

Talk About It

Use this book to answer the questions that follow.

1. What is the title of the book?
2. Who is the publisher?
3. On what page does the body of the book begin?
4. How many units are in this book?
5. What is listed first in the handbook?

Skills Practice

Use the table of contents on page 18 to answer each question. Write the answer.

1. What is the title of this book?
2. Who is the author?
3. What is the name of Chapter 2?
4. On what page does Chapter 4 begin?
5. Is there a chapter about rockets?

Use the index on page 18 to answer each question. Write your answer.

6. What pages tell about a sky map?
7. What page tells how to make a telescope?
8. What pages tell about space?

Sample Answer 1. Space Science is the title of this book.

Learning About Paragraphs

Sometimes you can tell or explain an idea in just one sentence. At other times you need to use several sentences to explain the idea.

> A **paragraph** is a group of sentences that tell one main idea.

A paragraph makes good sense when all the sentences work together. The first sentence usually states the most important idea of the paragraph. It is called the *main idea sentence*. The other sentences tell more about the main idea. They are called *detail sentences*.

> A **main idea sentence** states the most important idea of the paragraph.

> **Detail sentences** tell more about the main idea.

- Read this paragraph. What is the main idea sentence? What are the detail sentences?

Tina helped her mother paint the fence. First they removed the loose paint. Next they painted the fence. Third they put up a wet paint sign. Last they cleaned their paint brushes.

The first sentence is the main idea sentence. It tells you Tina helped her mother paint a fence. All the other sentences are detail sentences. They tell how the fence was painted. The words *first, next, third,* and *last* show what order the details follow.

Talk About It

Read the main idea sentence. Then read the detail sentences. Choose the detail sentences that belong with the main idea sentence.

Main idea: A date seed can make a pretty plant.

1. First plant the seed in a pot.
2. Potato plants do not start in pots.
3. Next keep the pot in a warm and dark place.
4. Potato plants start in the dark, too.
5. Third wait until a leaf appears.
6. Last put the plant in the light.

Skills Practice

Read the main idea sentence. Then read the detail sentences. Write the detail sentences that belong with the main idea sentence.

Main idea: Pete fried an egg for breakfast.

1. First he melted some butter in a frying pan.
2. Frying pans are also called *spiders*.
3. Next he cracked open the egg.
4. Third he put the egg in the pan.
5. His dog watched hungrily.
6. Finally he cooked the egg.

Direction Paragraphs

Thinking About Paragraphs

Imagine you bought a new game, but the rules were missing. You could not play without the directions. You need directions to know what to do.

Giving directions is very important. Sometimes you can give directions by writing them in a paragraph. Your paragraph must be clearly written so people will understand what to do. The sentences should be in an order that makes sense.

Follow these rules to write a paragraph that gives directions.

1. Begin with a main idea sentence. This sentence tells what the directions are for.
2. Next add detail sentences to explain how to do or make something. Each detail sentence gives one step of the directions. The sentences must be in order. They must tell what to do. You can use words like *first, second, third, next, then,* and *finally*.

● Read this paragraph. Find the main idea sentence and the detail sentences.

> Making a peanut butter and jelly sandwich is easy. First you take two pieces of bread. Next you spread one piece with peanut butter. Then you spread the other piece with jelly. Finally you put the pieces together with the peanut butter and the jelly sides facing each other. You have made a sandwich.

The first sentence in the paragraph gives the main idea. The paragraph tells how to make a peanut butter and jelly sandwich. The detail sentences give the steps in order. The words *first, next, then,* and *finally* tell the order of the steps.

The first word of the paragraph is moved in from the left margin. It is *indented*. This shows that a new paragraph is beginning.

Talking About Paragraphs

Read these sentences. One is a main idea sentence. Three are detail sentences. They are not in order. Put the sentences in an order that makes sense.

1. Second you tie the string to each cup.
2. Finally you talk and listen through the cup.
3. First you take two paper cups and some string.
4. Third you and a friend each hold a cup.
5. You can build your own telephone.

Writing a Paragraph

Read these sentences. First choose the main idea sentence. Then put the detail sentences in order. Write the paragraph. Remember to indent the first word.

1. First you take some sheets of paper.
2. Finally you tie a knot in each string.
3. Making a notebook is fun.
4. Then you put a piece of string through each hole.
5. Next you punch three holes through the paper.

A Class Paragraph

Thinking About Paragraphs

Your class is going to write a paragraph together that gives directions. The pictures will help you. They show how to build a sand castle. The pictures are in the right order to make sense.

Writing a Paragraph

Your teacher will write your paragraph on the board.

1. Your paragraph will start with a main idea sentence. The sentence is *A sandcastle is fun to build.*
2. Think of a detail sentence that tells what to do in the first picture. Use the word *first* to start your sentence.
3. Think of detail sentences for the next three pictures. Use words like *next, then,* and *last.*
4. Copy the paragraph on your paper. Remember to indent the first word.
5. Read the paragraph again. Could you build a sandcastle using the directions?

Practicing a Paragraph

Thinking About Your Paragraph

Now you are going to write your own paragraph that gives directions. The pictures will help you. They show how to fly a kite.

The Word Bank will also help you. It shows how to spell some of the words you may want to use.

Writing Your Paragraph

1. Your paragraph should start with a main idea sentence. Use this sentence: *Flying a kite is easy.* Write the sentence on your paper. Remember to indent the first word.
2. Look at the first picture. Write a detail sentence that tells what to do in the picture.
3. Write detail sentences for each of the other two pictures.
4. Save your paragraph.

Word Bank

first
string
next
then
sail
windy
soar
fly
last
finally

How to Edit Your Work

After you write a paragraph, you should edit it. *Edit* means "to read carefully and correct any mistakes." Good writers edit all of their writing. You should always edit what you write. Check for these things:

First make sure your paragraph says what you want it to say.

1. Are the detail sentences in an order that makes sense?
2. Did you use words like *first, next,* and *last*?
3. Does each sentence state a complete idea?

Next be sure other people can read and understand your paragraph.

4. Did you indent the first word of the paragraph?
5. Does each sentence start with a capital letter and end with the correct punctuation?
6. Did you spell all words correctly? Remember to use the Word Bank.

Read Bill's paragraph. What mistakes did Bill make? How did he correct them?

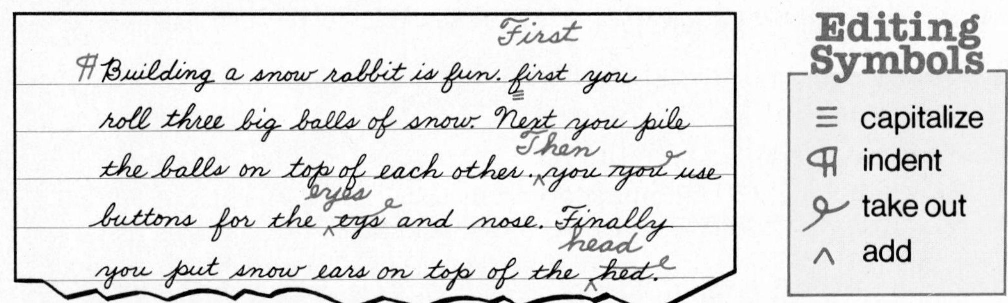

Edit Your Paragraph

Edit your paragraph about flying a kite. Use the six check questions and the editing symbols above to correct your mistakes. If you need to, write your paragraph again.

INDEPENDENT WRITING

A Direction Paragraph for a News Report

Prewriting You have learned that the order of sentences in direction paragraphs is very important. Sentences must be in an order that explains how to do or make something. Reporters for newspapers must also report the news in the exact order it happened. Imagine you are a reporter for the school newspaper. You have been asked to report on a trip you took to watch a craftsperson make something. Think about these questions and jot down notes. Whom did you visit? What did the craftsperson do first? What did he or she do next? What happened last?

Writing Write a paragraph that tells about your trip. Start your paragraph with a main idea sentence. Then write detail sentences that tell what happened in the exact order.

Editing Use the check questions and the editing symbols on page 26 to edit your paragraph.

Careers

Would you like to explore the bottom of an ocean? You may want to become an *oceanographer.* Oceanographers study many things about the oceans. They are interested in plants and animals that live in oceans. They study the rocks on the bottom of the ocean. They may even explore the earth below the bottom of the ocean. Oceanographers read all they can about oceans. They write about what they learn so all people will know more about oceans.

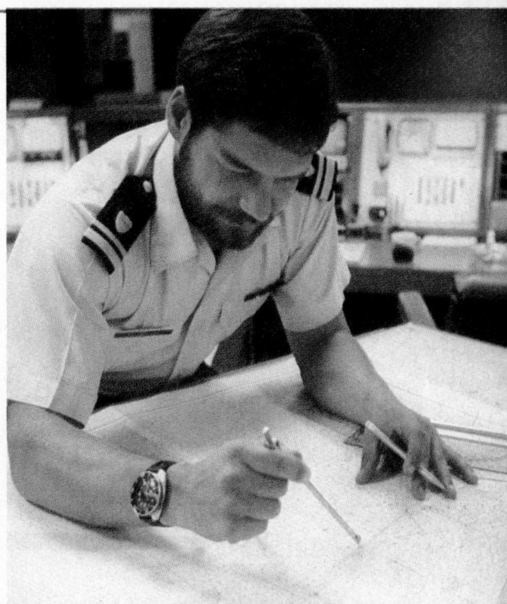

Unit Review

Read each group of words. Write **sentence** if the group of words is a sentence. Write **not a sentence** if the group of words is not a sentence. *pages 2–3*

1. Men reached the moon.
2. A large rocket.
3. Traveled through space.
4. Astronauts filmed the moon.
5. Gathered samples.
6. The men returned to Earth.

Read each sentence. Decide which kind of sentence each one is. Write **declarative, interrogative, exclamatory,** or **imperative.** *pages 4–5*

7. Collect plants and rocks.
8. How green that rock looks!
9. That rock comes from Mars.
10. Do plants grow there?
11. Does water float in space?
12. What odd plants grow here!

Some signals are missing in each sentence. Write each sentence so that it begins and ends in the right way. *pages 6–7*

13. everything weighs less on the moon
14. explorers lift big moon rocks
15. does the wind blow on the moon
16. how brightly the moon shines tonight
17. does the moon move around Earth
18. the moon changes the water level at the beach

Read each sentence part in the box. Write whether each one is a **subject part** or **predicate part.** *pages 10–11*

19. The planets [travel around the sun.]
20. [A scientist] discovered Pluto in 1930.
21. [People] look at Mars through a telescope.
22. Two moons [travel around Mars.]

23. People see thin rings around Saturn.
24. Hills cover the moon.
25. Neil Armstrong walked on the moon.
26. Water covers most of the Earth.

Write each sentence. Use commas where they are necessary. *pages 14–15*

27. The first manned flight into space was on Wednesday April 12 1961.
28. Jody who was the first American to fly in space?
29. Well I think it was Alan B. Shepard.
30. Yes you are correct.
31. John Glenn orbited the Earth on Tuesday February 20 1962.
32. I would like to travel in space one day Greg.

Read these detail sentences. They are not in the right order. Write them in an order that makes sense. *pages 22–27*

33. **a.** Next you put it in an envelope.
    b. Finally you drop the envelope in the mailbox.
    c. Then you seal the envelope and put on a stamp.
    d. First you write the letter.

Read these sentences. First choose the main idea sentence. Then put the detail sentences in an order that makes sense. Write the paragraph.

34. **a.** Second you bring the book to the librarian's desk.
    b. It is easy to get a book from the library.
    c. Last the librarian hands you your book and card.
    d. Then you give the librarian your card.
    e. First you find the book you want to read.

An Article

An *article* is writing that explains something to the reader. Articles are written for many reasons. Sometimes an article gives directions. The directions must be clear. They must also be in the right order.

This article tells how to care for goldfish. Some of the directions are numbered. Read the article carefully. Think about the important directions that the author gives.

These *Words To Think About* will help you understand the article.

Words To Think About

oxygen, a gas needed for breathing

algae, water plants

aquarium, a fish tank

How to Care for Goldfish

How a Fish Gets Air

All creatures need air in order to live. That is, they need the oxygen in the air. People need it too. We get it by breathing air into our lungs. But a fish can't breathe air. It has to take oxygen from the water.

All water has some oxygen, and a fish can take the oxygen out of the water with its gills. The gills are underneath the flaps which every fish has on the sides of its head.

When you see a goldfish gulping water with its big mouth, it's not drinking. It's breathing. The water passes over its gills and out through the flaps, leaving the oxygen behind.

That's why you must make sure that the water in your aquarium has enough oxygen. There are four ways to do this:

1. ***By having a big tank.*** The surface of the water gets oxygen from the air. The bigger the surface, the more oxygen it gets.

2. ***By having green water plants in the tank.*** As the plants grow, they give off oxygen. For this you need sand on the bottom to hold the plants.

3. ***By changing the water twice a week.*** The new water will have more oxygen. You don't need to do this if you have plants. If you *do* change the water, use a rubber tube (a siphon) so as not to disturb the fish.

4. ***By using an electric bubbler.*** It pumps air into the water. You don't need this either if the tank is big enough and has growing plants.

How Big a Tank?

You need one gallon of water for each fish one-inch long, not counting tails. So, a two-inch fish needs two gallons of water.

If you have a ten-gallon tank like ours, you can keep four goldfish, each two inches long. Always leave extra room. The fish will grow and the tank is never filled up to the top.

A round glass bowl will also do. Fill it only to the widest part. Then it has a bigger water surface to take in more oxygen.

Keep It Clean

It's important to keep your aquarium clean. Take out the fish waste and old food before they spoil the water. You can do this easily with a glass tube sold in pet stores.

If the walls of your tank become cloudy, that's because tiny green plants called *algae* are growing there. This happens if the tank gets too much sun or electric light. You can scrape off the algae.

It's good to keep two or three snails in the tank. They eat some of the algae and some of the leftover food. And they're interesting to watch.

A goldfish can become sick and die from too much food. A pinch of food each day is quite enough for one fish. Use special goldfish food.

Winifred and Cecil Lubell

Creative Activities

1. **Creative Writing** Imagine you are going on vacation. Think of something your friend will take care of for you. It might be your pet animal or your room. Write a paragraph with five directions for your friend. Make the directions clear. Write them in the right order.

2. Show the class how something is done. You might show how to shine your shoes or how to make book covers, for example. Explain the directions in the correct order.

3. Pet goldfish live in a bowl or tank. Think about other homes that pets have. For example, birds stay in cages. Dogs have doghouses. Find magazine pictures of animals in their homes. Bring them to class.

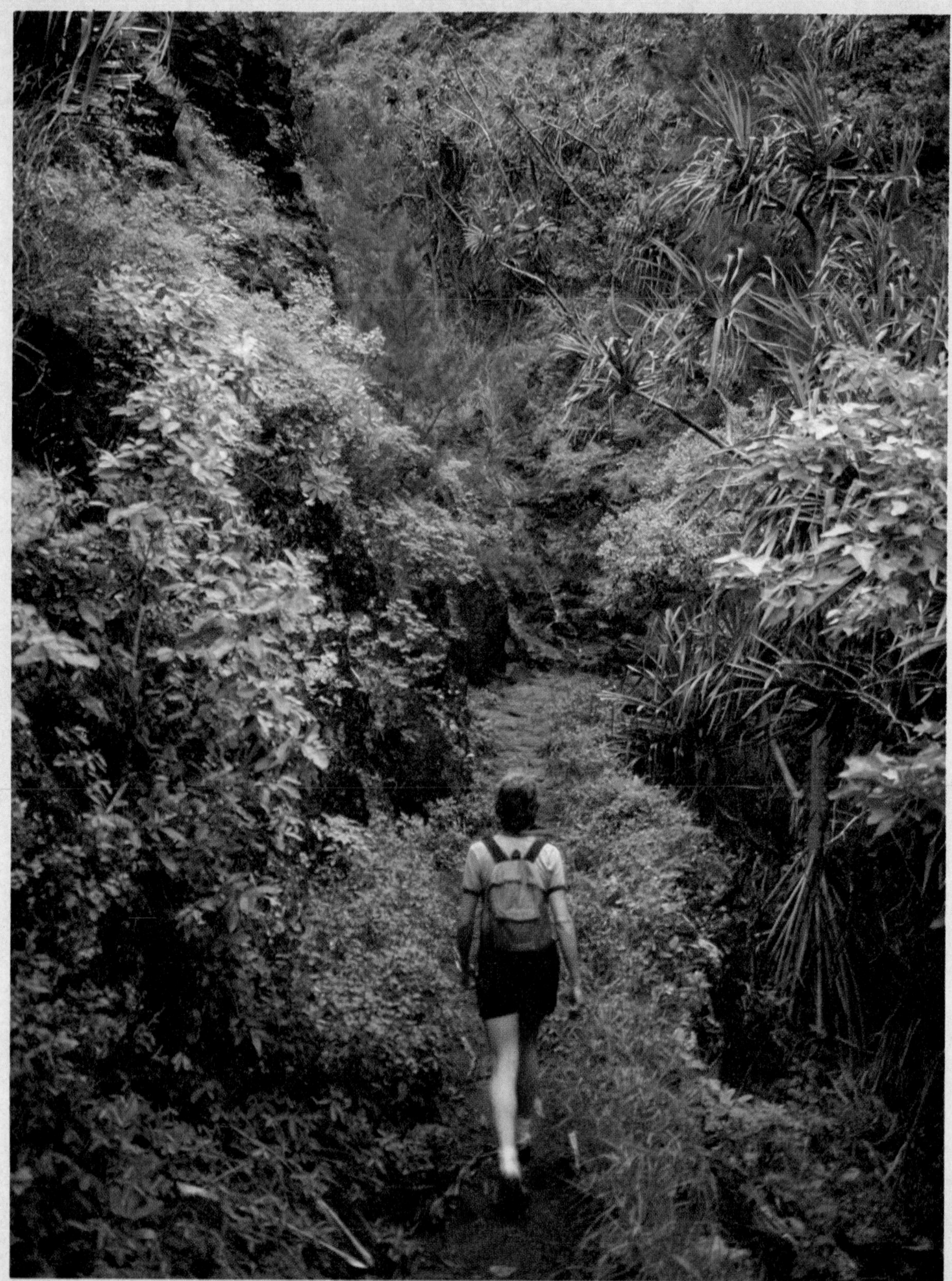

HIKER IN KAUII, HAWAII

Grammar and Related Language Skills

Nouns
Singular and Plural Nouns
Common and Proper Nouns
Possessive Nouns

Practical Communication

STUDY AND REFERENCE SKILLS
Using the Dictionary
COMPOSITION
Writing a Description Paragraph

Creative Expression

Poetry

Have you ever been on a hike? People who enjoy observing animal and plant life on long walks are sometimes called naturalists. Many naturalists keep a special journal to describe each hike. Where would you like to hike? What kinds of plants and animals would you find? Would any writing skills help you keep a hiking journal?

Learning About Nouns

When you look around you, you see many different things. You can name all the things you see. You can name people like *teacher* and *student*. You can name things like *book* and *desk*. And you can name places like *school* and *classroom*. A word that names a person, place, or thing is called a *noun*.

- Read each sentence below.

Snow fell last night.
The girl brings out a sled.
The child races to the hill.
A boy slides down the hill.

Find each noun. In these sentences *snow, night, girl, sled, child, hill,* and *boy* are all nouns.

A **noun** is a word that names a person, place, or a thing.

● Read each sentence below.

The girl looks at a snowball.
The child hides in the yard.
A face pops up above the wall.
A boy leaps out.

Find each noun. Tell whether each noun names a person, place, or thing.

Snowball, face, and *wall* are each nouns which name a thing. *Girl, child,* and *boy* are each nouns which name a person. *Yard* is a noun which names a place.

Talk About It

Read each sentence. Find each noun. Tell if each noun names a person, a place, or a thing.

1. A girl makes a house of snow.
2. A friend builds a wall.
3. A worker piles up snow.
4. A child makes a good door.
5. A boy builds a chimney.
6. A wind blows across the pond.
7. The girl finishes.
8. The friends leave.

Skills Practice

Read each sentence. Write the sentences. Then underline each noun.

1. The children play at the pond.
2. The neighbor puts on skates.
3. The pond shines like glass.
4. A girl arrives.
5. A man watches the dogs play.
6. One dog barks at the ice.
7. A dog rolls in the snow.
8. A child yells loudly.
9. A boy races with a friend.
10. The winner raises an arm.
11. An old man glides on the pond.
12. A girl catches up.
13. A fire crackles on the bank.
14. The sun shines on the skates.
15. Two boys build a snowman.
16. A girl finds her gloves.

Sample Answer 1. The <u>children</u> play at the <u>pond</u>.

Singular and Plural Nouns

Look around your classroom. How many other students do you see? How many desks or tables do you see? How many teachers do you see? Sometimes you use a noun to name only one person, one place, or one thing. At other times you may use a noun to name more than one person, place, or thing.

- Look at each underlined noun.

The man puts up the tent. A neighbor walks in the field.
The boys fish in the stream. Friends visit often.

Does the noun name one person, place, or thing? Or does it name more than one? *Man, tent, stream, neighbor,* and *field* are singular nouns. Each singular noun names *one* person, place, or thing. *Boys* and *friends* are plural nouns. Each plural noun names *more than one* person, place, or thing. You can make many nouns plural by adding *s* to the end of the singular noun.

A **singular noun** is a noun that names one person, place, or thing.

A **plural noun** is a noun that names more than one person, place, or thing.

Talk About It

Read each sentence. Find each noun. Tell if each noun is singular or if it is plural. Explain your answer.

1. Bears walk by the camp.
2. Many animals live here.
3. Birds call from trees.
4. A frog croaks.
5. Owls hoot.
6. The moon rises.
7. A boy tells scary stories.
8. Animals make strange noises.

Skills Practice

Write the plural form of each singular noun.

1. adventure
2. dime
3. needle
4. twig
5. apron
6. flag
7. hammer
8. tent
9. summer

Read each sentence. Write each noun. Write **singular** beside each singular noun. Write **plural** beside each plural noun.

10. Friends climb the mountain.
11. The girl steps over the rocks.
12. A bird sings.
13. Bears make a home in the cave.
14. A girl finds a stone.
15. The boys look for stones, too.
16. A squirrel runs up a tree.
17. The girls return.

Writing Sentences

Think about a time you walked or hiked someplace.

1. Write two sentences about what you saw on the way. Use plural nouns.
2. Write two sentences about where you walked. Use singular nouns.

Sample Answers **1.** adventures **10.** Friends, plural; mountain, singular

Spelling Plural Nouns

You cannot always make nouns plural by adding *-s*. It would be hard to say words like *lunch, box,* and *bus* with only an *s* at the end. You add *-es* to words like these.

- Look at the singular and plural forms of these nouns.

SINGULAR	PLURAL	SINGULAR	PLURAL
business →	businesses	sash →	sashes
bench →	benches	dish →	dishes
box →	boxes	witch →	witches

In each case *-es* was added to form the plural.

If a singular noun ends with **s, ss, x, ch, z,** or **sh,** add **-es** to form the plural.

Other nouns form the plural in still a different way. You have to learn the plural of these nouns.

- Learn the singular and plural forms of these nouns.

SINGULAR	PLURAL
child →	children
man →	men
woman →	women
foot →	feet
goose →	geese
tooth →	teeth
mouse →	mice

Talk About It

Read each sentence. At the end of each sentence is a singular noun. Say the plural form of the noun.

1. Two ____ at the art center begin. (class)
2. A boy finishes a picture of four ____. (mouse)
3. A girl makes two strange ____. (goose)
4. The girls make six little ____. (fox)
5. The friends work on two ____. (circus)

Skills Practice

Write the plural form of these nouns.

1. foot	4. glass	7. guess	10. mouse
2. dress	5. goose	8. tooth	11. ditch
3. wish	6. box	9. crash	12. man

Read each sentence. At the end of each sentence is a singular noun. Write each sentence with the plural form of the noun.

13. Two ____ bring friends to a picnic. (bus)
14. Many ____ fly kites. (child)
15. Some ____ catch a kite. (branch)
16. The three ____ rescue it. (woman)

Writing Sentences

Think about a day when you had fun with some friends.

1. Write two sentences about what you did with your friends. Use plural nouns.
2. Write two sentences about the best part of the day with your friends. Use singular nouns.

Sample Answers 1. feet 13. Two buses bring friends to a picnic.

More About Plural Nouns

Some nouns, like city and baby, end with a consonant and then *y*. You cannot simply add *-s* or *-es* to form the plural. You form the plural in a different way.

- Look at the singular and plural forms of these nouns.

SINGULAR	PLURAL	SINGULAR	PLURAL
library →	libraries	history →	histories
spy →	spies	story →	stories

The *y* was changed to *i* and *-es* was added to form the plural.

If a singular noun ends with a consonant and **y**, change the **y** to **i** and add **-es** to form the plural.

Talk About It

Say the plural form of each singular noun. Spell the plural form.

1. kitty
2. mystery
3. penny
4. puppy

Skills Practice

Write the plural form of each singular noun.

1. pony
2. party
3. baby
4. grocery
5. dairy
6. country
7. berry
8. sky
9. city
10. cherry
11. fly
12. laundry

Sample Answer 1. ponies

Compound Nouns

There are ways to form new nouns from words you already know. One way is to join two words to make a new noun. You can usually guess what the new noun means by looking at the two smaller words.

- Look at these words.

airplane skateboard

What two words have been joined to form each noun? *Skateboard* is formed from the words *skate* and *board*. A skateboard is a board you skate on. *Airplane* is formed from the words *air* and *plane*. An airplane is something you travel in through the air. Each new word is called a *compound noun*.

A **compound noun** is a noun that is formed from two smaller words.

Talk About It

Tell what two words have been joined to form each compound noun. Tell what each compound noun means. Look at the two smaller words for help.

1. snowball **3.** rainbow **5.** afternoon
2. birthday **4.** footprint **6.** windmill

Skills Practice

Write the meaning of each compound word.

1. barefoot **3.** wildcat **5.** snowstorm
2. raindrop **4.** blackbird **6.** Thanksgiving

Sample Answer 1. a foot that is bare

Skills Review

Read each sentence. Write each noun.

1. The sun shines.
2. The girl rushes to the park.
3. The boy goes too.
4. The friends play baseball.
5. A girl pitches.
6. A boy bats first.
7. The ball flies.
8. A player catches the ball.
9. Many batters strike out.
10. A boy runs to the base.
11. Some girls hit the ball.
12. The catcher gets a bat.
13. Our team bats now.
14. The player swings hard.
15. The bat hits the ball.
16. A player tags the base.
17. The girls enjoy the game.
18. The game ends.
19. The friends played well.
20. The pitchers shake hands.
21. The catcher holds a glove.
22. The friends talk.

Write each noun. Write **singular** beside each singular noun. Write **plural** beside each plural noun.

23. Tall trees grow in the park.
24. Ducks swim in a pond.
25. White swans sit on the banks.
26. The man likes geese.
27. The friends walk to the pool.
28. The children swim often.
29. The girl swims fast.
30. The boy floats on a raft.
31. The teacher arrives.
32. Classes begin.
33. A girl learns quickly.
34. Babies swim in a small pool.
35. The parents swim, too.
36. The woman floats on her back.

Read each sentence. At the end of each sentence is a singular noun. Write the plural form of the noun.

37. Two ____ walk to the park. (child)
38. Many ____ give shade. (branch)
39. Three ____ walk to the water. (goose)
40. Some ____ bring fruit. (woman)
41. A lady carries ____. (peach)
42. A man eats some ____. (cherry)
43. Many ____ see our food. (fly)
44. The children move to the two ____. (bench)
45. The child finds some trash ____. (box)
46. The baby finds some ____. (penny)

Write the meaning of each compound word.

47. wildflower
48. doorbell
49. bathtub
50. popcorn
51. sailboat
52. homesick

Some nouns in English do not change their form. These nouns have the same form in the singular and in the plural. Look at the noun *deer* in these sentences.

One deer sees a lake.	All the deer see it, too.

Deer stays the same for the singular and for the plural. *Trout, sheep, scissors, pants, moose,* and *fish* are other examples of this kind of noun. Can you think of some more of this kind of noun?

Common and Proper Nouns

If someone gave you a pet, you would probably not call it dog, cat, or bird. These nouns just name the kind of pet it is. You might name it *Blue, Tweety,* or *Smokey.* Each of these would be the name of one special pet.

- Read each sentence. Notice the underlined nouns.

The horse stands still.	Buttercup stands still.
A boy fixes the saddle.	Gene fixes the saddle.
Some friends leave the ranch.	Some friends leave Spur Ranch.

Horse, boy, and *ranch* name any person, place, or thing. They are *common nouns. Buttercup, Gene,* and *Spur Ranch* name a special person, place, or thing. They are *proper nouns.*

A **common noun** is a noun that names any person, place, or thing.

A **proper noun** is a noun that names a special person, place, or thing.

- Look at each proper noun.

Powells Trail	Penn Station	Illinois Central Railroad
Arrowhead Lake	North Pole	Hawthorn Melody Farms

Some proper nouns have more than one word, like *Spur Ranch.* Each word of these proper nouns begins with a capital letter.

- Read each sentence.

Barnum and Bailey Circus is a big traveling circus.
Richard the Lionhearted was the name of a king.
Many people live in the United States of America.

Some proper nouns have small words that are not important like *and, of,* and *the.* These words do not begin with a capital letter.

Begin each important word in a proper noun with a **capital letter.**

Talk About It

Look at each common noun in the list below. Think of a proper noun for each common noun.

1. city	**4.** boy	**7.** adult
2. dog	**5.** day	**8.** river
3. girl	**6.** cat	**9.** company

Skills Practice

Think of a proper noun for each common noun. Write the proper noun.

1. month	**3.** country
2. state	**4.** holiday

Write each sentence. Use capital letters where they belong.

5. The pathfinder club sets out.
6. The children meet the guide.
7. Arthur rides a horse named jumper.
8. Simon rode to hurp creek.
9. Arthur passes snake lake.
10. Who climbed smokey mountain?

Sample Answers 1. June (answers vary)
5. The Pathfinder Club sets out.

Capitalizing Proper Nouns

Often when you talk or write to adults, you do not call them by their first names. You use special titles with their last names. These titles are *Mr., Dr., Mrs., Miss,* and *Ms.* Each title begins with a capital letter.

Mr. is short for *Mister,* and *Dr.* is short for *Doctor. Mr.* can be used for a married or an unmarried man. *Miss* is used for unmarried women. *Mrs.* is used for married women. *Ms.* can be used for a married or an unmarried woman.

If you use the title *instead of* the name, you spell it out. You only use the short form *with* the person's name.

- Read each sentence. Notice how the titles are used.

Dr. Ash works with the nurses.
Ms. Ponte helps the doctor.
Mr. Chen works in an office.
Mrs. Gibson sees Miss James.

Dr., Ms., Mr., Mrs., and *Miss* come before the last name. *Miss* has no period. *Doctor* is spelled out in the second sentence because it is used instead of Dr. Ash.

Begin a title with a **capital letter.**
End most titles with a period.

There are other shortened words you often use when writing addresses. *St.* and *Ave.* are two of these words. These words are a short way of writing *Street* and *Avenue.*

- Look at each address. Notice the capital letters and periods.

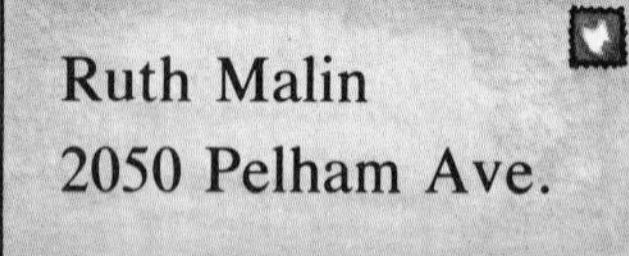

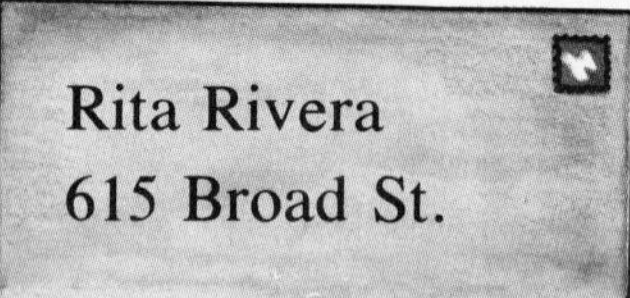

Begin each shortened word with a **capital letter.** End each shortened word with a period.

Talk About It

Read each proper noun. Tell what is missing from each.

1. dr Lee	**3.** Elm ave	**5.** miss Carr	**7.** mr Web
2. ms Roth	**4.** Wood st	**6.** mrs Olson	**8.** Oak st

Skills Practice

Write each sentence correctly.

1. ms Grew drove dr Taylor to Waltum Grocery.
2. The doctor bought mushrooms from miss Waltum.
3. mr and mrs Campos saw dr Taylor.

Write each address correctly.

4. dr Larry Taylor
   412 Rugby st

5. ms Elizabeth Harris
   223 Ogden ave

6. mrs Mollie Mankowski
   5748 Blackstone ave

7. mr and mrs Raymond Campos
   417 Arlen st

Writing Sentences

Imagine that your class took a special trip to a museum.

1. Write one sentence telling about the name of the museum. You may make up a name if you like.
2. Write one sentence telling the names of the adults in charge of the trip.

Sample Answers 1. Ms. Grew drove Dr. Taylor to Waltum Grocery.
4. Dr. Larry Taylor
412 Rugby St.

Possessive Nouns

Sometimes you may want to say that a person or thing has or *possesses* something. Then you use a special form of noun.

- Read each sentence.

Ben's tire rolls over a nail. Ben uses a friend's pump.

The nouns *Ben's* and *friend's* name who has something. Ben has a tire. The friend has a pump.

A noun that shows who has something is called a *possessive noun.* A special sign called an *apostrophe* (') shows that a noun is possessive.

> A **possessive noun** is a noun that names who or what has something.

Possessive nouns can be singular or plural. The apostrophe in a possessive noun can help you tell if it is a singular or plural possessive noun.

- Look at the possessive nouns in the box.

SINGULAR	PLURAL
boy's tires	boys' tires

Boy's tires means that one boy has all the tires. *Boy's* is a singular possessive noun. *Boys' tires* means that more than one boy has the tires. *Boys'* is a plural possessive noun.

> Add an **apostrophe** and **-s** (**'s**) to form the possessive of most singular nouns.
> Add an **apostrophe** (') to form the possessive of plural nouns that end with **s.**

Some nouns form their plural in unusual ways. The possessive form of these nouns is unusual, too.

- Look at the box. Notice how the plurals are formed.

SINGULAR	PLURAL	SINGULAR	PLURAL
child's	children's	man's	men's
goose's	geese's	woman's	women's

Talk About It

Read each sentence. At the end of each sentence is a noun. Tell if the noun is singular or plural. Tell the correct possessive form of each noun.

1. Don and Roger visit ____ museum. (Mae)
2. The friends walk to the ____ room. (children)
3. The ____ guide points to the sharks. (visitors)
4. The ____ special lights shine on the animals. (museum)

Skills Practice

Read each sentence. At the end of each sentence is a singular or plural noun. Write each sentence using the correct possessive form.

1. Don likes the room with ____ nests. (geese)
2. Roger and Don stare at the ____ supper. (snake)
3. Don looks at the ____ den. (lion)
4. A stuffed turkey is the ____ favorite bird. (friend)
5. Mae pays for the ____ lunches. (boys)
6. Later, they see ____ clothes from long ago. (women)
7. Roger enjoys ____ toys from the past. (children)
8. At last, Mae shows the ____ cave. (bears)

Sample Answer **1.** Don likes the room with geese's nests.

Making New Words

A compound noun is a word formed from two smaller words. You can also make new words by adding a letter or letters to the end of some words.

- Look at each word. What letters were added to form new words?

listen	listener	farm	farmer
direct	director	report	reporter

The letters *-er* and *-or* were added. They usually mean *a person who*. A *listener* is a person who listens. A *director* is a person who directs. A *farmer* is a person who farms. A *reporter* is a person who reports. The letters *-er* and *-or* are called *suffixes*.

A **suffix** is one or more letters added to the end of a word.

- Look at these words. Notice the spelling.

drive	operate
driver	operator

If a word ends in *e*, you must drop the *e* before you add the suffix *-er* or *-or*.

You will find that most words add the suffix *-er*. Only a few words add the suffix *-or*.

- Look carefully at the spelling of each word below.

visitor　　operator　　inventor　　sailor

Talk About It

Add an *-er* or *-or* suffix to these words to form new words. Spell the new words. Tell the meaning of each new word.

1. write
2. visit
3. speak
4. nibble
5. sail
6. gather

Skills Practice

Read each pair of sentences. Look at the underlined word in the first sentence. Add the suffix *-er* or *-or* to the underlined word to complete the second sentence. Write the second sentence in each pair.

1. Mrs. James visited today.
Mother enjoys a ____.

2. Tracy sails on a boat.
The ____ goes on a boat.

3. The Wilsons run a farm.
A ____ works hard.

4. Elena drives to work.
A ____ goes to work.

5. Ms. Feld directs the band.
The band likes its ____.

6. Paula listens to music.
A ____ enjoys music.

7. Earl operates the saw.
The ____ uses the saw.

8. Mr. Ford teaches school.
The ____ read Jean's paper.

9. Jeff works on a ranch.
A ____ wakes up early.

10. Fong rides a horse.
A ____ uses a saddle.

Writing Sentences

Write three sentences. In each sentence tell about a worker and his or her job. Use words with the suffix *er* or *or*.

Sample Answer 1. Mother enjoys a visitor.

Skills Review

Write a proper noun for each common noun.

1. day
2. month
3. city
4. doctor
5. girl
6. boy

Write each proper noun. Use capital letters where they belong.

7. The friends leave saturday.
8. The boys meet at grant park.
9. Then mei arrives with sally.
10. The hike and camp club sets off.
11. A squirrel races by buffy.
12. The dog walks beside hal.
13. Hal passes apple creek.
14. Dan crosses link bridge.
15. Snow covers mount green.
16. Yukio sees rothko cave.

Write each sentence correctly.

17. Dad called dr frank.
18. The doctor lives near ms mason.
19. mr and mrs roberts walk home.

Read each sentence. Capital letters are missing from each address. Periods are missing, too. Write each address correctly.

20. Mayer's bakery
    1429 Olympic ave
21. ms Luisa alba
    336 Armitage st
22. The vitto Family
    781 annawan ave

Read each sentence. Write the possessive noun in each sentence.

23. Pete's class goes to a zoo.
24. Ms. Ray's students hurry.
25. The seal's fur shines.
26. Joe hears a lion's growl.
27. Elephants' trunks curl.
28. Al enjoys a bird's colors.

Skills Review

At the end of each sentence is a singular or plural noun. Write the correct possessive form of each noun.

29. The ____ teacher calls the class. (children)
30. Some friends looked at the ____ rattles. (snake)
31. ____ friend touches a snake. (Phil)
32. Glenda points at the ____ stripes. (zebra)
33. The zookeeper walks around the ____ tails. (alligators)
34. Linda thinks the ____ tail is ugly. (alligator)
35. The zookeeper brings the ____ food. (monkeys)
36. The class laughs at a ____ tricks. (monkey)

Look at the underlined word in the first sentence. Add the suffix *-er* or *-or* to the underlined word to complete the second sentence. Write the second sentence in each pair.

37. Sarah visits Rosa often.
Rosa talks to the ____.

38. Bob operates the machines.
The ____ runs the machines.

39. Jill invented a toy.
The ____ showed the toy.

40. Laura visits a ranch.
A ____ raises cattle.

Exploring Language

Some of the nouns you use today as common nouns were once proper nouns. Here are some examples.

The **teddy bear** was named after President Teddy Roosevelt who loved bears.

The **sandwich** is named after the Earl of Sandwich who first made one.

Do you know of any other common nouns that come from names?

Alphabetical Order

All the letters in the alphabet follow a special order. This is called *alphabetical order.*

A B C D E F G H I J K L M N O P Q R S T U V W X Y Z

Many kinds of lists are in alphabetical order. The names in an address book or a telephone book are in alphabetical order. The words in a dictionary are in alphabetical order. Things listed in an index are also in alphabetical order.

Alphabetical order is helpful when you have a long list of words. You know exactly where to find each word if your list is in alphabetical order.

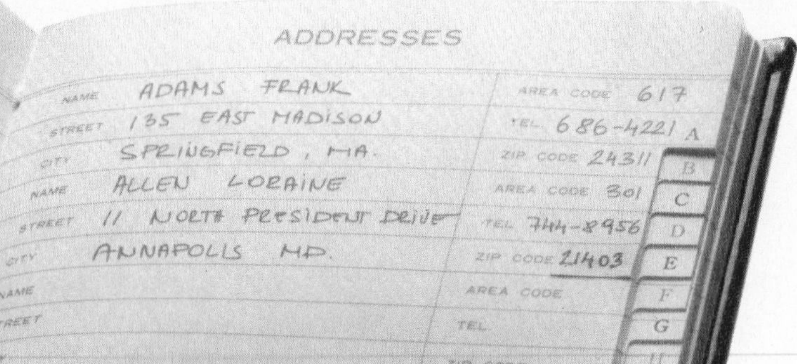

- Look at the words in each list. What is the first letter of each word? Look at the alphabet. Are these words in alphabetical order?

hammock	party	clever
grand	evening	interesting
owl	time	same
cozy	drain	trust

Many words begin with the same letter. Then you must look at the second letter. When all the second letters are the same, you must look at the third letter.

- Look at the words in each list. Look at the alphabet. Are these words in alphabetical order?

smart	reel	kettle
snake	relief	kitchen
sock	receive	kind
station	review	kneel

Talk About It

Put the words in each list in alphabetical order.

1.	2.	3.	4.
comic	defend	light	sparrow
cobbler	groom	lotion	speck
couch	castle	lantern	speech
cone	equal	least	sprinkle

Skills Practice

Write the words in each list in alphabetical order.

1.	3.	5.	7.
ignore	peek	loaf	tub
icicle	pelican	jacket	trade
illness	petal	drawer	truth
idle	pepper	knife	ten

2.	4.	6.	8.
emotion	glory	cricket	jealous
emit	glue	crawl	joke
empire	glisten	crease	jingle
emerald	glass	crowd	jewel

Sample Answer 1. icicle idle ignore illness

Learning About the Dictionary

You often hear or read words you are not familiar with. You can use a dictionary to find out more about these words.

The dictionary is a very long list of words. Each word in the list is called an entry. The entries are arranged in alphabetical order.

The dictionary tells what the words mean. Many words have two meanings. When a word has two meanings, the dictionary gives both meanings. You will find **1.** in front of the first meaning. You will find **2.** in front of the second meaning. Sometimes an example sentence follows a meaning. An *example sentence* helps make the meaning clear.

- Look at the dictionary page. What are the entries? Read the second meaning of the word *market*. Read the example sentence for this meaning.

magic/melody

mag · ic (maj′ ik) The art or skill of doing tricks or of making strange or unusual things happen.

man · ner (man′ ər) **1.** The way in which something is done. *Fill out the form in the following manner.* **2.** Polite ways of behaving or acting. *You have good table manners.*

mar · ket (mär′ kit) **1.** A place where food and other things are bought and sold **2.** To shop for things. *Father and I will market for supplies tomorrow.*

meal (mēl) **1.** The food eaten at one particular time. *Our family eats three meals a day.* **2.** A kind of grain.

mel · o · dy (mel′ ə dē) A pleasing arrangement of sounds. *Can you hum that melody?*

at; **ā**pe; c**ä**r; **e**nd; m**ē**; **i**t; **ī**ce; h**o**t; **ō**ld; f**ô**rk; w**oo**d; f**o͞o**l; **oi**l; **ou**t; **u**p; t**ur**n; si**ng**; **th**in; **th**is; **hw** in **wh**ite; **zh** in trea**s**ure. The symbol **ə** stands for the sound of **a** in **a**bout, **e** in tak**e**n, **i** in penc**i**l, **o** in lem**o**n, and **u** in circ**u**s.

A dictionary tells you what a word means. It also shows you how to say, or pronounce, a word. The pronunciation of *market* looks like this—(mär′ kit). It comes between the entry and the meaning. Every dictionary has a *pronunciation key* to help you say the word. A pronunciation key may look like this.

> **at**; **ā**pe; c**ä**r; **e**nd; m**ē**; **i**t; **ī**ce; h**o**t; **ō**ld; f**ô**rk; w**oo**d; f**o͞o**l; **oi**l; **ou**t; **u**p; t**ur**n; si**ng**; **th**in; **th**is; **hw** in **wh**ite; **zh** in trea**s**ure. The symbol **ə** stands for the sound of **a** in **a**bout, **e** in tak**e**n, **i** in penc**i**l, **o** in lem**o**n, and **u** in circ**u**s.

The entries and pronunciations are broken up into parts called *syllables*. The *syllables* also help you to pronounce words. The word *market* has two syllables.

Talk About It

Use the sample dictionary to answer each question.

1. Which entries have one meaning?
2. What are the example sentences for the word *manner*?
3. How many syllables does the word *magic* have?

Skills Practice

Use the sample dictionary to answer each question. Write the answer.

1. Which entries have two meanings?
2. What is the example sentence for the word *meal*?
3. Which meaning of *meal* does the sentence show?
4. How do you write the pronunciation for *melody*?
5. How many syllables does the word *melody* have?

Sample Answer 1. manner market meal

Using Words That Describe

Thinking About Words That Describe

You have five senses. They are sight, sound, smell, taste, and touch. Your senses help you to experience the world around you. Sometimes words can describe how your senses work. These sense words can make things come alive in your mind.

You can use sense words to compare two different things. When you compare, you show how two different things are alike.

Sometimes you use the word *like* or *as* when you compare. This kind of comparison is called a *simile*.

> A **simile** is a comparison that shows how two different things are alike. A simile always uses the word **like** or **as.**

The ice was <u>as</u> smooth <u>as</u> glass.
My shoes squeaked <u>like</u> rusty hinges when I walked.

You can also compare two things without using *like* or *as*. In this kind of comparison, you say that one thing *is* another thing. This kind of comparison is called a *metaphor*.

> A **metaphor** is a statement that compares two different things without using the words **like** or **as.**

<u>The racing car</u> was a <u>roaring lion</u>.
<u>The white clouds</u> were <u>huge puffs of cotton</u>.

The racing car is being compared to a roaring lion. The clouds are compared to a mountain of cotton balls.

Talking About Words That Describe

Think of a word to complete each sentence. Tell whether each sentence contains a simile or a metaphor.

1. Mike walked like a ____ in his tight shoes.
2. The baby was as sticky as a ____.
3. Ants marched across the picnic rug like ____.
4. The comet was a fiery ____.

Writing About Words That Describe

Think of a word to complete each sentence. Write the sentence. If the completed sentence contains a simile, write **simile.** If it contains a metaphor, write **metaphor.**

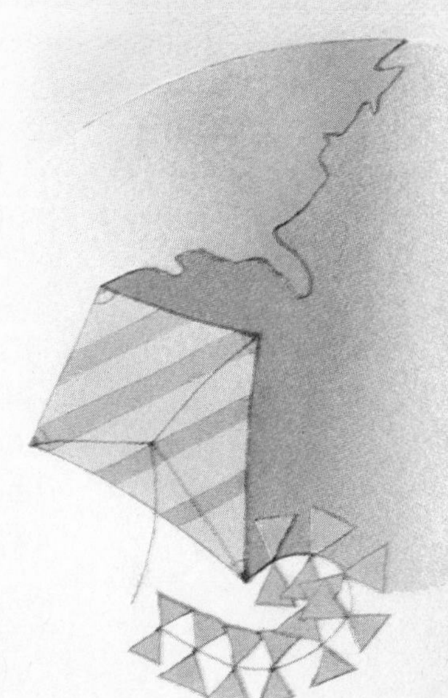

1. The kite soared like a ____.
2. My wet shoes felt like ____.
3. The pudding was as lumpy as ____.
4. The desert was a blazing ____.
5. The old tuba honked like a ____ when I blew into it.
6. Paula is a ____ when she is angry.
7. The burned chocolate smelled like ____.
8. After shoveling snow, my frozen toes were ____.
9. The stale cookies tasted like ____.
10. The shooting star was a flashing ____.

Writing Sentences

Write two sentences that use similes. Write one sentence that uses a metaphor.

1. Write a sentence telling how *sharp* a thing is.
2. Write a sentence telling what an *old violin* might sound like.
3. Write a sentence calling the *moon* by another name.

Description Paragraphs

Thinking About Paragraphs

You describe things for many reasons. Sometimes you want to tell a friend about a person, place, or thing you have seen. You can write a paragraph that describes something.

A paragraph that describes has a main idea sentence and detail sentences. The main idea sentence tells whom or what the paragraph is about. The detail sentences use words that describe the person, place, or thing. The words tell how someone or something looks, sounds, tastes, smells, or feels.

Andy went on a camping trip. Read the paragraph he wrote about the place where he camped.

> I found a good place to camp. The large lake has clear water. You can hear the wind whistle through the trees. The wind feels soft and cool. The snow on the mountains tastes sweet. The flowers smell fresh.

In Andy's paragraph the first sentence is the main idea sentence. It tells what is being described. One detail sentence tells what something looks like. Another detail sentence tells how something sounds. Other detail sentences tell how things feel, taste, and smell.

Talking About Paragraphs

Read the paragraph that Andy wrote.

1. What is the main idea sentence?
2. Which words tell how the lake looks?
3. Which word tells how the wind sounds?
4. Which words tell how the wind feels?
5. Which word tells how the snow tastes?
6. Which word tells how the flowers smell?

Writing a Paragraph

Pretend you are at a baseball game. Read each sentence. Use a word in the blank that describes the baseball game. Write the sentence.

1. The players look ____ before the game.
2. The grass on the field smells ____.
3. The baseball feels ____.
4. The fans sound ____ during the game.
5. The roasted peanuts taste ____.

A Class Paragraph

Thinking About Paragraphs

Have you ever lost something? What did you do to try to find it? You probably looked for the thing yourself. Perhaps you asked other people to look. If you did, you needed to describe what you lost. That way people would know if they found it.

If you lose something in school, you might put a paragraph on the bulletin board in the hall. The paragraph describes the thing you have lost. Other people read the paragraph and can help you look for what is missing.

Your class is going to write a paragraph together. Pretend you have lost a rabbit that was kept in the classroom. You want to put a notice on the bulletin board in school. You need to describe your rabbit so other people will know if they see it.

This picture will help you describe the rabbit.

Writing a Paragraph

1. Your paragraph will start with this main idea sentence: *Our class has lost a rabbit.* Your teacher will write it on the board.
2. Think of one sentence that tells about the color of the rabbit's fur.
3. Think of a sentence that tells about the marks on the rabbit's back.
4. Think of a sentence that tells about the rabbit's ears.
5. Think of a sentence that tells what the rabbit feels like when you pet it. Your teacher will write the sentences on the board.

Careers

Recreation therapists help people who have been sick or hurt. They teach people to make many things. Sometimes people hurt their hands. A recreation therapist can help people to use their hands again. Therapists must be able to describe how to do many things. They must write and speak so people understand them.

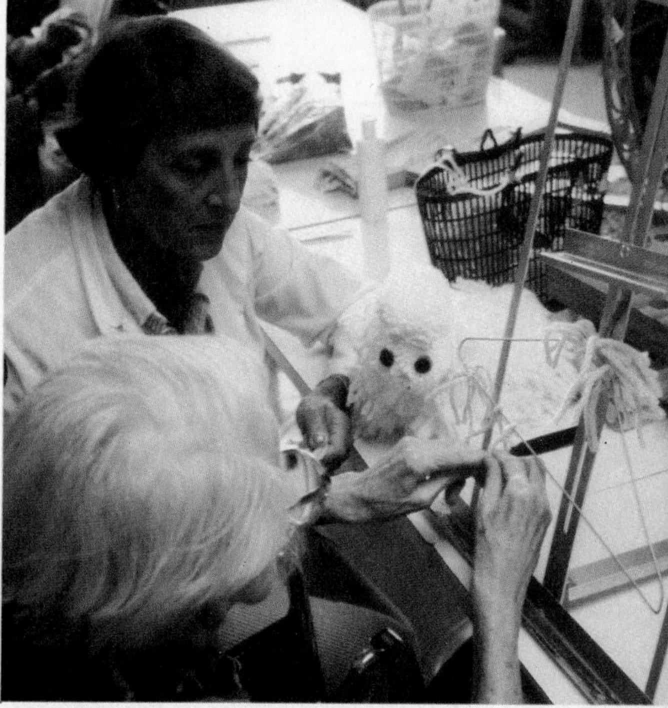

Practicing a Paragraph

Thinking About Your Paragraph

You can write your own paragraph. Pretend you lost your baseball shirt. You want to put a paragraph on the bulletin board at school. Your paragraph will describe the shirt.

The pictures show how the shirt looks from the front and back.

Writing Your Paragraph

1. Your paragraph will start with a main idea sentence. You may use the main idea sentence below. You may wish to write a different main idea sentence. Write the sentence. Indent the first word.

   Please help me find my baseball shirt.

2. Write a detail sentence that tells the color of the shirt. The Word Bank can help you.
3. Write a detail sentence that tells about the buttons on the front.
4. Write a detail sentence that tells the name of the team.
5. Write a detail sentence that tells about the numeral on the back.

Word Bank

team
shirt
color
white
red
stripes
seven
buttons
ten

Edit Your Paragraph

Read your paragraph again. Think about these questions.

1. What words did you use to describe the main idea?
2. What nouns did you use in your paragraph? Are they common nouns or proper nouns? Did you capitalize each important word in the proper nouns?
3. Did you indent the first word of the paragraph?
4. Did you begin each sentence with a capital letter? How did you end each sentence?
5. Did you begin each proper noun with a capital letter?
6. Did you spell words correctly? Check the Word Bank.

Editing Symbols

≡ capitalize
¶ indent
ℓ take out
^ add

Correct your mistakes. If you need to, write your paragraph again.

INDEPENDENT WRITING

A Description Paragraph

Prewriting Your five senses help you describe how things feel, taste, look, smell, and sound. Suppose a Martian came to visit your classroom. You must describe simple objects such as erasers, pencils, or rulers to the creature as clearly as you can. Choose an object in your desk or classroom. Use your five senses and jot down ideas that describe the object.

Writing Write a paragraph that describes an object in your desk or classroom. Start your paragraph with a main idea sentence that names the object. Then write detail sentences that describe the object clearly.

Editing Use the check questions and the editing symbols above to edit your paragraph.

Unit Review

Read each sentence. Write each noun. Write **singular** beside each singular noun. Write **plural** beside each plural noun. *pages 38–42*

1. The sun warms the sand.
2. Waves crash on the beach.
3. A gull comes by.
4. Friends dig in the sand.
5. A man swims.
6. A crab bites the toes.

Read each sentence. At the end of each sentence is a singular noun. Write the plural form of the noun. *pages 38–42*

7. I brushed my ____. (tooth)
8. The workers dug two ____. (ditch)
9. The ____ worked on the ranch. (woman)
10. Four ____ brought the children. (bus)

Think of a proper noun for each common noun. Write the proper noun. *pages 46–47*

11. city **12.** country **13.** girl **14.** boy

Write each sentence correctly. Use capital letters where they belong. *pages 48–49*

15. The girls meet at lake george.
16. Jan gives david a book.
17. Ray joins scout club.

Write each address correctly. *pages 48–49*

18. mr Tyronne Singer
368 Salmon st

19. dr Nona Ash
19 kings ave

Read each sentence. Write the possessive noun in each sentence. *pages 50–51*

20. Wendy points at the gull's beak.
21. The waves hit June's legs.
22. The friends' buckets fill with sand.

Read each sentence. At the end of each sentence is a singular or plural noun. Write each sentence using the correct possessive form. *pages 50–51*

23. The ____ hands dig under the castle. (children)
24. The boys hear the ____ motors. (boats)
25. The ____ noise disappears. (motor)
26. The children hear the ____ roar. (ocean)

You are going to write a paragraph that describes the ocean. Here is the main idea sentence: *Last week our family visited the ocean*. Here are words you may use in your detail sentences. *pages 60–67*

blue	foamy	cold	roaring
crashing	salty	fresh	

27. Write the main idea sentence of the paragraph.
28. Write a sentence that tells how the ocean looked.
29. Write a sentence that tells how the water felt.
30. Write a sentence that tells how the waves sounded.
31. Write a sentence that tells how the water tasted.
32. Write a sentence that tells how the ocean smelled.

A Poem

Did you ever think the moon looks like a freckled snowball? Have you ever seen a cloud that looks just like a polar bear? Writers of poetry often use such examples in their poems. Some poetry has rhymes like the old Mother Goose rhymes you know. Some poetry does not rhyme. All poetry tries to use words that describe something so clearly you can see it for yourself.

Listen to these poems as your teacher reads them aloud. Perhaps you would like to read them to yourself. Think about the pictures the writer describes.

These *Words to Think About* may help you understand the poem.

Words To Think About

haunches, legs
strands, threads
cease, to stop
skeins, threads
shoon, shoes
casements, windows
thatch, straw roof
couched, asleep
cote, shelter
scampering, running
reeds, tall grass

Night

Night is a purple pumpkin,
Laced with a silver web,
And the moon a golden spider,
Wandering through the strands.
At dawn the purple pumpkin,
Rolling slowly around,
Leans against the star-web,
Moving the spider down.
The silver web slides slowly,
Slowly across the sky,
And the spider moon creeps slowly,
Slowly by.
The twinkling stars cease spinning
Their skeins of silver gray,
The spider moon
Crawls down the strands
And night turns into day.

Patricia Hubbell

Silver

Slowly, silently, now the moon
Walks the night in her silver shoon;
This way, and that, she peers, and sees
Silver fruit upon silver trees;
One by one the casements catch
Her beams beneath the silvery thatch;
Couched in his kennel, like a log,
With paws of silver, sleeps the dog;
From their shadowy cote the white breasts peep
Of doves in a silver-feathered sleep;
A harvest mouse goes scampering by,
With silver claws, and silver eye;
And moveless fish in the water gleam,
By silver reeds in a silver stream.

Walter de la Mare

Fog

The fog comes
on little cat feet.

It sits looking
over harbor and city
on silent haunches
and then moves on.

Carl Sandburg

Creative Activities

1. **Creative Writing** Two of these poems describe the night. Try to write your own poem about the night. Remember that not all poems have to rhyme.

2. Listen to the poems again. What pictures do you see in your mind? Choose one poem or a few lines from one poem. Make your own picture by drawing, painting, or whatever you like to do best.

LOS ANGELES FREEWAY

Grammar and Related Language Skills

Verbs
Verbs in the Present and the Past
Irregular Verbs
Spelling Verbs

Practical Communication

STUDY AND REFERENCE SKILLS
Reading Graphs and Tables

COMPOSITION
Writing a Factual Paragraph in a Friendly Letter

Creative Expression

A Story

People who read maps and help give directions are called navigators. Would you need a navigator to help find your way on a superhighway? Do you think you could read a map correctly? Could you explain directions to someone else? What speaking skills must a good navigator have? What writing skills does a navigator need?

Verbs

Many sentences tell about things that happen. These sentences show action. Special words in the sentences name the action. You know many of these action words already. They are words like *run, sit, walk,* and *build.*

- Read the sentences below. Find the action word in each sentence.

The Johnsons traveled to Holland.

The family walked to the stores.

The children visited a tiny city.

The action words are *traveled, walked,* and *visited.*

An **action verb** is a word that names an action.

Action verbs are in the predicate part of a sentence. The *predicate part* tells what action the subject does. Look again at each sentence above. The predicate part is in a red box.

- Read these sentences.

Carl runs to the bus.

Alison finds a seat.

Nina writes letters.

Look at the predicate part of each sentence. What is the action verb?

Talk About It

Read each sentence. Tell what the verb is in each sentence.

1. People built this tiny city in Holland.
2. The builders made tiny buildings.
3. Little flags wave in the air.
4. Guards stand outside the palace.
5. A man drives a golden coach.

Skills Practice

Write each sentence. Underline each verb.

1. Tiny trains carry people.
2. Small cars crowd a street.
3. Little roses grow in a lane.
4. Cows nibble hay on a farm.
5. Boats sail on the river.
6. A band plays music.
7. Drummers march in a parade.
8. People walk to a castle.
9. Tiny people build tents.
10. Girls ride little bicycles.
11. Pilots fly airplanes.
12. Animals live in a zoo.
13. A little windmill turns.
14. People shop in tiny stores.

Writing Sentences

Think about waking up in a strange place. You are a giant in a tiny city where tiny people live.

1. Write two sentences telling how people act when they see you. Be sure to use action verbs.
2. Write two sentences telling what you do in the little city. Use action verbs.

Sample Answer **1.** Tiny trains carry people.

Verb Tenses

You use a verb to name an action. A verb also tells when an action happens. Sometimes you talk about things that happen now. Sometimes you talk about things that already happened. Sometimes you talk about things that will happen in the future.

- Look at the verbs in these sentences.

The animals run fast. The driver sings.

The verbs *run* and *sings* name actions that happen now. These actions take place in the present time.

The **present tense** of a verb names an action that happens now.

- Read these sentences. Notice the verbs *has* and *have*.

The driver has a fur hat. The children have fur hats, too.

The verbs *has* and *have* are different from other verbs. They tell about owning something. They are in the present tense.

- Look at the verbs in these sentences.

A dog chased the sled. The children laughed.

The verbs *chased* and *laughed* name actions that already happened. These verbs are in the past tense.

The **past tense** of a verb names an action that already happened.

Verbs in the past tense have a special form. Add *-ed* to most verbs to make a verb in the past.

- Now look at the verbs in these sentences.

The race will start soon. The horse will pull the sled.

The verbs in these sentences name actions that will happen at a future time. These verbs are in the future tense.

The **future tense** of a verb names an action that will take place in the future.

Verbs that show action in the future have a main verb and the helping verb *will* or *shall.*

A **helping verb** is a verb that helps the main verb to name an action.

Talk About It

Find the verb in each sentence. Tell whether the verb is in the past, present, or future tense.

1. Sam will visit Lapland soon.
2. My father talked loudly.
3. The ground freezes quickly.
4. Many people have sleds.

Skills Practice

Write each verb. Then write if it is in the **past, present,** or **future** tense.

1. People will meet at noon.
2. The people carried jackets.
3. The people have scarves.
4. Sleds will race across snow.
5. Some children ski down the hill.
6. Boys skated on the lake.
7. The girls will ski later.
8. Children yelled excitedly.
9. Clouds moved quickly.
10. It will snow all night.
11. A driver passes a cabin.
12. He waves to the children.
13. The cabin has a fireplace.
14. Everyone will rest inside.

Sample Answer 1. will meet, future

Using the Present Tense

Nouns are often in the subject part of a sentence. The *subject part* names whom or what the sentence is about. Some nouns in the subject part name one person, place, or thing. Other nouns name more than one person, place, or thing.

> A **singular noun** names one person, place, or thing.
>
> A **plural noun** names more than one person, place, or thing.

- Read each sentence. Look at the noun in the subject part. Then look at the verb.

Mary travels to India.	The friends travel to India.

The sentences show that a verb works with the noun in the subject part. When the noun and the verb work together, they *agree*. The verb has one form to agree with a singular noun. The verb has another form to agree with a plural noun.

- Read each pair of sentences.

A woman dances to the music.	People dance at fairs in India.
Lisa comes to the fair.	The children come to the fair.

In the first column each verb agrees with a singular noun. In the second column each verb agrees with a plural noun.

Most verbs in the present tense end in *-s* when they agree with a singular noun. Most verbs in the present tense do not end in *-s* when they agree with a plural noun.

The verbs *has* and *have* are present tense verbs. The verb *has* agrees with a singular noun. The verb *have* agrees with a plural noun.

- Read these sentences.

The town has a fair every year.	Some fairs have dancers.

Talk About It

Choose the correct verb for each sentence.

1. Boats ____ during one fair. (race, races)
2. The villagers ____ beautiful snake boats. (sail, sails)
3. The village ____ a colorful boat. (have, has)
4. The boat ____ through the water. (move, moves)

Skills Practice

Write each sentence. Use the correct verb for each sentence.

1. The village ____ a fair today. (have, has)
2. The fair ____ early in the morning. (begin, begins)
3. People ____ to music. (dance, dances)
4. Many cooks ____ food. (prepare, prepares)
5. A clown ____ the crowd. (cheer, cheers)
6. Several groups ____ songs. (sing, sings)
7. Some children ____ on the beach. (play, plays)
8. A boy ____ a tree. (climb, climbs)
9. An actor ____ a show. (give, gives)
10. Storytellers ____ stories. (tell, tells)
11. The crowd ____ to the storyteller. (listen, listens)
12. The people ____ a good time. (has, have)

Writing Sentences

Make believe you and two friends go on a trip. You may go anywhere you want.

1. Write two sentences about what *one* friend does there.
2. Write two sentences about what *two* friends do together.

Use verbs that name actions that happen in the present.

Sample Answer 1. The village has a fair today.

Spelling and the Present Tense

The verb in a sentence agrees with the noun in the subject part. Verbs in the present tense have different forms. Some agree with singular nouns. Others agree with plural nouns.

- Find the noun in the subject part of each sentence.

Paul travels. Bert takes trips.
Polly visits Ireland. Andrea likes airplanes.

The noun in each subject part is singular. The verb agrees with the noun in the subject part. Add *-s* to most verbs in the present tense when the verb agrees with a singular noun.

- Read each sentence. How is each verb spelled?

Paul wishes for a vacation. Paul watches shows about Ireland.

If a verb ends in **s, ss, x, ch, z,** or **sh,** add **-es** to the verb to make it agree with a singular noun.

Talk About It

What form of the verb belongs in each sentence? Spell each verb.

1. The plane ____ in Ireland. (land)
2. Bert ____ outside. (rush)
3. The captain ____. (wave)
4. Bert ____ the boat. (catch)

Skills Practice

Write each sentence. Use the correct form of the verb in the present tense.

1. A cart ____ the castle. (pass)
2. The cart ____. (break)
3. A girl ____ the cart. (push)
4. A boy ____ the cart. (fix)
5. The boy ____ the cart. (pull)
6. The man ____ the cart. (paint)

Sample Answer 1. A cart passes the castle.

Making New Words

Sometimes you can give a new meaning to a word. You can add a prefix to the beginning of it. A *prefix* is a letter or group of letters added to the beginning of a word.

- Read the sentences. Look at the verbs. What prefix was added to the verb? How does the prefix change the meaning of each verb?

  Tracy *packed* a trunk for the trip.
  Tracy *unpacked* the trunk on the ship.

The prefix *un-* often means *the opposite of*. When you *pack* a trunk, you put things into the trunk. When you *unpack*, you do the opposite. You take things out of the trunk.

- Read each sentence.

  The family *packed* the suitcases too soon.
  The children *repacked* the suitcases.

The prefix *re-* means *again*. To *repack* a suitcase means to pack it again.

Talk About It

Tell the meaning of each verb. Use each verb in a sentence.

1. reopen **2.** uncover **3.** untie

Skills Practice

Write the meaning of each verb.

1. resell **3.** unlock **5.** unfasten
2. unzip **4.** repay **6.** reheat

Sample Answer 1. sell again

Skills Review

Read each sentence. Write each verb.

1. The Wynns visited New York.
2. The plane traveled quickly.
3. Mae likes the city.
4. Many people rush to the buildings.
5. Trucks hurry through the streets.
6. Taxi drivers beep horns.
7. The Wynns ride the subway.
8. A boat takes the Wynns up the East River.
9. The Wynns see the Statue of Liberty.
10. A light shines in the statue.
11. Eric finds the stairs.

Write the verb that appears in each sentence. Then write whether each verb is in the **past**, **present**, or **future** tense.

12. Mae spots a tall building.
13. The Wynns rested all evening.
14. Eric will count the bridges on the East River.
15. Mr. Wynn traveled to New York last year, too.
16. Mr. Wynn has a friend in New York.
17. Mr. Wynn visited the friend.
18. Some children will meet Mr. Wynn in the hall.
19. Many families have apartments in this building.
20. Mr. Wynn will wait for the elevator.

Write the correct verb for each sentence.

21. New York ____ many buildings. (have, has)
22. Cars ____ the streets. (fill, fills)
23. A shopper ____ many stores. (find, finds)

24. A band ____ in parks. (play, plays)
25. A subway ____ under the ground. (roar, roars)
26. The bridges ____ lights. (have, has)
27. A ship ____ on the river. (sail, sails)
28. The ship ____ from England. (come, comes)
29. Lights ____ on the ship. (blink, blinks)

Read each sentence. Write the correct form of the verb in the present tense.

30. Juan ____ the city lights. (enjoy)
31. Rosa ____ the lights, too. (watch)
32. One person ____ after a bus. (race)
33. A car ____ in front of a store. (pass)
34. Juan ____ a shoelace. (break)
35. Rosa ____ the shoelace. (fix)
36. Rosa ____ Mrs. Garcia. (visit)

Write the meaning of each verb.

37. redo
38. refill
39. remake
40. unpin
41. rewash
42. unmake

Exploring Language

Some verbs name noises. Many of these verbs sound like the noises they name. Look at these sentences.

The bees buzz. The cat meows.
The saws whirr. The waves splash.
The snakes hiss. The bubbles pop.

Can you think of any more verbs that sound like the noises they name?

Verbs in the Past Tense

Action verbs can be used to show actions that happen now. These verbs are in the present tense. But sometimes you want to tell about actions that already happened. Verbs can also show that an action happened in the *past*.

The **past tense** of a verb names an action that already happened.

- Read the sentences below. Look at the verbs.

> Last year Ron visited Africa.
> Ron traveled to many cities.
> Ron enjoyed the bush country.
> Ron also liked African music.

Each underlined verb names an action that already happened. These verbs are in the past tense.

Add **-ed** to most verbs to form the past tense.

If a verb ends in **e,** drop the **e** and add **-ed** to form the past tense.

- Look at the sentences again. Notice how the past tense of each verb has been formed by adding *-ed*.

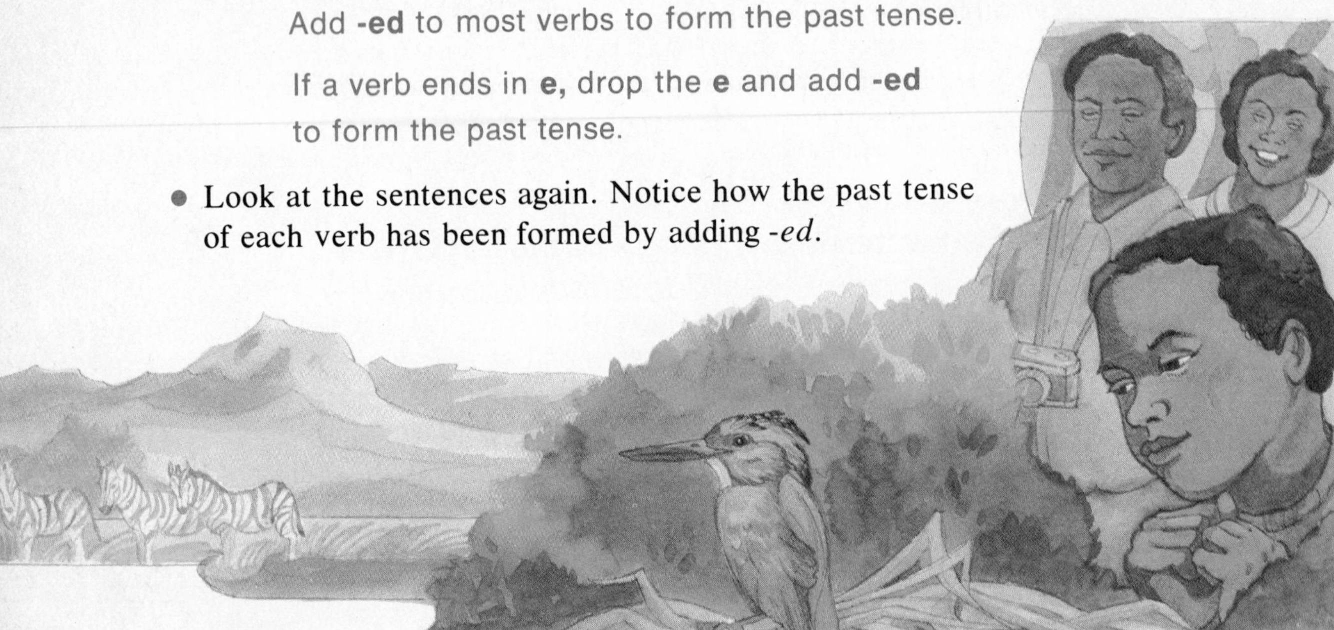

Talk About It

Read each sentence. Complete each sentence by telling the correct form of the verb in the past tense.

1. Ron ____ to the bush country. (travel)
2. Farmers ____ vegetables there. (plant)
3. The farmers ____ Ron to a feast. (invite)
4. Ron ____ many new foods. (taste)
5. The people ____ around the fire. (dance)

Skills Practice

Write each sentence with the correct form of the verb in the past tense. Underline the verb.

1. Ron ____ to a park with Lucy. (walk)
2. The children ____ the wild animals. (watch)
3. A giraffe ____ to reach the leaves. (stretch)
4. Some zebras ____ by. (race)
5. Some animals ____ Ron. (frighten)
6. The guide ____ to a baby elephant. (call)
7. Lucy ____ at the elephant. (laugh)
8. Two monkeys ____ to the top of the tree. (climb)
9. A lion ____ loudly at the people. (roar)
10. The day ____ too quickly. (end)

Writing Sentences

Imagine that you have been lost in the desert for two weeks. You have only a camel, a little water, and a little food. Each night you write down in a notebook what has happened that day. Write four sentences from your notebook telling about your days in the desert. Use verbs in the past tense.

Sample Answer 1. Ron walked to a park with Lucy.

The Past with Have and Has

You know that verbs in the past tense show action that already happened. Some actions happened in the past, but they had no real ending time. Other actions began in the past and they continue in the present.

- Look at these sentences.

  The driver *has parked* the bus at the lake.

  The children *have played* for a long time.

In the first sentence the verb in the past with *has* names an action that started in the past. The action has no real ending time. In the second sentence the verb in the past with *have* names an action that began in the past and continues in the present.

- Look again at the verbs in the sentences above. One word in each verb shows action. The word *parked* shows action. *Parked* is the *main verb.* The other word helps the main verb. It is a *helping verb.* In these sentences *have* and *has* are helping verbs.

  A **helping verb** is a verb that helps a main verb to name an action.

The past tense of the main verb usually works with the helping verbs *have* and *has.* You add *-ed* to most verbs to form the past tense.

- Look at the chart. The first column shows the verb. The second column shows the past tense of the verb. The third column shows the past with *have* or *has.*

VERB	PAST	PAST WITH HAVE OR HAS
jump	jumped	have or has jumped
arrive	arrived	have or has arrived
wash	washed	have or has washed

Talk About It

Read each sentence with the correct form of the main verb.

1. Kim has ____ from Mexico. (arrive)
2. Kim's class has ____ about Mexico. (learn)
3. The children have ____ about many things. (talk)
4. Kim has ____ them many pictures. (mail)

Skills Practice

Write each sentence. Use the correct form of the main verb.

1. Many people have ____ Mexico. (visit)
2. Kim has ____ a trip to Mexico. (want)
3. Kim's aunt and uncle have ____ to Mexico. (move)
4. They have ____ there for five years. (live)
5. Kim's parents have ____ a long time for this trip. (wait)
6. Kim's brother has ____ for two years. (work)
7. Kim's parents have ____ for two years. (save)
8. Kim and her brother have ____ Spanish. (learn)
9. Kim has ____ information about Mexico. (collect)
10. Kim has ____ a diary about their trip. (start)

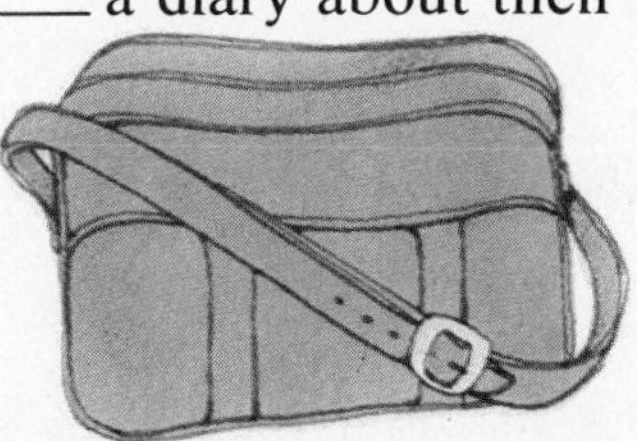

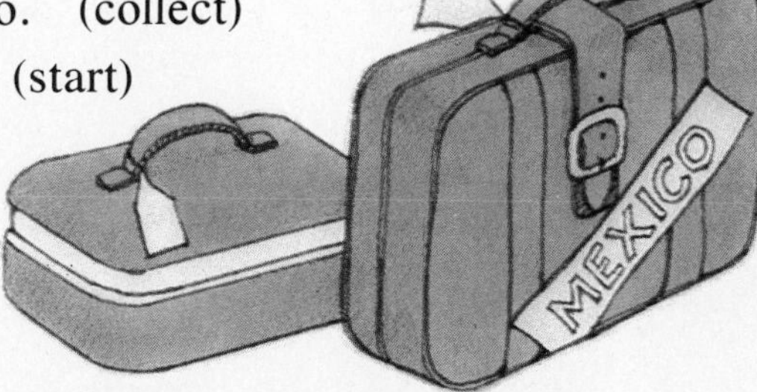

Writing Sentences

Think about a place you visited with a friend. Write four sentences telling what you or your friend did. Use the helping verbs *have* or *has* with the main verb in each sentence.

Sample Answer **1.** Many people have visited Mexico.

More About the Past

You add *-ed* to most verbs to form the past. You also add *-ed* to most verbs to show past action with *have* or *has*.

past Sue painted the living room yesterday.

past with has The family has painted the entire house this year.

Some verbs change in different ways to form the past and the past with *have* or *has*.

past The Paynes saw China last week.

past with have The Paynes have seen Iran, Turkey, and India.

The main verb in the first sentence is *saw*. *Saw* is the past tense of the verb *see*. In the second sentence the main verb is *seen*. The helping verb is *have*. Notice how the main verb changes when it is used with a helping verb.

The chart shows some verbs. For these verbs, the past tense is not formed by adding *-ed*. The first column shows the present tense. The second column shows the past tense. The third column shows the past tense with *has* or *have*. There is no rule for forming the past tense and the past tense with *have* or *has* for these verbs. You must memorize them.

VERB	PAST	PAST WITH HAVE OR HAS
begin	began	have or has begun
bring	brought	have or has brought
come	came	have or has come
do	did	have or has done
draw	drew	have or has drawn
drive	drove	have or has driven
eat	ate	have or has eaten
fall	fell	have or has fallen

find	found	have or has found
fly	flew	have or has flown
go	went	have or has gone
make	made	have or has made
ride	rode	have or has ridden
run	ran	have or has run
say	said	have or has said
see	saw	have or has seen
speak	spoke	have or has spoken
teach	taught	have or has taught
throw	threw	have or has thrown
write	wrote	have or has written

Talk About It

Read each sentence with the correct form of the main verb.

1. Lee has ____ home. (write)
2. Yesterday José ____. (come)
3. Last May Pat ____ to Texas. (ride)
4. My family has ____ back. (fly)

Skills Practice

Write the past and past with have or has for these verbs.

1. begin 2. make 3. see 4. find 5. say 6. speak

Write each sentence. Use the correct form of the main verb.

7. Lee has ____ his work. (do)
8. Jane ____ Jan last year. (bring)
9. Sam has ____ a picture. (draw)
10. Dad ____ yesterday. (drive)
11. Al has ____ to work. (go)
12. Bob has ____ a horse. (ride)
13. Jack ____ yesterday. (speak)
14. Tom has ____ it away. (throw)
15. Greg finally ____ his hat (find)
16. Mom has ____ us to swim. (teach)
17. Yesterday Sam ____ a kite. (fly)
18. The baby has ____ already. (eat)
19. Jim has ____ the boys. (see)
20. Sue ____ last week. (begin)

Sample Answer 1. began, have or has begun

Spelling Verbs

You show the past tense of most verbs by adding *-ed* to the verb. Sometimes you double the last letter when you add *-ed*.

- Look at the verbs in the box below.

VERB	PAST	PAST WITH HAVE OR HAS
hop	hopped	have or has hopped
stop	stopped	have or has stopped

Each verb ends with a consonant, vowel, consonant. To form the past tense, you double the last consonant and add *-ed*.

> If a one-syllable verb ends with consonant, vowel, consonant, double the last consonant and add **-ed** to make the past tense.

Talk About It

Form the past tense of each verb. Spell each new word.

1. tap **2.** tag **3.** strap **4.** drag

Skills Practice

Write the past tense of each verb.

1. clap **4.** flop **7.** pop **10.** step
2. pin **5.** hug **8.** flag **11.** hum
3. jam **6.** grab **9.** plan **12.** beg

Sample Answer 1. clapped

More About Spelling Verbs

Some verbs also change spelling when *-ed* or *-es* is added.

- Find the verb. How does the spelling change?

PRESENT TENSE	**PAST TENSE**
The boys fry eggs.	The girl fried eggs.
The boy fries eggs.	The children fried eggs.

In these verbs, you change the *y* to *i* and add *-es* or *-ed*.

If a verb ends in a consonant and **y,** change the **y** to **i** and add **-es** to form the present tense.

If a verb ends in a consonant and **y,** change the **y** to **i** and add **-ed** to form the past tense.

- Look at the sentences again. In the present tense, the verb *fry* agrees with a plural noun. *Fry* changes to *fries* to agree with a singular noun. In the past tense *fried* does not change.

Talk About It

Complete each sentence. First use the verb in the present tense. Then use the past tense. Spell each verb.

1. The boy ____. (worry)
2. The girl ____. (try)
3. The dog ____. (hurry)
4. The horse ____. (whinny)

Skills Practice

Write each sentence two times. First use the verb in the present tense. Then use the verb in the past tense.

1. The woman ____. (marry)
2. The sink ____. (empty)
3. The baby ____. (cry)
4. The paint ____. (dry)

Sample Answer 1. The woman marries. The woman married.

Skills Review

Read each sentence. Write the correct form of the verb in the past tense.

1. My family ____ New England. (visit)
2. Mother ____ in Maine once. (live)
3. Her father ____ every day. (fish)
4. The house ____ the sea. (face)
5. The family ____ to the city. (move)
6. Her father ____ there. (work)
7. Everyone ____ the sea. (miss)
8. Mother ____ back to the sea. (travel)
9. The family ____ the old house. (enjoy)
10. The children ____ in the sand. (play)

Read each sentence. Write the correct form of the main verb.

11. The vacation has ____. (end)
12. Judy has ____ the house. (clean)
13. John has ____ all the windows. (close)
14. Jack has ____ off the water. (turn)
15. Mom and dad have ____ the bags. (pack)
16. Dad has ____ the car. (prepare)
17. John and Judy have ____ the shells. (collect)
18. Jack has ____ the games. (gather)
19. Mom and John have ____ the furniture. (cover)
20. Dad has ____ the doors. (lock)
21. The Lanskys have ____ the trip west. (begin)
22. The family ____ to a ranch. (go)
23. Betty ____ huge herds of cattle. (see)
24. Linda has ____ a horse many times. (ride)
25. Bert ____ off one horse. (fall)
26. Mary Lansky has ____ to Uncle Frank. (write)
27. People have ____ great things about the ranch. (say)

28. The sisters have ____ everything. (do)
29. Bert ____ a special rope. (make)
30. Bert has ____ after the cows everyday. (run)
31. Father ____ an old arrowhead yesterday. (find)
32. The family has ____ ranch food. (eat)
33. The children ____ home tired on Friday. (come)

Write the correct form of the verb in the past tense.

34. tap
35. mop
36. dip
37. nip
38. sip
39. map
40. hop
41. skip

Read each sentence. First write the verb in the present tense. Then write the verb in the past tense.

42. The farmer ____ . (worry)
43. The dancer ____ . (hurry)
44. The egg ____ . (fry)
45. The clown ____ . (cry)
46. The grass ____ . (dry)
47. The child ____ . (study)
48. The singer ____ . (try)
49. The man ____ . (spy)

Some verbs are strange. The past tense of some verbs can be formed in different ways. Americans form the past tense in one way. British people form the past tense in another way. Look at the verb *dive*.

	VERB	PAST	PAST WITH HAVE OR HAS
(British)	dive	dove	dove
(American)	dive	dived	dived

British people usually use *dove* for the past tense. Most Americans say *dived*. Which form do you use?

Reading Graphs and Tables

You can get information from many places. You can read books or ask questions. You can also read a graph. A *graph* shows information in picture form.

- Look at this graph.

The numerals on the left tell the number of animals. The words on the bottom tell what kind of animals are in the pet store. Look at the column for *dogs*. Go up to the top of the column. Now look at the numeral on the left. You can see that 15 dogs are in the pet store.

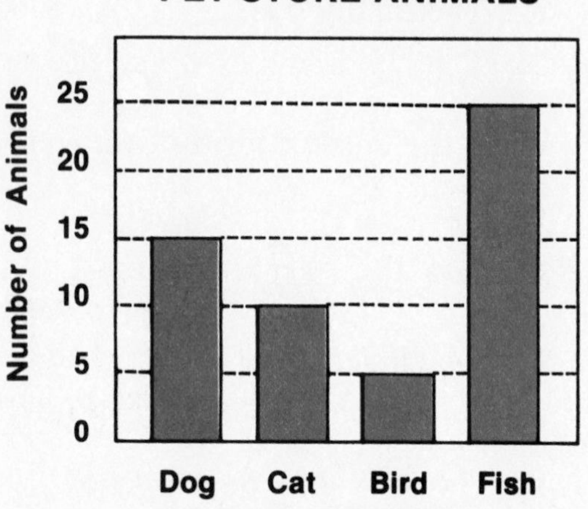

- Look at the graph. What four animals are being counted? How many cats are there?

There is another way to get information. A *table* shows information, too.

This table shows the number of children in three different classes.

Class	Number of Children in Each Class
Art	16
Gym	30
Math	18

- Look at the table above. There are 16 children in art class. How many children are in math class?

Talk About It

Graph A

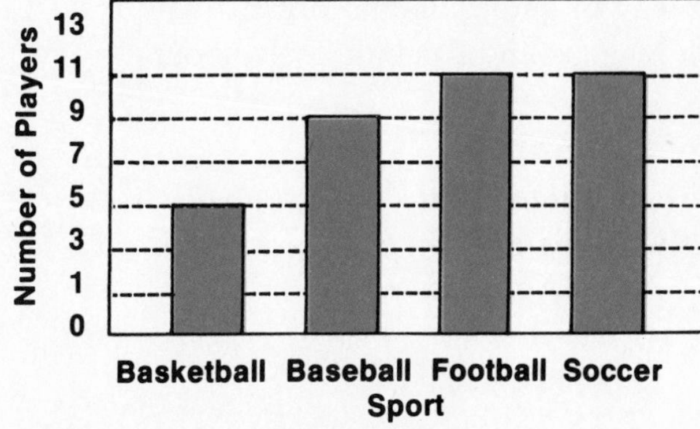

Table B

Children	Number of Blocks We Live from School
Henry	5
Kim	7
Lilly	3
Ray	4

Answer these questions about *Graph A*.

1. What do the numerals on the left side tell?
2. What do the words on the bottom tell?

Answer these questions about *Table B*.

3. What kind of information does the table show?
4. Which child lives the farthest from school?

Skills Practice

Answer these questions about *Graph A*. Write your answers.

1. How many players are on a baseball team?
2. Which sport has the least number of players?
3. Which two sports have the same number of players?

Answer these questions about *Table B*. Write your answers.

4. Which child lives the closest to school?
5. Who lives 4 blocks from school?
6. How many blocks from school does Henry live?

Sample Answer 1. There are nine players on a baseball team.

Making A Survey

Very often you need to gather information. After the information is gathered, you must organize it so that it is helpful to you. A *survey* is a way of gathering and organizing information. It often shows how a group of people feels about something.

Mr. Gold wants to divide his class into groups to do art work. He made a survey to find out what his class likes to work with the best.

1. First he asked the children to choose either crayons, paints, clay, or chalk.
2. Next he wrote down what everyone chose.
3. Last he made a graph to show what he learned.

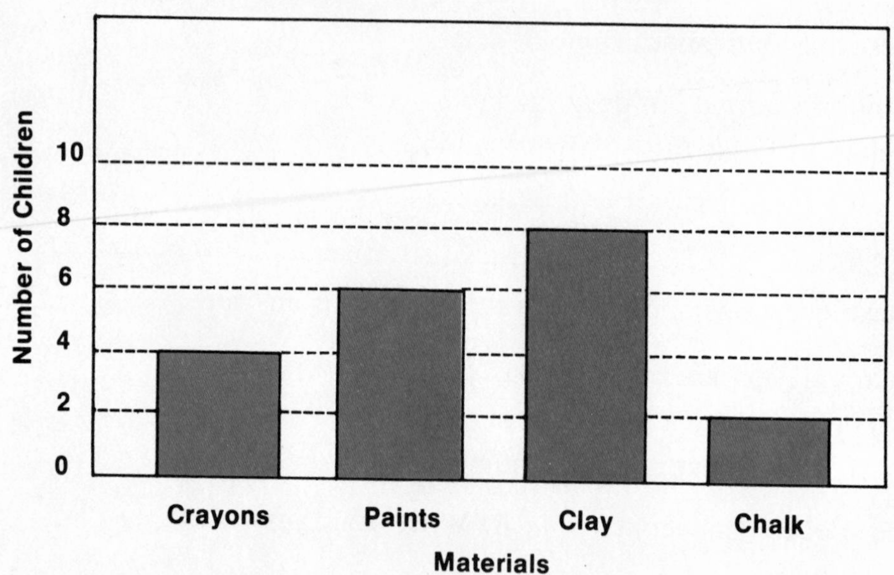

- Look at the graph. How many children chose paints? How many chose clay? What do the children like to work with the best?

Talk About It

1. Make a survey of your class. Ask everyone these questions.

   a. Who likes sports?
   b. Who likes collecting things?
   c. Who likes making things?
   d. Who likes playing games?

2. Ask your teacher to help you make a graph.

Skills Practice

Cheryl made a survey of her class. The graph shows the information she gathered.

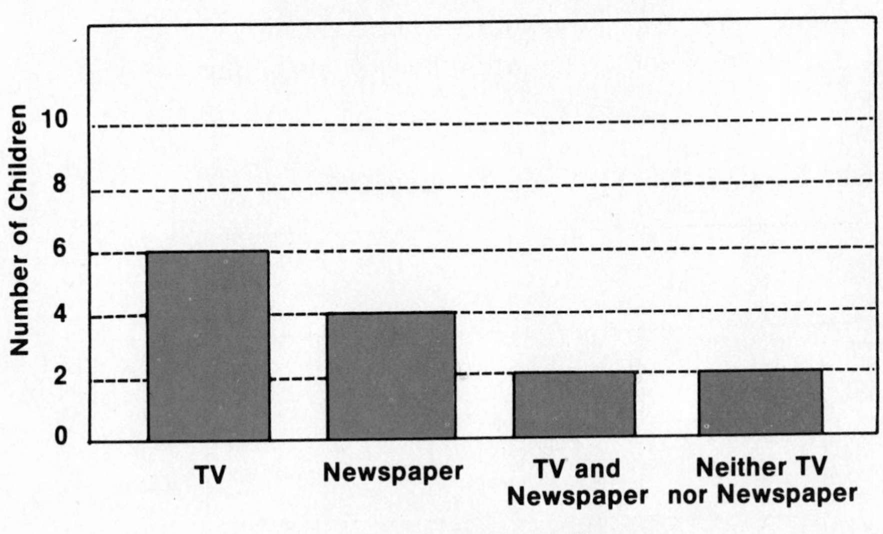

Use the graph to answer each question. Write the answer.

1. How many watch the news only on TV?
2. How many read the news only in newspapers?
3. How many learn the news from TV and newspapers?
4. How many do not watch or read the news?

Sample Answer **1.** Six children watch the news only on TV.

A Factual Paragraph

Thinking About a Factual Paragraph

People write paragraphs for many reasons. Some paragraphs give directions. Other paragraphs describe something.

Another kind of paragraph tells about something you have learned. This kind of paragraph uses facts.

Facts give you information about a topic. You can find facts by reading a book. You can ask people who know about a subject. You can also read a graph. Remember that a graph shows facts in picture form. Always be sure to check that facts are correct before you use them.

Mr. Pearson's class asked questions to find out how students traveled to school. The graph shows what they found.

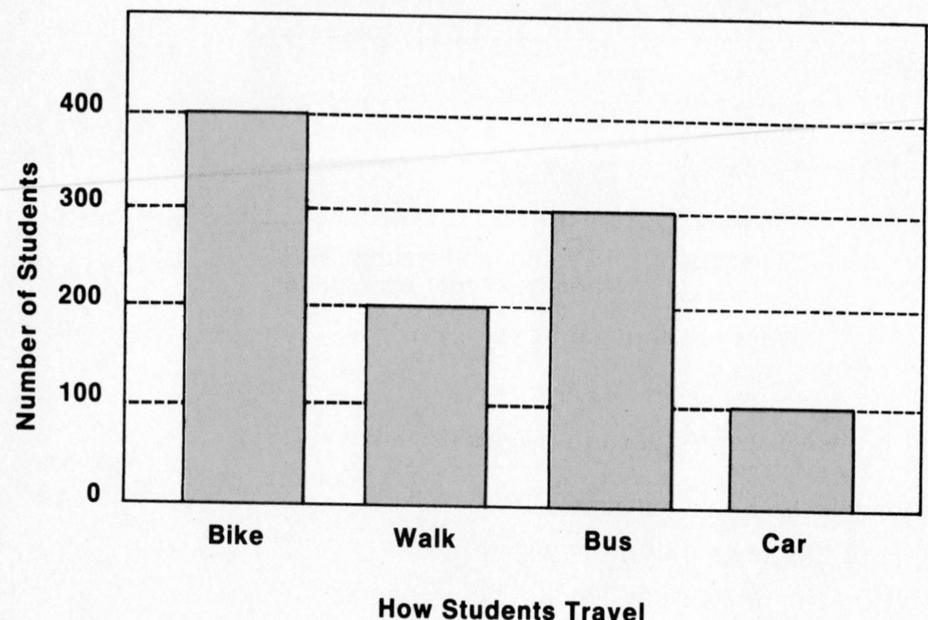

Edit Your Letter

Read your letter again. Use the questions below.

1. Have you checked all the facts in the body of your letter?
2. Does your letter have the date, a greeting, a closing, and your name?
3. Do the verbs agree with the subject in your sentences?
4. Are capital letters, commas, and periods used correctly?
5. Are all words spelled correctly? Check the Word Bank.

Editing Symbols

≡ capitalize
¶ indent
take out
^ add

Correct any mistakes. If you need to, write your paragraph again.

INDEPENDENT WRITING

A Friendly Letter

Prewriting One important kind of a friendly letter is a thank-you letter. Suppose the school librarian brought several books to your class. You might write a thank-you letter to the librarian. Jot down notes that tell facts such as how many students read each kind of book, which kind of book was most popular, and why the students liked that kind.

Kind of Books	Number Read
sports	12
travel	4
mystery	14
history	6

Writing Write a thank-you letter to the librarian. Reread your notes and use the chart to help you. Review the friendly letter on page 102 to make sure all the parts of your letter are written correctly.

Editing Use the check questions and the editing symbols above to edit your letter.

Unit Review

Read each sentence. Write the verb. *pages 76–77*

1. People sell many things.
2. Weavers make rugs.
3. A man plays music.
4. Children sing along.
5. The girls dance.
6. The visitors watch.

Write the verb that appears in each sentence. Then write whether each verb is in the past, present, or future tense. *pages 78–79*

7. People climb mountains.
8. Visitors will walk.
9. No cars pass through.
10. Elena visited India.
11. Tom enjoyed the trip.
12. The friends will return.

Write the correct verb for each sentence. *pages 78–82*

13. Many people ____ in Japan. (live, lives)
14. My friends ____ a house by the water. (have, has)
15. Mei often ____ fish. (catch, catches)
16. Miko ____ tea for us. (prepare, prepares)
17. We ____ Japan every year. (visit, visits)

Write the correct form of each verb in the present tense. *page 82*

18. Ann ____ the water. (splash)
19. Joe ____ the boats. (watch)
20. Kim ____ the boat. (fix)
21. Ted ____ the ball. (catch)
22. Ed ____ the bat. (pass)
23. Bob ____ home. (rush)

Write the correct form of each verb in the past tense. *pages 86–87*

24. People in China ____ a way to make paper. (invent)
25. The Chinese ____ the first books. (print)
26. People from Europe ____ Asia long ago. (visit)
27. People ____ to Europe with many new ideas. (return)

Write the correct form of the main verb. *pages 88–91*

28. Doris has ____ about Japan all year. (talk)
29. Mr. Jones has ____ in Japan for a month. (live)
30. Mrs. Jones has ____ for a Japanese company. (work)
31. Doris and Jack have ____ several plays. (attend)
32. The Jones family has ____ many interesting things. (do)
33. The Garcias have ____ to Mexico for a month. (go)
34. Mr. Garcia has ____ good things about it. (say)
35. Mrs. Garcia has ____ many friends. (find)
36. The Garcias have ____ new foods. (eat)
37. The children have ____ some famous places. (see)

Read each sentence. First write the verb in the present tense. Then write the verb in the past tense. *page 93*

38. The ink ____. (dry)
39. The father ____. (worry)
40. Jan ____ to school. (hurry)
41. Lana ____ very hard. (try)

Now you will write a friendly letter.

42. The parts of a letter are below. The parts are not in order. Put the parts in the right order. Then write the letter. *pages 102–105*

a. Mary
b. This morning we began our vacation. We got in the car and traveled for four hours without stopping. My brother and I played tic-tac-toe. Later we ate lunch at a state park.
c. December 22, 19__
d. Your Friend,
e. Dear Randy,

A Story from Outer Space

Would you like to take a trip to Mars? Astronauts have already landed on the moon. The planet Mars may be the next landing place for earth travelers.

In this story Miss Pickerell goes to Mars. In this chapter she is learning to travel in outer space. Look at the *Words to Think About*. They will help you understand the story.

Words to Think About

orbit, the path of a planet as it moves around other planets

calculate, to figure out something ahead of time

re-calibrate, to check or mark a scale more than once

Destination Mars

A strange change took place in Miss Pickerell. All this time she had been wanting to get home to her cow and her rock collection. She had been impatient. She had been bored. She had looked forward to nothing but her return to the earth.

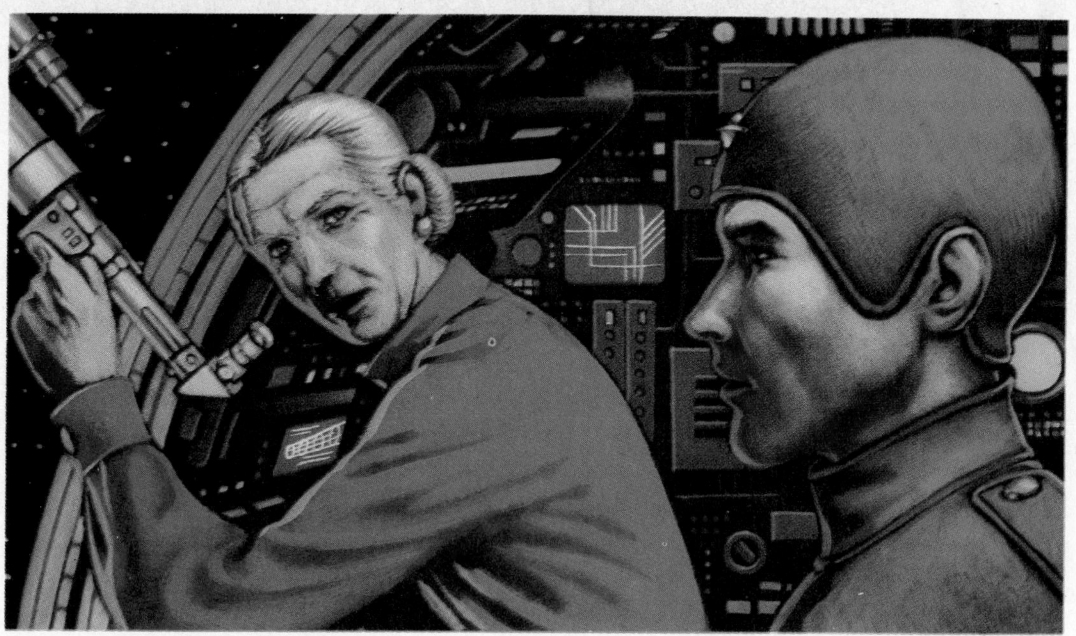

Now, however, she suddenly found herself wanting to go on. She no longer wished to go back. She felt a wild excitement of anticipation. Miss Pickerell knew now how explorers must feel. She almost ached with eagerness. She felt that if they couldn't somehow get to Mars, the disappointment would be so great she wouldn't be able to stand it.

"That is Mars, isn't it?" she asked Mr. Killian hopefully, when he came to relieve her at the eyepiece.

"Oh, sure," said Mr. Killian.

Miss Pickerell sighed with relief. "About how far away would you say it was, Mr. Killian?"

"About 10 or 15 million miles," Mr. Killian said airly.

"Oh...Well, then, I suppose it will be quite a little while before we get there."

"*If* we ever do!"

"You mean we might run out of—out of fuel?" Miss Pickerell was alarmed.

"Don't have to worry about that. Using atomic fuel."

"Oh, good!" said Miss Pickerell. She remained hovering in the air behind Mr. Killian, too excited to go back to her bunk and rest. "As long as Mars is in such plain sight why can't we just point the ship directly at it?"

"Wouldn't work," Mr. Killian said. "On account of the orbit. You know about orbits?"

"I know the earth has an orbit," Miss Pickerell said. "I know that the earth travels around the sun. And I know it takes the earth a whole year to go all the way around its orbit"

"Mars does the same thing," Mr. Killian said. "All the planets do. All the planets move in orbits around the sun. Some of them have bigger orbits because they are farther away from the sun. And some of them take longer."

"How long does it take Mars to go around its orbit?" Miss Pickerell asked.

"Almost twice as long as the earth takes. Mars is farther away from the sun than the earth is."

Miss Pickerell thought about this for a minute. "Mr. Killian, if the earth is moving all the time in an orbit, and if Mars is moving all the time in its orbit, then, at this very minute, we must be right between the earth's orbit and Mars's orbit."

"That's right."

"I begin to understand now," Miss Pickerell said. "Of course we can't point the ship right at Mars, because by the time we got where Mars is now, Mars would be somewhere else—somewhere else along its orbit."

"Sure. Another thing makes it complicated. An orbit isn't round. More like a hoop that's been squeezed in on two sides."

"Dear me!" Miss Pickerell said. "It *is* very complicated, isn't it? Oh, I *do* hope we'll be able to figure out just the right place to steer toward, so that this ship and Mars will get there at the same time."

"Nobody could do that but Haggerty," Mr. Killian said, "because we're moving so fast ourselves. This ship has

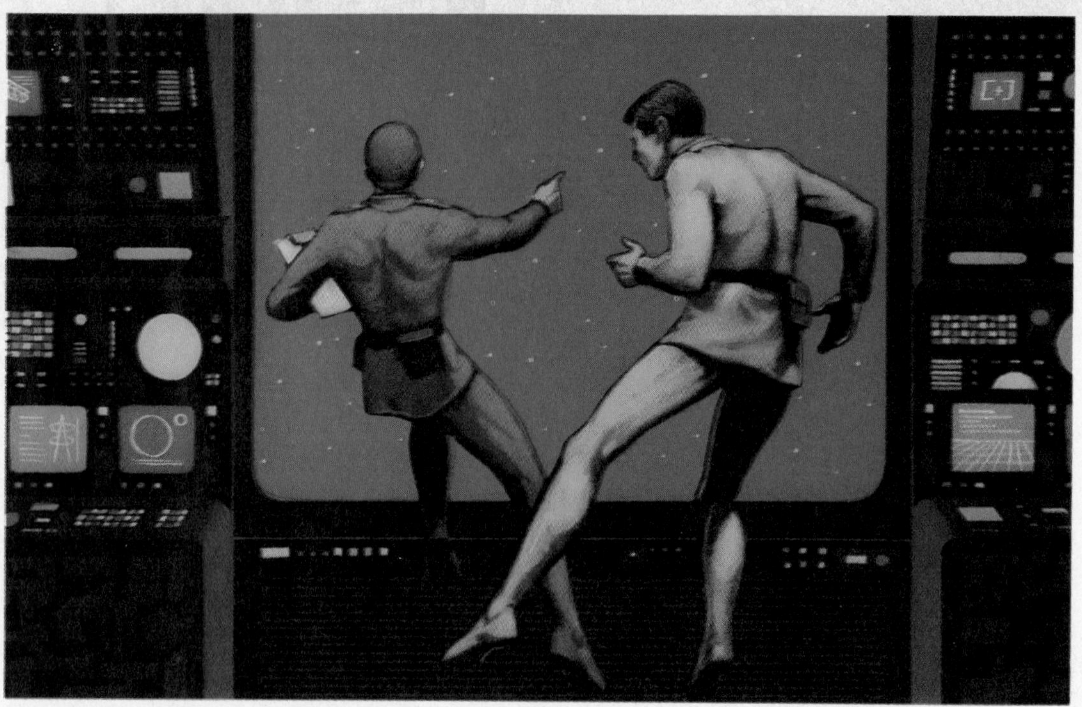

a sort of orbit, too. Only hope is that the original calculations were correct."

Their suspense about original calculations came to an end that very day, when the last of the instruments had been re-calibrated and reset into the panel.

Mr. Killian made a number of adjustments, and the captain hovered right behind him.

"Well," the captain asked. "What about it, Mr. Killian? Are we on our course? Will we get to Mars?"

Mr. Killian moved away from the panel and referred to a chart fastened to the wall. He returned and took readings from the instruments.

"Yes," he said. "We're on our course, sir. We'll get to Mars all right."

"Oh, good!" Miss Pickerell said, pressing her hands tightly together.

The captain turned and looked at her oddly. “I was under the impression, Miss Pickerell, that you wanted to get home as fast as possible.”

“Oh, well!” Miss Pickerell said. “That was before. I didn't think such a thing was possible then. But now—why, now I wouldn't miss going to Mars for anything in the world. I don't even mind if we get back too late for the state fair.”

“We will,” Mr. Killian said. “Much too late.”

Ellen MacGregor

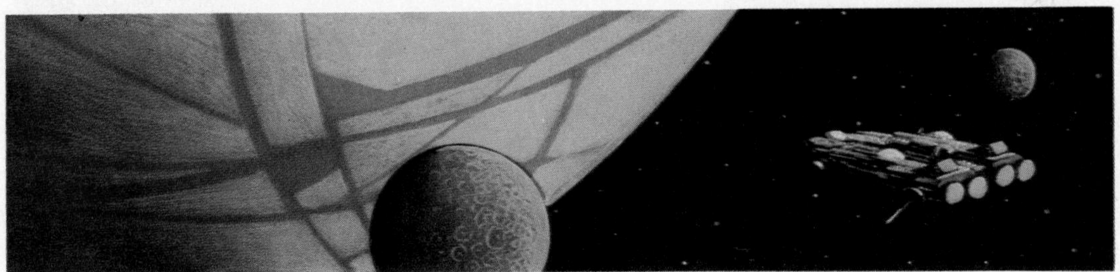

Creative Activities

1. **Creative Writing** Miss Pickerell will be away for a long time. Write a letter to Miss Pickerell. Tell her what is happening on Earth while she is away.

2. **Creative Writing** Write a paragraph to tell how Miss Pickerell feels about going 10 to 15 million miles away to Mars. Write another paragraph to tell how you would feel if you were going to Mars.

3. The other planets are Mercury, Venus, Jupiter, Saturn, Uranus, Neptune, and Pluto. Earth and Mars are between Venus and Jupiter. Your class can make a model of all the planets in orbit around the sun.

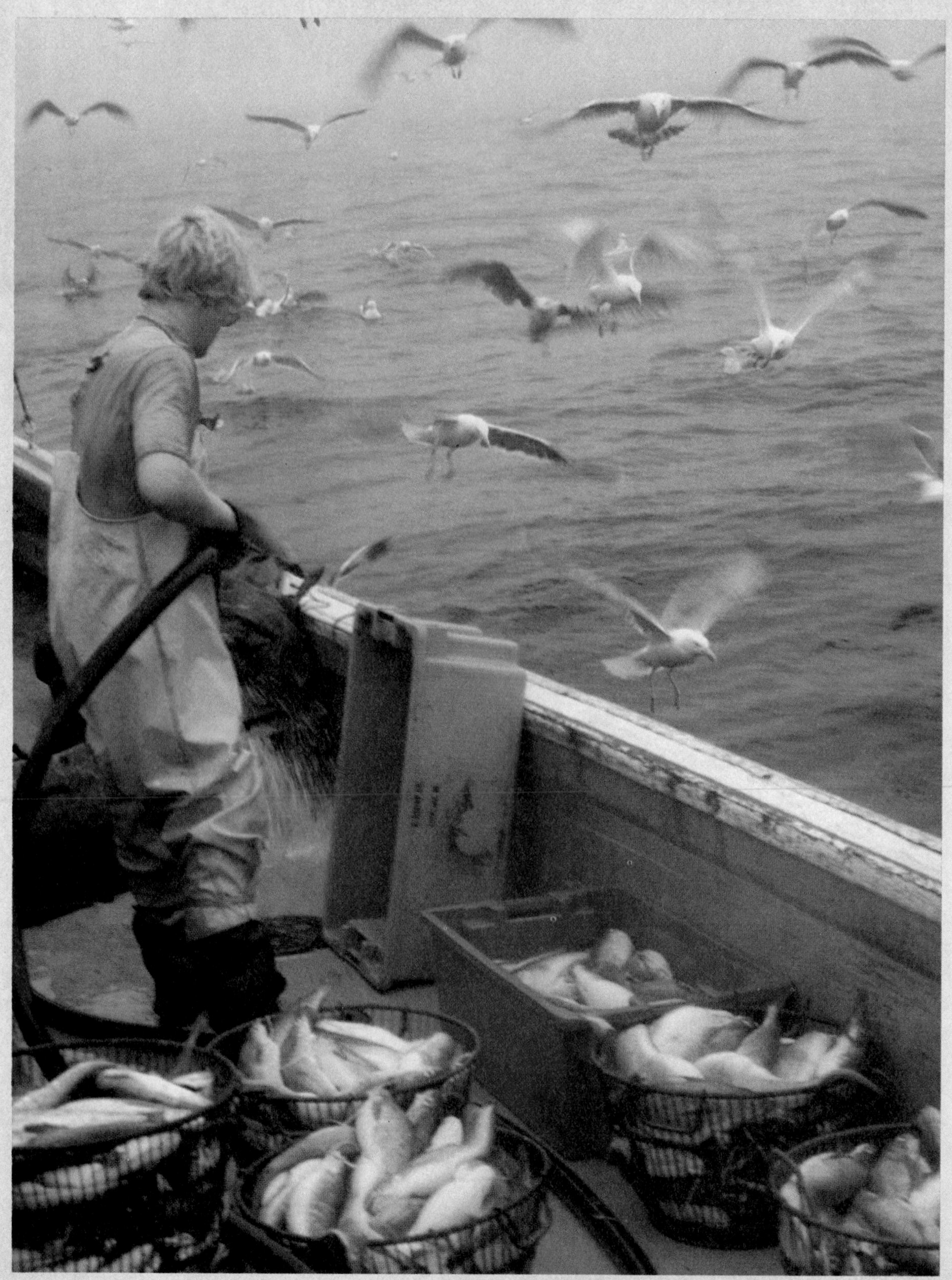

FISHING OFF THE COAST OF MAINE

Grammar and Related Language Skills

Pronouns
Using Pronouns
Pronouns with Verbs
Possessive Pronouns
Using Pronouns After Verbs

Practical Communication

STUDY AND REFERENCE SKILLS
Using the Library

COMPOSITION
Writing a Story

Creative Expression

A Legend

Fishing is an old and important profession. Fishers and other workers need to keep up with changes in their professions. Have you read or heard about the kinds of modern equipment used in fishing today? What speaking skills would help you describe new methods of fishing? What listening, speaking, and writing skills help people who do this kind of work?

Pronouns

A *noun* is a word that names a person, a place, or a thing. Special words can be used in place of nouns. They are called *pronouns*.

> A **pronoun** is a word that takes the place of one or more nouns.

- Suppose your name were Adam. Without pronouns you would have to speak about yourself like this:

  Adam cooks many different kinds of food. Then Adam serves the food that Adam cooks.

- Now read these sentences. The sentences are different in one way.

  I cook many different kinds of food.
  Then I serve the food that I cook.

This time the pronoun *I* is used in place of the noun *Adam*. Notice how much better the sentences sound.

- Look at the words in the box below. The words on the left are pronouns. These pronouns are used in sentences.

I	My name is José. I drive a bus.
you	Do you drive a bus, too?
he	Miguel drives a bus. He drives a city bus.
she	Juana drives a bus. She drives in the country.
it	The bus stops often. It stops on every street.
we	Miguel and I drive in lots of traffic. We don't like all the traffic.
you	Do you drive taxis?
they	Juana and Sheila drive in the country. They don't meet much traffic.

Talk About It

Read each pair of sentences below. Find the pronoun in the second sentence of each pair.

1. Paul Anders drives a truck. I drive a truck, too.
2. The truck carries things. It travels very fast.
3. Paul's truck carries mail. He drives a small truck.
4. Some people drive in the city. They drive on busy streets.

Skills Practice

Read each pair of sentences. Write the second sentence of each pair. Underline the pronoun in each sentence.

1. Kevin and Lisa baked together. They baked bread.
2. Kevin heated a pan. Then he melted some butter.
3. Lisa counted the eggs. She cracked them into a bowl.
4. Kevin mixed the flour. Then he added other things.
5. Kevin added yeast. It rose in the bowl.
6. Lisa turned on the oven. She turned the oven up high.
7. The bread baked slowly. It turned golden brown.
8. Lisa and Kevin felt hungry. They ate some bread.
9. Lisa and Kevin cleaned the kitchen. They worked hard.
10. Lisa washed the dishes. She dried the dishes, too.
11. Kevin scrubbed the pans. He scrubbed for a long time.
12. Lisa put the pans away. Then she packed the bread.

Sample Answer **1.** They baked bread.

Using Pronouns

A pronoun takes the place of one or more nouns. Now you must choose the correct pronoun for the job.

Suppose you need a pronoun for the noun *bus*. The noun *bus* names one thing. The pronoun *it* takes the place of one thing. The noun *bus* agrees with the pronoun *it*.

- Read each pair of sentences below. Which pronouns take the place of the underlined words?

Uncle Max walks downtown. He owns a bakery.

The bakers help Uncle Max. They bake good things.

Mary visited Uncle Max. She traveled by train.

A man baked bread. He used a huge oven.

The pronouns are in blue boxes. They agree with the underlined words.

- Read the following pair of sentences.

Mary and I visited the city. We traveled by car.

In the second sentence the pronoun *we* takes the place of the noun *Mary* and the pronoun *I*.

The sentences in the box tell you how to choose a pronoun.

> Use I to talk about yourself.
> Use we to talk about one or more persons and yourself.
> Use you to talk directly to one or more persons.
> Use she to talk about one female.
> Use he to talk about one male.
> Use it to talk about one thing.
> Use they to talk about two or more persons or things.

Talk About It

Read each pair of sentences. Tell which pronoun takes the place of the underlined word or words. Explain your answer.

1. Jake bakes the bread. ___ makes corn bread, too.
2. Mrs. Brown makes muffins. ___ makes the muffins quickly.
3. One muffin falls to the floor. ___ breaks into pieces.
4. Jane and I eat some bread. ___ eat too much.

Skills Practice

Read each pair of sentences. Write the second sentence of each pair. Use the pronoun that takes the place of the underlined word or words.

1. Three bakers baked bread. ___ made many kinds.
2. Uncle Max smiled. ___ baked a surprise.
3. A box sat near the oven. ___ held many rolls.
4. One roll fell down. ___ rolled on the floor.
5. Jake baked something good. ___ made corn muffins.
6. Jane and I ate several muffins. ___ drank milk, too.
7. The bakers sliced bread. ___ sliced many pieces.
8. Jane tasted some bread. ___ ate and ate.

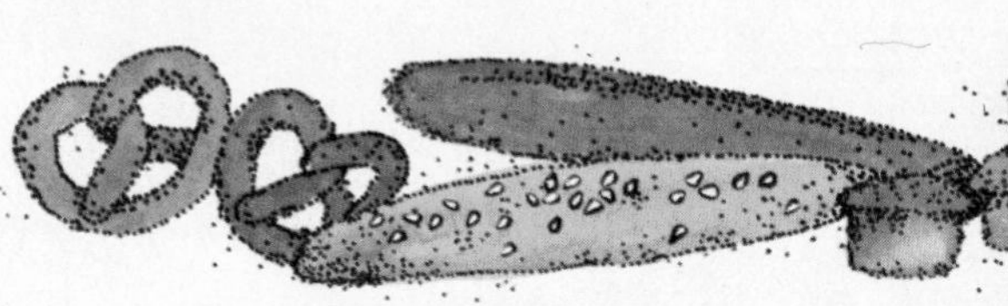

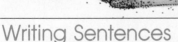

Writing Sentences

Imagine that you are a famous doctor. You work with a group of other doctors. Write four sentences telling about the ways all of you help people. Use the pronouns *I, he, she,* and *we* in your sentences.

Sample Answer **1.** They made many kinds.

Pronouns with Verbs

The pronouns *I, you, she, he, it, we,* and *they* are used in the subject part of a sentence. The *subject part* of a sentence names whom or what the sentence is about. A sentence also has a *verb,* or action word.

- Look at the underlined verbs in the following sentences.

Roberto works in a pet store.
He feeds the animals.

I help in the pet store.
Sometimes you help, too.

The action happens now. The verbs are in the present tense.

Pronouns and verbs must work together in a sentence. They must *agree.*

- Look at the following sentences.

I work in a pet store.
You feed the animals.

We watch the fish.
They swim in a tank.

Notice that no endings have been added to the verbs. A verb in the present tense does not change when it agrees with the pronouns *I, you, we,* or *they.*

- Now look at the sentences below.

He feeds a toad
It jumps around.

She watches a bird.
It catches a worm.

Notice that the verbs end with *-s* or *-es.* The pronouns *he, she,* and *it* work with verbs that end in *-s* or *-es.*

If a verb ends in **s, ss, x, ch, z,** or **sh,** add **-es** to make the correct form of the present tense.

Add **-s** to most other verbs to make the correct form of the present tense.

Talk About It

Read each pair of sentences. Say the present tense form of the verb that agrees with the pronoun. Spell the verb.

1. Ed and I work in a pet store. We ____ on Saturday. (work)
2. Karen and Anna work too. They ____ the puppies. (feed)
3. I feed the birds. I ____ the bird seed. (buy)
4. Ed gets his coat. He ____ home. (rush)

Skills Practice

Write the second sentence of each pair. Use the form of the verb in the present tense that agrees with the pronoun.

1. Pedro looks around. He ____ a lot of animals. (see)
2. Karen feeds the toad. She ____ food for the turtles. (fix)
3. Ed and I watch the toad. We ____ the toad. (watch)
4. The toad looks for more food. It ____ for worms. (wish)
5. The kittens play, too. They ____ in a big cage. (climb)

Writing Sentences

Do you know someone who has an interesting job? Write four sentences telling about that person's work. Use pronouns whenever you can.

Sample Answer **1.** He sees a lot of animals.

More About Using Pronouns

You know that a pronoun takes the place of one or more nouns. But you must be careful when using pronouns. A pronoun can only be used when its meaning is clear.

- Look at the pair of sentences below.

  Wanda feeds the hungry cow.
  Then <u>she</u> walks around the barnyard.

Notice that the meaning of the underlined pronoun is unclear. In the second sentence it isn't clear whether Wanda or the cow walks around the barnyard. In this case either the noun *Wanda* or *cow* should have been repeated. The pronoun *she* should not have been used. The second sentence above should have said:

Then <u>Wanda</u> walks around the barnyard.

- Look at these pairs of sentences. Tell whether you should use the underlined pronoun in the second sentences.

Carlos fed the rooster.
<u>He</u> ate quickly.

Michelle fed the pigs.
<u>They</u> like vegetables.

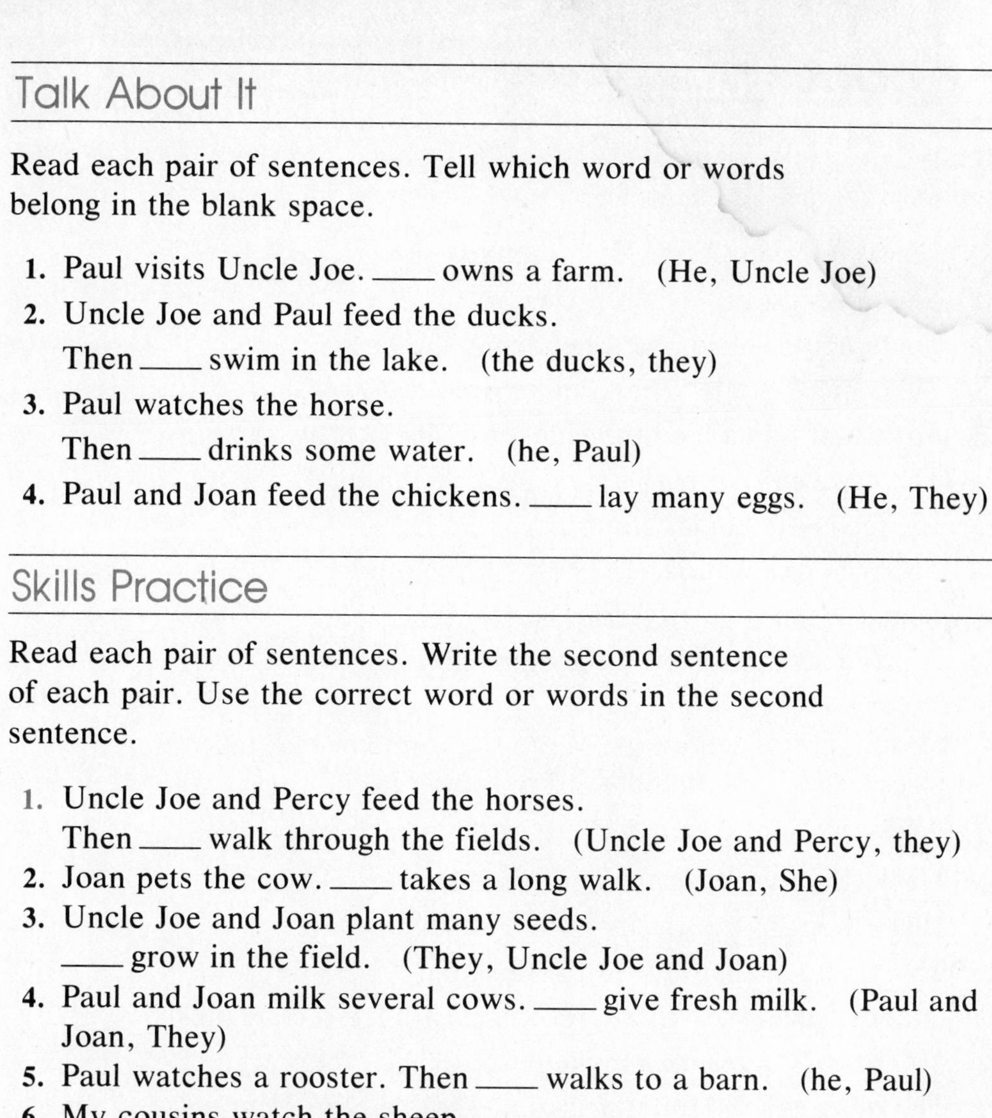

Talk About It

Read each pair of sentences. Tell which word or words belong in the blank space.

1. Paul visits Uncle Joe. ____ owns a farm. (He, Uncle Joe)
2. Uncle Joe and Paul feed the ducks.
   Then ____ swim in the lake. (the ducks, they)
3. Paul watches the horse.
   Then ____ drinks some water. (he, Paul)
4. Paul and Joan feed the chickens. ____ lay many eggs. (He, They)

Skills Practice

Read each pair of sentences. Write the second sentence of each pair. Use the correct word or words in the second sentence.

1. Uncle Joe and Percy feed the horses.
   Then ____ walk through the fields. (Uncle Joe and Percy, they)
2. Joan pets the cow. ____ takes a long walk. (Joan, She)
3. Uncle Joe and Joan plant many seeds.
   ____ grow in the field. (They, Uncle Joe and Joan)
4. Paul and Joan milk several cows. ____ give fresh milk. (Paul and Joan, They)
5. Paul watches a rooster. Then ____ walks to a barn. (he, Paul)
6. My cousins watch the sheep.
   ____ drink some water. (They, The sheep)
7. Sandra sees the cow.
   Then ____ walks away. (she, the cow)
8. Joan and Sandra pick some wild flowers.
   ____ dance in the grass. (They, Joan and Sandra)
9. Paul helps Uncle Joe. ____ carries the milk. (He, Paul)
10. Joan gives Sandra some bread. ____ likes bread. (She, Sandra)

Sample Answer 1. Then Uncle Joe and Percy walk through the fields.

Skills Review

Read each pair of sentences. Write the pronoun in the second sentence of each pair.

1. Joe works on a farm. He often cuts the grass.
2. The grass grows fast. It grows very tall.
3. Sonja helps Uncle Joe. She cleans the barn.
4. Susie helps Sonja. They both work very hard.
5. Susie and Sonja feed the chickens. They throw the corn.
6. The chickens eat corn. They peck at the food.
7. Joe feeds the horse. He brushes the horse, too.
8. The pigs roll around. They roll in the mud.
9. Sonja watches quietly. She laughs at the pigs.
10. A crow screams a lot. It screams all day.

Read each pair of sentences. Write the pronoun that takes the place of the underlined word or words in the first sentence.

11. Uncle Dan works in the circus. ____ trains elephants.
12. Diane went to the circus. ____ saw Uncle Dan.
13. Many animals live there. ____ do funny tricks.
14. Other people work there, too. ____ care for the animals.
15. Mr. Rogers cares for monkeys. ____ feeds them well.
16. The monkeys did funny tricks. ____ stole Kim's hat.
17. Kim and I saw a clown. ____ both like clowns.
18. Uncle Dan pointed up. ____ pointed to a wire.
19. A lady walked on the wire. ____ smiled from high up.
20. The wire swings. ____ moves back and forth.

Read each pair of sentences. Write the form of the verb in the present tense that agrees with the pronoun.

21. Jan and I visit Ms. Sato. We ____ Ms. Sato. (watch)
22. Ms. Sato works hard. She ____ telephone lines. (fix)

23. Ms. Sato likes her job. It ____ her busy. (keep)
24. Jan waves to Ms. Sato. She ____ from the ground. (watch)
25. Ms. Sato finishes with the tools. They ____ into a sack. (go)
26. Jan and I meet Mr. Crow. He ____ skyscrapers. (build)
27. Mr. Crow works high up.
    He ____ at the top of skyscrapers. (work)
28. Jan and I talk about the job. It ____ hard. (look)
29. Jan sees the elevator. It ____ Mr. Crow up. (take)

Read each pair of sentences. Write the correct words to complete the second sentence.

30. The girls sell books. ____ spend the money. (The girls, They)
31. The cook calls the customer. ____ answers. (He, The customer)
32. The kitten sees the mouse. ____ runs inside. (The mouse, It)
33. My friends climb trees. ____ are tall. (The trees, They)

Unclear pronouns can often give you a strange or funny picture of something. Read each pair of sentences below. What kind of funny picture do you get from these sentences?

My uncle feeds the pig.
Then he rolls in the mud.

Betty feeds the cow some hay.
Then she drinks grape juice.

Exploring Language

Possessive Pronouns

Special pronouns show who or what has something. They are called *possessive pronouns*. A possessive pronoun must agree with the noun or nouns it replaced.

- Look at this example.

Mr. Brown owns a store. His store sells clothing.

Mr. Brown is one man. The possessive pronoun *his* shows what Mr. Brown has or owns.

- Look at the pairs of sentences below.

Ms. Gray runs a tugboat.
Her boat helps large ships.

Meg and I sailed with Ms. Gray.
Meg and I liked our trip.

Captains waved from far off.
Their ships passed by.

The whistle blew.
Its sound rang out.

The second sentence in each pair has a possessive pronoun. That pronoun agrees with the underlined word or words in the first sentence.

These sentences tell you how to choose a possessive pronoun.

> Use my to tell what you, yourself, have.
> Use your when you are talking directly to one or more people and telling them what they have.
> Use his to tell what one male has or owns.
> Use her to tell what one female has or owns.
> Use its to tell what one thing has.
> Use our to tell what you and one or more other people have.
> Use their to tell what two or more people have.

Talk About It

Read each pair of sentences. Use the correct possessive pronoun to fill in each blank space.

1. Mr. Trent flies an airplane.
   ____ plane flies fast.
2. You rode in the plane.
   ____ ride lasted a long time.
3. The plane made noise.
   ____ noise finally stopped.
4. Eva and I rode in the plane.
   ____ trip was fun.

Skills Practice

Read each pair of sentences. Write the second sentence with the correct possessive pronoun.

1. Dave's pipes broke.
   ____ basement flooded.
2. Cindy saw the flood first.
   ____ warning helped Dave.
3. The dog swam by.
   ____ tail wagged.
4. The plumber brought her case.
   She removed ____ tools.
5. We looked around.
   ____ job begins now.
6. The Smiths brought snacks.
   ____ help was needed.

Writing Sentences

Imagine that you and your friends find an old chest in your grandmother's cellar or attic. Your grandmother lets you share what is inside with your friends.

Write four sentences about the things you and your friends find. Try to use possessive pronouns.

Sample Answer **1.** His basement flooded.

Using Pronouns After Action Verbs

Some pronouns are used in the subject part of a sentence. They are *I, you, she, he, it, we, you,* and *they.* They come before an action verb.

You can also find pronouns in the predicate part of a sentence. Here is a list of pronouns. They come after an action verb.

me	us
you	you
him, her, it	them

A pronoun in the predicate part must agree with the noun it replaces.

- Read each pair of sentences. The predicate part of each sentence is in a pink box. Notice which pronouns take the place of the underlined nouns in the predicate part.

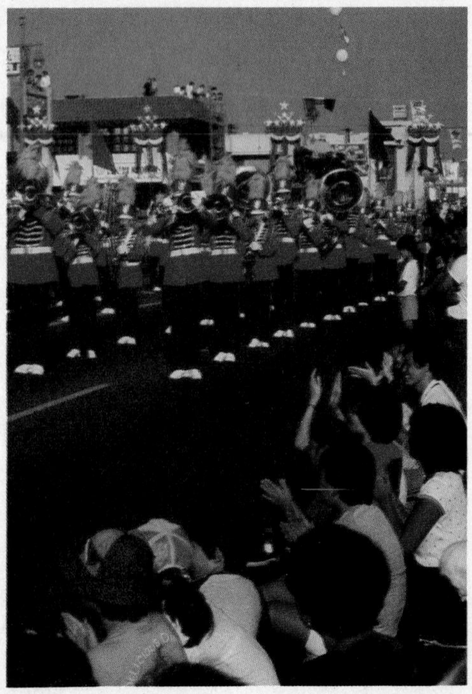

Al and Jay call the bandleader.

The players call him.

A sound startles Patty.

The tuba startles her.

The drummer sees Tom and me.

The drummer sees us.

Tony plays the drum.

Tony plays it.

Peter greets the musicians.

Peter greets them.

Talk About It

Read each pair of sentences. In the first sentence of each pair, some words are underlined. Tell which pronouns can be used in the second sentence to replace the underlined words.

1. Tanya helped Mary.
   Tanya helped ____ .
2. Sam sees Jim and me.
   Sam calls ____ .
3. Mr. Miller sees Joan and Bill.
   Mr. Miller watches ____ .
4. Jody brought the package.
   Jody carried ____ .

Skills Practice

Read each pair of sentences. In the first sentence of each pair, some nouns are underlined. Write the second sentence. Use the correct pronoun in place of the underlined words.

1. Mr. Reda calls the musicians.
   Mr. Reda calls ____ .
2. Tyrone checks the drum.
   Tyrone adjusts ____ .
3. Mr. Reda hears Jody and me.
   Mr. Reda hears ____ .
4. Mary and Jan see Mr. Reda.
   The girls call ____ .
5. Jack lost the music.
   Tom found ____ .
6. The band marches past Stacy.
   The band marches past ____ .
7. Stacy sees Greg and me.
   Stacy sees ____ .
8. Mike drops the drumsticks.
   Sam grabs ____ quickly.
9. Mike thanks Sam.
   Mike thanks ____ .
10. The band pleases Mrs. Jones.
    The band pleases ____ .

Words Often Confused

Some words sound exactly alike. These words are called *homonyms. Homonyms* sound alike but have different spellings and different meanings.

- Read the following sentences. Look at the underlined words.

The farmers finished their jobs.
They put the hay over there.

How are these words different? They have different spellings and different meanings. *Their* shows what two or more people have. It is a possessive pronoun. *There* means *in that place.*

- Read the following sentences.

Two farmers fed the horses.
They fed the cows, too.
Then the farmers went to the field.

Look at the underlined words in the above sentences. *Two* means the numeral *2. Too* means *also* or *more than is needed. To* means *in the direction of.*

- Now read these sentences. Look at the underlined words.

It's closing time at the zoo. The elephant closes its eyes.

In the first sentence you see *it's* spelled with an apostrophe ('). *It's* is a short word for *it is.* In the second sentence *its* has no apostrophe. *Its* is the possessive pronoun. *Its* means the eyes *of the elephant.*

Talk About It

Read each sentence. Tell the correct word for each blank space. Spell each word.

1. Pedro has a job at the zoo. ____ a hard job. (It's, Its)
2. He fed the monkeys ____ bananas. (there, their)
3. I fed them some bananas, ____. (to, too, two)

Skills Practice

Write each sentence. Use the correct word for each blank space.

1. The monkeys ate ____ bananas quickly. (to, too, two)
2. One monkey ate ____ many bananas. (to, too, two)
3. Uncle Pedro took us ____ the elephants. (to, too, two)
4. He went inside to give them ____ bath. (their, there)
5. The smaller tiger played with ____ friend. (its, it's)
6. ____ time to go home. (Its, It's)
7. We visited ____ for three hours. (there, their)

Writing Sentences

Write four sentences. Use each word below in one sentence.

1. their
2. there
3. to
4. too

Sample Answer 1. The monkeys ate two bananas quickly.

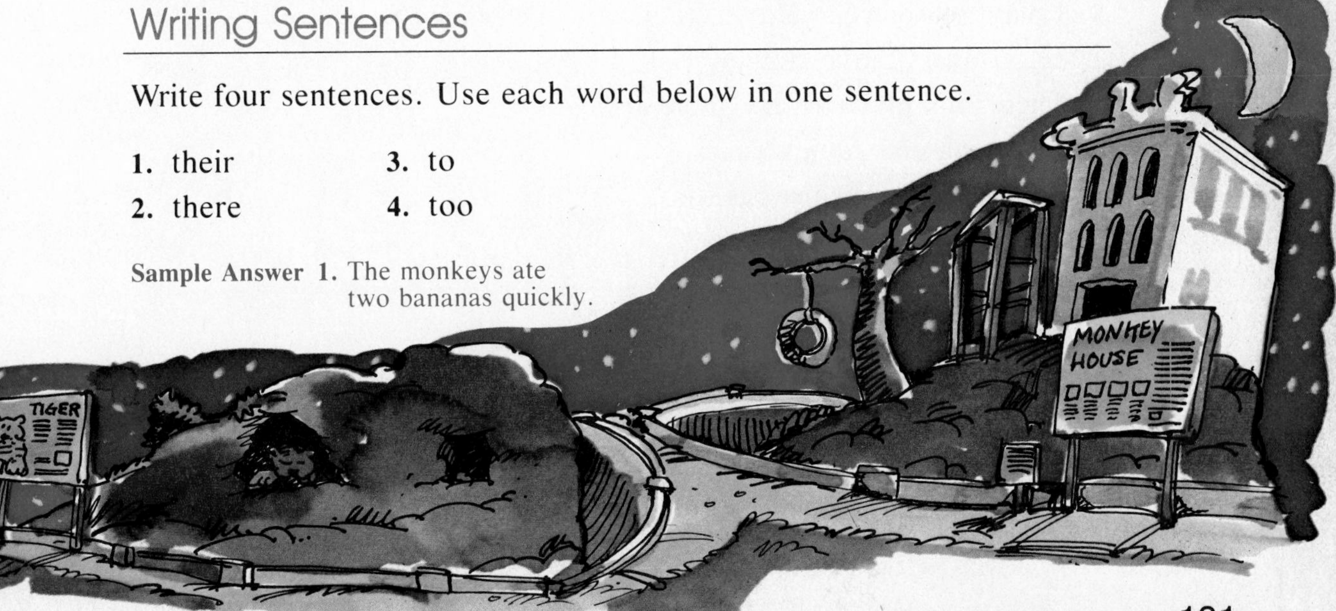

Skills Review

Read each pair of sentences. Write the correct possessive pronoun to fill in each blank space.

1. Mr. and Mrs. Rosen grow vegetables every year.
   ____ farm grows fruit, too.
2. Mr. Rosen just bought a new tractor.
   ____ tractor makes a lot of noise.
3. The cows watch Mr. Rosen.
   ____ heads turn as Mr. Rosen rides by.
4. I often work for Mr. Rosen.
   ____ job is to help at the fruit stand.
5. Mrs. Rosen also teaches music.
   ____ students learn a lot.
6. Sam and Tom play many songs together.
   ____ fingers move very quickly.
7. Jeff and I listen to Sam and Tom.
   We clap ____ hands.
8. Sandra plays a song and sings.
   ____ voice is very nice.
9. I play two pieces next.
   ____ fingers move slowly.
10. Then John plays a very short march.
    ____ song ends quickly.
11. Mrs. Rosen writes songs, too.
    She often plays ____ songs.
12. You play now.
    It's ____ turn.
13. We enjoy the lessons.
    ____ teacher waves good-by.

Skills Review

Read each pair of sentences. In the first sentence of each pair, some nouns are underlined. Write the pronoun to fill in each blank space. Use the correct pronoun in place of the underlined words.

14. Mother baked bread.
    We enjoyed eating ____ .
15. Mr. Smith helped Tom.
    Mr. Smith showed ____ how.
16. Ms. Mario called Sue and me.
    Ms. Mario asked ____ .
17. We heard Stacy and Jay.
    We heard ____ .
18. Mrs. Edwards thanked Jane.
    Mrs. Edwards thanked ____ .
19. Leon repaired the bikes.
    Leon fixed ____ .

Read each sentence. Write the correct word for each blank space.

20. Mae and Ron finished ____ work. (there, their)
21. The books are over ____ . (there, their)
22. Mae works ____ or three hours each day. (to, too, two)
23. ____ pleasant work for her. (It's, Its)
24. The office has ____ own library. (it's, its)
25. She walks ____ the office every day. (to, too, two)
26. Ron usually walks, ____ . (to, too, two)

Some words in the English language sound alike. But the words have different spellings and meanings. Here is a list of some pronouns that sound like other words. Try to make up a sentence using each word.

PRONOUN	SOUND ALIKE	MEANING
I	eye	
you	ewe	female sheep
we	wee	very small

Using the Library

A library is a good place to read, to study, and to prepare for reports. It is divided into three main parts to help you find books quickly and easily.

One part of the library has books that are fiction. *Fiction* tells stories about people and things that are not real. All fiction books are arranged in alphabetical order by the author's last name.

You will find nonfiction books in another part of the library. *Nonfiction* books tell facts. They are arranged by subjects. Books about history are arranged together. Books about science are arranged together. Other subjects are arranged together in this way, too.

Reference books are in the third part of the library. *Reference books* give facts about many different subjects. The dictionary, encyclopedia, and atlas are reference books that you can find in the library.

Every library has a file of all its books. The file is called the *card catalog*. The card catalog has drawers with many cards. All the cards are arranged in alphabetical order. When you want to find a certain book, you use the card catalog. There are three kinds of cards.

- Look at these sample cards:

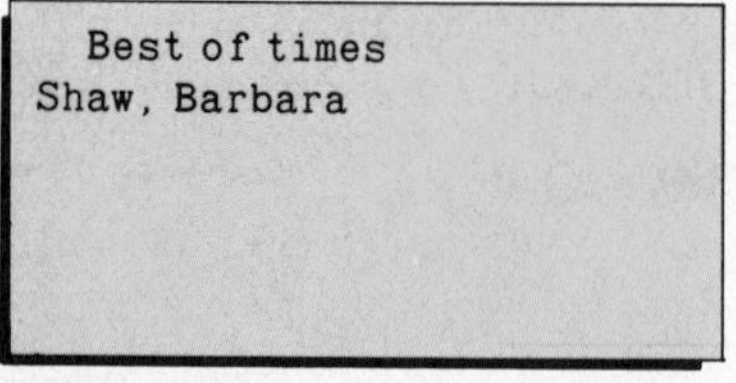

1. The *title card* lists a book by its title.

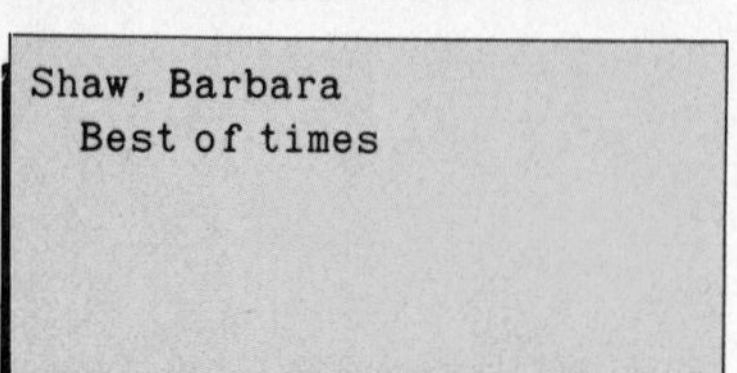

2. The *author card* lists a book by the author's last name.

```
FARM LIFE--FICTION
Shaw, Barbara
  Best of times
```

3. The *subject card* lists a book by the subject of the book.

Talk About It

Answer each question about the library.

1. How are fiction books arranged?
2. How are nonfiction books arranged?
3. What are some reference books?

Would you use a *title card,* an *author card,* or a *subject card* to find each book?

4. A book about gardens
5. A book called *Winnie the Pooh*
6. A book by Lewis Carroll

Skills Practice

In what part of the library would you find each book? Write **fiction, nonfiction,** or **reference.**

1. A story of Paco's dream
2. An encyclopedia
3. A book about insects
4. A story about Ben's club
5. A dictionary
6. A story of Tamu's adventures

What card in the card catalog helps you find each book? Write **title card, author card,** or **subject card.**

7. A book by Pamela Travers
8. A book about spiders
9. A book called *Henry Huggins*
10. A book about wolves

Sample Answers 1. fiction; **7.** Author card

Interviewing Skills

Thinking About Interviews

There are many ways to learn about people. Suppose your class has been studying interesting people in your town. One way to find information is by interviewing the person. In an interview one person asks questions about something the other person has done. The person who asks the questions is called an *interviewer*.

The first step in planning your interview is to invite the person to be interviewed. An *invitation* tells the day, time, and place for the interview. You should also give your phone number. Then the person can call and say if he or she is coming.

Can you come for an interview?

Name: Rafael Perez

Place: 10 Park Lane, Room 227

Date: April 14, 19–

Time: 2 o'clock **Phone No.** 568-0993

You have been asked to interview a famous author who lives in your town. First you would send the author an invitation like the one above. Then you would prepare a list of questions to ask. Your list might have the following questions:

When did you become interested in writing?
Did you have any special training?
How did you decide what to write about?

Talking About Interviews

1. What is the first step in planning an interview?
2. What information would you include in the invitation?
3. What famous person would you like to interview?
4. What questions would you ask that person?

Preparing for an Interview

Think of someone you would like to interview. Do the following things to prepare for the interview:

1. Write an invitation. Be sure to include the person's name and a day, time, and place for the interview. Remember to give your phone number.
2. List questions you would use in the interview.

Careers

Some people make a living by interviewing other people. An *interviewer* might work for a newspaper, a magazine, or a TV or radio station. Sometimes people write books based on interviews. Interviewers must be able to organize many things. They must study about many subjects. Interviewers must speak and write very well. They must also be good listeners.

A Story

Thinking About a Story

Think of all the stories you hear, see, and read each day. Your friend might tell you a story in school. You may watch a story on television. You also might read a story in a book.

Every story has a plot. The *plot* is the action of the story. Everything that happens to the characters is part of the plot.

A story is often divided into two parts. The first part tells who the characters are. It also tells when and where the action takes place. The second part tells what happens as the action continues. Often a character faces a problem. The story ends by telling what finally happens to the characters.

Here is a two-paragraph story:

One morning Dave was driving his truck along a busy road. There was a long line of cars behind him. Dave came to a low, overhead bridge. His truck was a little too high to pass under the bridge. Dave stopped and got out of the truck. The drivers behind him started to honk their horns.

Dave rested against the truck. He wondered what he should do. Finally he got an idea. He let a little air out of the tires. Then the truck was low enough to pass under the bridge. The other drivers smiled as Dave finally started to travel again.

Talking About a Story

Read the story on the other page.

1. Who are the characters in the story?
2. When and where does the story take place?
3. What problem does Dave have? Which paragraph of the story tells about the problem?
4. How does Dave solve his problem? Which paragraph tells how he solves his problem?

Writing a Story

Below are seven sentences that tell a story. The sentences are not in the right order. Change the order of the sentences so the story has a beginning, a middle, and an end. Then write the whole story on your paper. Remember to indent the first sentence.

1. Sam liked the idea.
2. He began carrying large stones down the hill.
3. Slow Sam decided one morning to build a house at the bottom of a hill.
4. So he carried each stone back up the hill and then rolled it down.
5. The stranger suggested that Sam roll down the stones instead of carrying them.
6. A stranger watched what Sam was doing.
7. He wanted to use large stones to build his house.

Practicing a Story

Thinking About Your Story

You can write a two-paragraph story. Look at the pictures below. Decide on an idea for the plot of your story. Remember to think about the characters in the story. Think about a problem your characters may have.

Writing Your Story

1. Begin your first paragraph by writing two sentences that describe the characters in your story.
2. Continue the paragraph with one or two sentences that tell when and where the story takes place.
3. Add three or four sentences that tell about a problem the characters have.
4. Begin your second paragraph with two or three sentences that tell how the characters try to solve the problem.
5. Complete the second paragraph with two sentences that tell what finally happens to the characters.

Edit Your Story

Read your story again. Use the questions below.

1. Does your story describe your characters clearly?
2. Did you describe when and where the story takes place?
3. Do your sentences clearly tell what happened to the characters?
4. Did you use pronouns correctly?
5. Did you indent the first word in each paragraph?
6. Are capital letters and periods used correctly?
7. Did you spell all words correctly?

Correct your mistakes. If you need to, write your story again.

Editing Symbols

≡ capitalize
¶ indent
take out
∧ add

INDEPENDENT WRITING

A Two-Paragraph Story

Prewriting Think of the different kinds of stories you can write. Do you like mysteries or adventure stories? Do you prefer sports stories or tall tales? Look at these titles for four kinds of stories. Choose one or use your own idea.

MYSTERIES	ADVENTURE
The Case of the Vanishing House	*Alone on an Island*
SPORTS STORIES	TALL TALES
The Day We Lost the Big Game	*Flippo the Floppy Fly*

Then make notes about the characters and the plot.

Writing Write a story using your notes. If you need help in writing, you can follow the plan on page 140.

Editing Use the check questions and the editing symbols above to edit your story.

Written and Oral Book Reports

Thinking About a Report

You have probably read many interesting books about people. Suppose you wanted to tell your class about a particular book. You might write a report or give an oral report about the person in the book.

When you write your own book report, use this form to help you.

Name________________________

My Book Report

Title________________________

Author________________________

____

____

____

____

____

1. Write your name, the book's title, and the author.
2. Write a main idea sentence about the main character.
3. Write four or five detail sentences that tell what the main character thinks, says, or does.

Sometimes you will give an oral report. Write notes about the things you will say. Read your notes again. Put them in an order that makes sense. Use the written book report form as your guide. Before you speak, practice with a friend or a tape recorder. Remember to use these rules when you speak.

1. Face your listeners. Look at them as you speak.
2. Stand up straight.
3. Make sure your voice is loud and clear so that everyone can hear you.
4. Speak slowly and carefully so that everyone can understand you.
5. Tell your listeners where they can get the book if they want to read it.

Talking About a Book Report

Read what Sandra said about a book she read.

The name of the book I read was *Martin Luther King* by Jack Smith. It tells about the life of Martin Luther King, Junior. He wanted all people to be free. He often talked about his dreams of freedom. Dr. King hoped that someday everyone would be treated in the same way. He worked with many people. He asked both rich and poor people to join in the fight for equal rights. Martin Luther King was a very important man. If you want to read the book about him, you will find it in the school library.

1. How did Sandra begin her oral report?
2. What is the title of her book? Who is the author?
3. Who is the main character in the book?
4. Which sentences tell details about the character?
5. How did Sandra end her report?

Writing or Presenting a Book Report

You may do an oral or a written book report. Think about a book you have read. Decide which character to speak or write about. Make notes about the things you will say. Put your notes in order.

1. Give the book's title and author.
2. Give one sentence that presents a general idea of the character in the book.
3. Give three other sentences that tell what the character thought, said, or did in the book.

If you decide to give an oral talk, remember to review the rules for speaking in front of a group.

Unit Review

Read each pair of sentences. Write the pronoun in the second sentence of each pair. *pages 116–117*

1. Some people fish for fun. They fish for a living.
2. Stan likes to fish. He fishes in a small boat.
3. Kate often fishes, too. She uses worms for bait.
4. Anna and Ken use fly hooks. They use worms, too.

Read each pair of sentences. Write the pronoun that takes the place of the underlined word or words. *pages 118–119*

5. <u>Maria</u> catches fish. ____ fishes on a boat.
6. <u>The boat</u> moves fast. ____ sails over waves.
7. <u>Maria and I</u> fish all day. ____ fish until dark.
8. <u>Juan and Maria</u> make dinner. ____ fry the fish.

Read each pair of sentences. Write the form of the verb in the present tense that agrees with the pronoun. *pages 120–121*

9. Tim and Pam own a bakery.
   They ____ hard. (work)
10. Pam prepares the dough.
    She ____ it well. (mix)
11. Tim lights the ovens.
    He ____ the bread. (bake)
12. Mike and I buy a loaf.
    We ____ the bread. (enjoy)

Write the second sentence of each pair. Use the correct word or words to fill in the blank space. *pages 122–123*

13. John and Ellen feed the ducks.
    Then ____ go for a swim. (they, the ducks)
14. John and Ellen pick some flowers.
    Then ____ walk to the house. (they, John and Ellen)
15. The cat watches a bird.
    Then ____ flies away. (it, the bird)
16. The dog follows the chicken.
    Then ____ returns to the house. (it, the dog)

Read each pair of sentences. Write the correct possessive pronoun to fill in each blank space. *pages 126–127*

17. Anne drives a train. ____ work is interesting.
18. The train goes fast. ____ engine chugs.
19. Tim calls Anne. ____ voice is loud.
20. Ed and I drive trains, too. ____ jobs are hard.

Read each pair of sentences. In the first sentence of each pair, some nouns are underlined. Write the second sentence. Use the correct pronoun in place of the underlined words. *pages 128–129*

21. Yesterday we bought tomatoes. Today we ate ____.
22. Tom and George saw the kitten. They followed ____.
23. Mother covered Tim. Mother covered ____.
24. The librarian called Bob and me. The librarian called ____.
25. Mrs. Arenas thanked Mary. Mrs. Arenas thanked ____.

Read these sentences from a story. They are not in order. Change the order so the story has a beginning, a middle, and an end. Then write the story. *pages 138–141*

26. a. Then Lou got an idea.
    b. Sid held the money for the peaches in his hand.
    c. He took a long stick and put gum on the end of it.
    d. One afternoon Sid and Lou were walking to town.
    e. That is how the boys got the money out of the hole.
    f. They planned to buy peaches for their dinner.
    g. He tripped and the money rolled into a deep hole.
    h. Lou lowered the stick into the hole and pressed the gum against the money.
    i. Sid could not reach the money in the hole.

A Legend

Legends are a kind of folk tale. They tell about real or imaginary people and places. Legends about real people tell about their special qualities. Legends about imaginary heroes describe their unusual abilities.

The legend of Paul Bunyan describes an imaginary character with amazing size and strength. It tells how he used these abilities to help clear America's great forests. Try to imagine each event as you read the story.

There may be some words that are new to you. Look at the *Words to Think About*. They will help you understand the story.

Words to Think About

mighty, having great power

lumberjack, one who cuts down trees

logger, one who cuts down trees

tidal waves, swift powerful ocean waves

rapids, part of the river where the water is swiftest

sawmill, place where logs are sawed into lumber

feat, act or deed

crowbar, bar of iron or steel

Paul Bunyan and His Boyhood

Many tales are told of Paul Bunyan the giant woodsman. Mightiest hero of the North Woods! A man of great size and strength who was taller than the trees of the forest. He had such strength in his huge arms that they say he could take the tallest pine tree and break it in two with his bare hands. They tell of his mighty deeds and strange adventures from Maine to California.

He could outrun the swiftest deer, and cross the wildest river in one stride! Even today lumberjacks who work in the woods find small lakes and point out, saying:

"Those are the footprints of Paul Bunyan that have been filled with water."

A giant logger was Paul and he chopped down whole forests in a single day. And he and his woodsmen logged off North Dakota in a single month! His axe was as wide as a barn door and had a great oak tree for a handle. It took six full-grown men to lift it!

They say that he was born in Maine and even as a baby

he was so large that his mother and father had to have fourteen cows to supply milk for his porridge. Every morning when they looked at him he had grown two feet taller. They built a huge cradle for Paul and floated it in the ocean off the coast of Maine. The ocean waves would rock him to sleep.

One day he started bouncing up and down in his cradle and started a seventy-foot tidal wave that washed away towns and villages. After that Paul's folks gave up the idea of a floating cradle and took Paul with them into the Maine woods. Here they felt he could be kept out of mischief.

Paul spent his boyhood in the woods and helped his father cut down trees. They sawed the trees into logs and tied them together into large rafts which were floated down the river to the sawmills. Even as a boy he had the strength of twelve men and could ride a raft through the wildest rapids in the river.

One day the man at the sawmill refused to buy the logs. They were too large for his mill to cut up into lumber. So Paul chained them together again and pulled the raft back up the river to his father's camp. Imagine his dad's surprise to see young Paul wading up the river towing the great raft of logs behind him!

Everybody liked young Paul, and for miles around they told of his great feats of strength: of how he took an iron crowbar and bent it into a safety pin to hold together a rip in his trousers; of how at another time he came to the end of the field he was plowing with two oxen and having no room to turn the plow and oxen around, picked up the plow, oxen and all, and turned them around to start back the other way.

Yet Paul never boasted. When people asked him how strong he was he just laughed. And when Paul laughed the folks in the villages ran into their houses and hid in the cellars, thinking it was a thunderstorm!

In spite of his huge size, Paul was as quick as lightning. They say he was the only man in the woods who could blow out a candle at night and hop into bed before it was dark.

Being so quick on his feet was once his undoing. He was out in the woods hunting one day and shot at a bear. Paul was anxious to see if he had hit, and ran lickety-split toward it, only to get there before the shot he had fired. The result was that he received a full load of his own buckshot in the seat of his breeches.

When Paul was full grown he decided he wanted to become the greatest lumberjack in America and perform great feats of logging. He dreamed of leading his men through wondrous adventures in the great forests of the West.

Creative Activities

1. **Creative Writing** Imagine being introduced to Paul Bunyan. Think of questions to ask him. Write an interview between you and Paul Bunyan.

2. A *collage* is a picture made of small pieces of paper or cloth. It can also be made from pictures cut from old magazines. Try making a collage that shows an event from Paul Bunyan's boyhood.

Mid-Year Review

Read each group of words. Write **sentence** if the group of words is a sentence. Write **not a sentence** if the group of words is not a sentence. *pages 2–3*

1. Travels through space.
2. Two astronauts.
3. A spaceship lands on Mars.
4. The astronauts explore.
5. Collects information.
6. Scientists report to Earth.

Read each sentence. Decide which kind of sentence each one is. Write **declarative, interrogative, exclamatory,** or **imperative.** *pages 4–5*

7. Ask about the journey.
8. How long did it take?
9. It took nearly ten months.
10. How red the rocks are!
11. Do you feel cold?
12. Take this pack.

Some signals are missing in each sentence. Write each sentence so that it begins and ends in the right way. *pages 6–7*

13. would you go in a spaceship
14. look at the spaceship
15. what a strange sight it is
16. scientists learn many things
17. will you help the scientist
18. read this report

Read each sentence part in the box. Write whether each one is a **subject part** or a **predicate part.** *pages 10–11*

19. [A rocket] blasts off.
20. [Many people] watch.
21. The spaceship [travels fast.]
22. Space explorers [work hard.]
23. [Astronauts] study space.
24. The stars [shine.]

Write each sentence. Use commas where they are necessary. *pages 14–15*

25. Did John leave on Monday October 25 1982?
26. No he left on the following day.
27. Susan when did he return from his trip?

Mid-Year Review

Write each noun. Write **singular** beside each singular noun. Write **plural** beside each plural noun. *pages 38–42*

28. Sparrows fly to branches.
29. The robin sees the worms.
30. The crows have feathers.
31. A nest sits in a tree.
32. The birds sing all day.
33. The bees gather nectar.

Read each sentence. Following each sentence is a singular noun. Write the plural form of the noun. *pages 38–42*

34. Jan washes the ____. (dish)
35. The ____ bark. (puppy)
36. The ____ laugh. (child)
37. Ann has the ____. (box)
38. The ____ peek out. (mouse)
39. Tom sees the ____. (bear)

Write each sentence correctly. Use capital letters. *pages 48–49*

40. My sister visits peter.
41. Jason climbs pikes peak.
42. José sees niagara falls.
43. Lee lives near lake erie.
44. Judy saw the pacific ocean.
45. Jim flew to denver.

Write each address correctly. *pages 48–49*

46. ms Catherine Wilson
16 wesley rd

47. miss Sharon Hill
56 tall trees rd

48. dr Ming Chen
63-14 river st

49. mr Joe Hinds
22 spring ave

Following each sentence is a singular or plural noun. Write each sentence using the correct possessive form. *pages 50–51*

50. The ____ pets jumped into the pond. (children)
51. The ____ toys fell into the water. (boys)
52. ____ dog lost a bone. (Joan)
53. A ____ eggs sit in the nest. (bird)
54. The children looked for the ____ boat. (men)

Mid-Year Review

Write the correct form of the verb in the present tense. *pages 78–82*

55. Edward ____ out. (rush)
56. A baby ____ water. (splash)
57. Taro ____ down. (dig)
58. Theresa ____ sand. (mix)
59. She ____ castles. (build)
60. She ____ them over. (push)

Write the correct form of the verb in the past tense. *pages 86–87*

61. They ____ off. (stroll)
62. The ship ____ away. (sail)
63. The waves ____ out. (move)
64. He ____ his sister. (help)
65. Water ____ us all. (splash)
66. Lunch ____ good. (taste)

Write the correct form of the main verb. *pages 88–91*

67. The friends have ____ to Bermuda. (go)
68. Stephen has ____ some letters to his sister. (write)
69. Most of the people have ____ on a ferryboat. (ride)
70. The children have ____ their breakfast. (eat)

Read each sentence. First write the verb in the present tense. Then write the verb in the past tense. *pages 92–93*

71. James ____ the meal. (plan)
72. Beth ____ the salad. (try)
73. Amy ____ the food. (carry)
74. Tom ____ a plate. (drop)

Read each pair of sentences. Write the pronoun that takes the place of the underlined word or words. *pages 118–119*

75. Jeff plays the piano. ____ practices daily.
76. The piano sounds beautiful. ____ looks pretty, too.
77. Allison sings well. ____ voice is lovely.
78. Jeff and Allison perform. ____ will have a concert.
79. Toni and I listen to them. ____ enjoy their music.

Mid-Year Review

Read each pair of sentences. Write the form of the verb in the present tense that agrees with the pronoun. *pages 120–121*

80. Jane works Saturdays. She ____ bicycles. (fix)
81. The Smiths have a shop. They ____ clothes. (sell)
82. Abe works in a forest. He ____ for fires. (watch)

Write the second sentence of each pair. Use the correct word or words to fill in the blank space. *pages 122–123*

83. Janet sees Tina. ____ calls to her friend. (She, Janet)
84. The dog chases a rabbit. ____ runs fast. (The rabbit, It)
85. Luis and Maria call the boys. ____ say hello. (Luis and Maria, They)
86. Sandra watches Sue. Then ____ takes a walk. (Sandra, she)

Read each pair of sentences. Write the possessive pronoun that belongs in each blank space. *pages 126–127*

87. The Isaacs own a store.
____ store sells sweaters.

88. You write plays.
____ plays are funny.

89. Peter bought a flute.
____ flute is new.

90. Julia flies airplanes.
____ days are long.

Read each pair of sentences. In the first sentence of each pair, some nouns are underlined. Write the second sentence. Use the correct pronoun in place of the underlined words. *pages 128–129*

91. We bought flowers.
We liked ____ .

92. Dad took Greg and me.
Dad drove ____ .

93. The crowd cheered Ann.
The crowd cheered ____ .

94. I lost my sweater.
Jody found ____ .

95. Carlos answered James.
Carlos wrote ____ .

96. We saw Tim and Jed.
We called ____ .

TELEVISION CAMERA CREW

Grammar and Related Language Skills

Review of Sentences
Simple and Compound Subjects
Subjects and Verbs
Building Sentences
Using Commas
Punctuating Conversations

Practical Communication

STUDY AND REFERENCE SKILLS
Test-Taking Skills

COMPOSITION
Writing a Conversation

Creative Expression

A Play

Do you know how people produce a television program? A camera operator must listen well to the directions of the program's director. The operator must act quickly to shoot a scene correctly. Many camera operators shoot scenes in unusual places. What listening and speaking skills would help a camera operator do a job well?

Reviewing Sentences

You sent your first message when you were born. You cried. Now you can send your messages with sentences instead of tears. A *sentence* is a group of words that state a complete idea.

- Read each group of words. Which groups are sentences?

A baby.	A baby sends a message.
Our class.	Our class writes news articles.

A message may use more than one kind of sentence. Each kind of sentence states an idea in a different way.

A **declarative sentence** is a sentence that tells something. Declarative sentences end with a period (**.**).

An **interrogative sentence** is a sentence that asks something. Interrogative sentences end with a question mark (**?**).

An **exclamatory sentence** is a sentence that shows excitement or strong feeling. Exclamatory sentences end with an exclamation mark (**!**).

An **imperative sentence** is a sentence that tells or asks someone to do something. Imperative sentences end with a period (**.**).

Remember,

Use a **capital letter** to begin the first word of every sentence.

Every sentence has a subject part and a predicate part. The *subject part* names whom or what the sentence is about. The *predicate part* tells what action the subject does.

- Read each sentence. Find the subject part and the predicate part.

Mark | writes the news.   His friend | takes pictures.

The subject parts are in blue boxes. The predicate parts are in red boxes.

Talk About It

Tell what kind of sentence each one is. Tell how each sentence should begin and end.

1. what a big day this is
2. what happens today
3. give me a clue
4. our newspaper comes out

Skills Practice

Write each sentence. Make each sentence begin and end in the right way.

1. who takes the pictures
2. hand Tim the funnies
3. what a story she tells
4. this artist draws well
5. how nice the news looks
6. who wrote the sports page

Read each sentence below. Look at the part in the box. Write **subject part** if it is a subject part. Write **predicate part** if it is a predicate part.

7. My sister Rita | seeks more news for the paper.
8. Her teacher | helps her.
9. The school librarian | tells her about some new books.
10. Some of the children | read the books about plants.

Sample Answer 1. Who takes the pictures?

Simple Subjects

In some sentences the subject part has only one word. In other sentences the subject part may have several words. The *subject part* of a sentence names whom or what the sentence is about.

- Read these sentences. The subject part of each sentence is in a blue box.

Children work. The busy children work hard.

In the second sentence the subject part has several words. Children is the main word. The other words in the subject part are *The* and *busy*. They tell something about *children*. The main word, *children*, is called the simple subject.

> The **simple subject** is the main word in the subject part.

- Read each sentence below. The subject part is in a blue box. The simple subject is underlined.

The students walk into the busy newsroom.

My friend sits at a desk.

Our whole class visits the newsroom.

The reporters work hard.

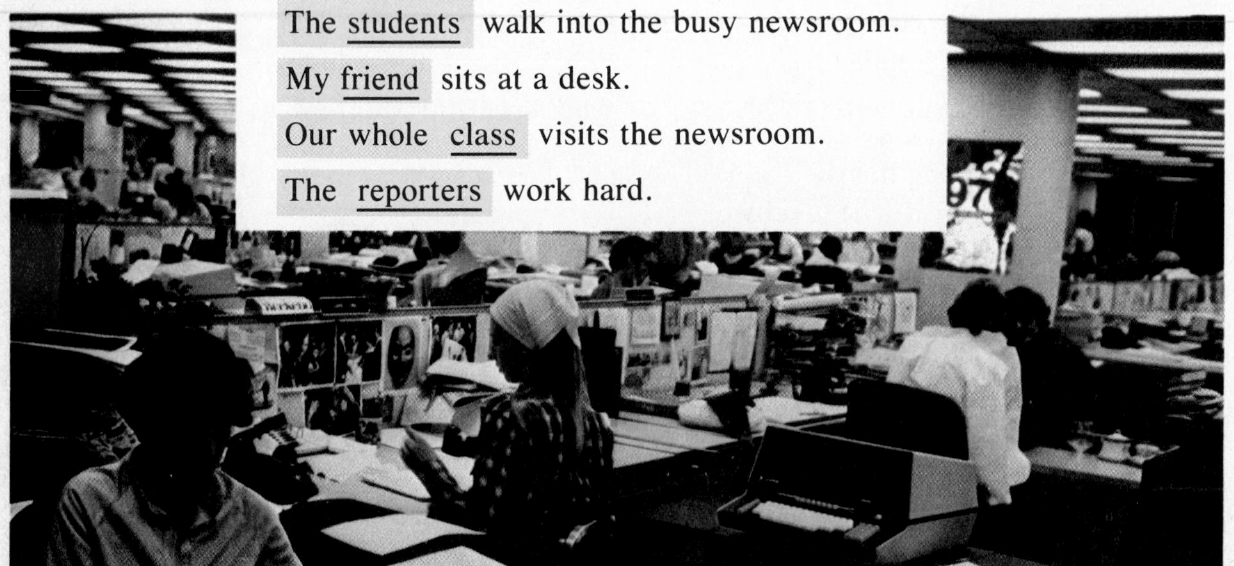

Talk About It

Read each sentence. What is the subject part? What is the simple subject?

1. One woman types a story.
2. Her fingers move quickly.
3. Another reporter watches.
4. Three telephones ring.
5. A lion escaped from the zoo.
6. Two reporters rush out.

Skills Practice

Write each sentence. Draw one line under the subject part. Draw a second line under the simple subject.

1. A woman throws some pictures on a desk.
2. A tall man chooses one of the pictures.
3. People work hard upstairs.
4. Busy artists draw new ads.
5. A man shows his art work.
6. The workers start the huge presses.
7. Big wheels whirl on the presses.
8. The busy printers hurry with the newspaper.
9. One machine folds the newspapers.
10. Big trucks deliver the newspapers.

Writing Sentences

Imagine that a lion escapes from a zoo. You are a reporter. Write four sentences. In each sentence use *lion* as the simple subject. Use *escapes* as the verb. Make up a different subject part for each sentence. Underline the subject part. For example, you might write: A big, fierce lion escapes from the zoo.

Sample Answer 1. A woman throws some pictures on a desk.

Compound Subjects

The simple subject is the main word in the subject part of a sentence.

- Look at these sentences. The simple subjects are underlined.

New machines break sometimes. New wires break sometimes.

A sentence sometimes has two or more main words in the subject part. A subject part with two or more simple subjects is called a *compound subject*.

- Look at these sentences. Each subject part is in a blue box. The two simple subjects that make each compound subject are underlined. The word *and* joins the two simple subjects.

New machines and wires break sometimes.
Men and women fix them.

A **compound subject** has two or more simple subjects.

Sometimes you will find pronouns in compound subjects. The pronouns that are used in the subject part are *I, you, she, he, it, we,* and *they*. These pronouns help you to tell about people, places, and things without repeating names.

- Read these sentences. Sometimes you use a pronoun with a noun in a compound subject. At other times you use two pronouns in a compound subject.

Max and I watch the workers. He and I wave to one worker.

- Read each sentence again. Notice that the pronoun *I* always comes last in a compound subject.

Talk About It

What is the subject part? Name the simple subjects.

1. Ms. Jackson and Mr. Sacks make telephones.
2. She and Mr. Sacks work together.
3. Carlos and Maria visited their company.
4. He and Maria met other inventors.

Skills Practice

Write each sentence. Draw a line under the subject part. Draw a second line under the simple subjects.

1. My aunt and her friend fix telephone lines.
2. She and Mr. Lansky like their jobs.
3. Dawn and I watched one day.
4. They and we had a picnic at lunchtime.
5. A man and a cat climbed a telephone pole.
6. He and it became frightened.
7. Aunt Grace and Mr. Lansky helped them down.
8. She and he face many problems.
9. Snow and ice bring trouble.
10. Wires and poles fall in a storm.

Writing Sentences

There are many different ways to send messages. You can use a telephone to send a message. You can write a letter to send a message.

Write two sentences telling ways to send a message. Use a compound subject in each sentence. In one sentence, use a pronoun in the compound subject. For example, you might write, "Terry and I made a telephone call."

Sample Answer 1. My aunt and her friend fix telephone lines.

Subjects and Verbs

You know that the simple subject works together with the verb in a sentence. This means that the simple subject and the verb *agree* with one another.

- Look at these sentences. The verbs are in the present tense.

Sarah sends a message. I send a message.

In each sentence above the verb agrees with the underlined simple subject. *Sends* agrees with *Sarah*. *Send* agrees with *I*.

You know that a *compound subject* has two or more simple subjects. A verb must also agree with the compound subject in a sentence.

- Look at this sentence.

Sarah and I send messages.

In the sentence above the compound subject is *Sarah and I*. *Send* is a verb in the present tense. The verb *send* agrees with the compound subject.

- Look again at the sentence in the box. Notice that the compound subject is joined by *and*. When a compound subject is joined by *and*, a verb in the present tense does not change.

- Now read these sentences. The verbs are in the past tense.

William talked on the telephone.

William and Maria talked on the telephone.

In the first sentence *William* is a simple subject. In the second sentence *William and Maria* is a compound subject. The verb *talked* agrees with both subjects. A verb in the past tense does not change.

Talk About It

Read each sentence. Choose the form of the verb that belongs in the blank. Explain your answer.

1. Maria and William ____. (shout, shouts)
2. She and he ____ flags. (wave, waves)
3. Al and I ____ mirrors. (shine, shines)
4. He and Maria ____. (whispers, whisper)
5. Men and women ____. (talks, talk)
6. Boys and girls ____. (listens, listen)

Skills Practice

Write each sentence. Use the correct form of the verb.

1. William and Maria ____ smoke signals. (uses, use)
2. Mary and Selma ____ on the telephone. (calls, call)
3. The girl and her friend ____ a message. (tapes, tape)
4. Letters and tapes ____ through the mail. (travels, travel)
5. Tapes and letters ____ for answers. (waits, wait)
6. William and his friend ____ Maria. (telephones, telephone)
7. You and I ____ on the picturephone. (talks, talk)
8. You and I ____ each other. (watches, watch)

Sample Answer 1. William and Maria use smoke signals.

Skills Review

Write each sentence. Make each sentence begin and end in the right way.

1. what does Mr. Garcia do
2. he works at the radio station
3. mr. Garcia is an announcer
4. how interesting his job is
5. have you heard him speak on the radio
6. we listen to him every day

Read each sentence. Look at the part in the box. Write **subject part** if it is a subject part. Write **predicate part** if it is a predicate part.

7. Our whole class | makes a newspaper.
8. A reporter | finds good stories.
9. The artists | draw the ads.
10. My best friend | takes pictures.
11. Judy's cousin | writes the sports page.
12. Mr. Wilson | helps the whole class.

Read each sentence. Write each subject part. Draw a line under each simple subject.

13. My rock group plays loud music.
14. My older sister sings with us.
15. My sister's friend listens.
16. The drummer beats his drums.
17. The fussy neighbors complain.
18. The new piano player leaves.

Read each sentence. Write the subject part.
Underline the simple subjects.

19. My father and my mother read newspapers.
20. My brother and I read the best parts out loud.
21. Lisa and John write letters.
22. Her brother and my brother write postcards.
23. A bear and its cubs growl.
24. A baby and a kitten make little noises.

Read each sentence. Write the form of the verb that belongs in the blank.

25. Letters and postcards ______. (arrives, arrive)
26. A sailor and a pilot ____ special radios. (uses, use)
27. Toby and Asahi ____ messages by telephone. (delivers, deliver)
28. Luis and Nadia ____ a message. (tapes, tape)
29. My friend and I ____ in sign language. (talks, talk)

Exploring Language

When you use compound subjects, you probably follow a certain rule without even thinking about it. Look at these compound subjects. Can you guess the rule?

You say:

cats and dogs,	but not	animals and dogs.
apples and oranges,	but not	apples and fruit.
roses and daisies,	but not	roses and flowers.

Simple Predicates

You know that the *subject part* of a sentence tells whom or what the sentence is about. The *predicate part* of a sentence tells what action the subject does. The predicate part may have one word or more than one word.

- Look at these sentences. The predicate parts are in red boxes.

Charlie Cowan writes.

Charlie Cowan writes well.

Charlie Cowan writes well each day.

There is one word in each predicate part that is the most important of all. It names the action. That word is *writes*. The word *writes* is called the verb or *simple predicate*.

> The **simple predicate** is the main word or group of words in the predicate part.

- Now read these sentences.

My sister fixes radios.

She repairs TVs.

I watch her often.

In each sentence above, the predicate part is in a red box. The simple predicate is underlined for you.

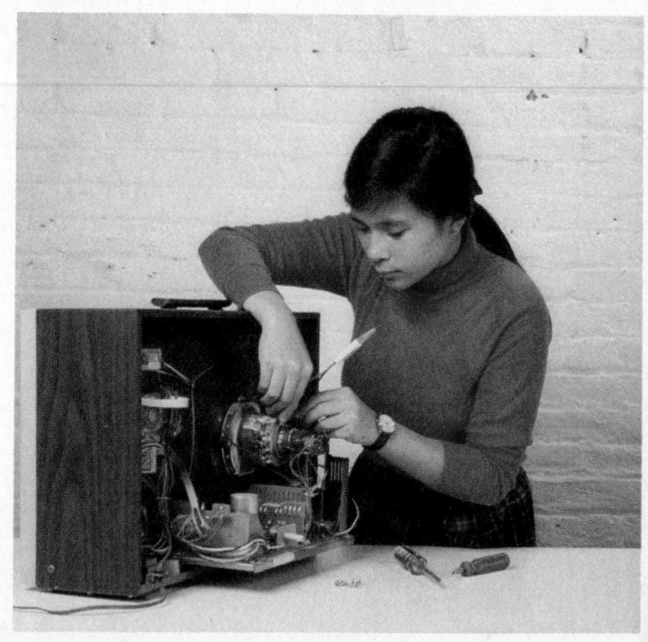

Talk About It

Read each sentence. What is the predicate part? What is the simple predicate?

1. I hear the radio.
2. I hear good stories.
3. I hear the news report.
4. Mom changes the station.
5. She wants some good music.
6. Dad and I listen to the music.

Skills Practice

Write each sentence. Draw a line under the predicate part. Draw a second line under the simple predicate.

1. My mother likes a detective show.
2. She listens carefully.
3. She hears the clues.
4. My mother solves many cases.
5. My sister owns a new radio.
6. She likes loud music.
7. Friends visit after school.
8. My uncle works on a radio show.
9. People telephone him.
10. They ask many questions.

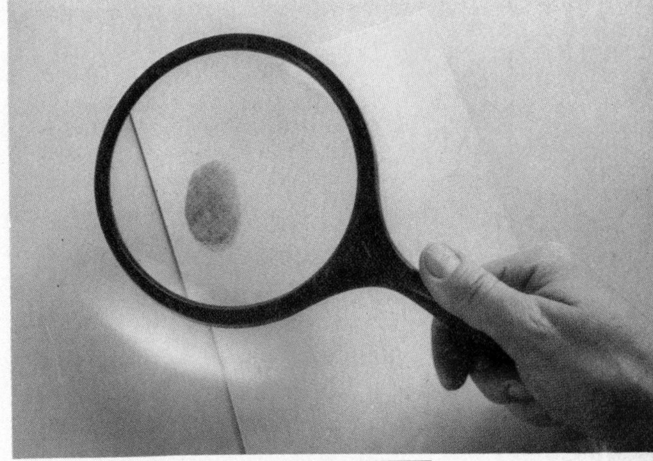

Writing Sentences

Choose four of these simple predicates. Add more words to each simple predicate to make an interesting sentence. Try to tell a story.

peek	type	snoop	rub	squeeze
surprise	finish	touch	shout	knock

Sample Answer 1. My mother likes a detective show.

Building Sentences

You know that every complete sentence must have a *subject part* and a *predicate part*. Some sentences have only one subject and one predicate.

Sometimes you can combine two short sentences to avoid repeating the same words over and over. For example you can combine the subject parts of two sentences to form one sentence.

- Look at these sentences.

Mr. Bell	called.

Mr. Watson	called.

The subject parts in the two sentences are different, but the predicate parts are the same.

- Now read this sentence.

Mr. Bell and Mr. Watson	called.

Notice how the subject parts have been combined to form a new sentence by using the word *and*. The two subject parts form a *compound subject*.

You can also combine the predicate parts of two sentences to form one sentence.

- Look at these sentences.

The inventor	imagined.

The inventor	experimented.

The subject parts in the two sentences are the same, but the predicate parts are different.

- Now read this sentence.

The inventor	imagined and experimented.

Notice how the predicate parts have been combined to form a new sentence by using the word *and*. The two predicate parts form a *compound predicate*.

Talk About It

Read each set of sentences. Tell how to combine subject parts or predicate parts to form one new sentence.

1. Mr. Bell studied. Mr. Watson studied.
2. Mr. Watson listens. Mr. Watson hears.
3. The telephone rings. The telephone works.
4. The scientist talks. The helper talks.

Skills Practice

Combine the subject parts or the predicate parts of each sentence to form one new sentence. Write the new sentence.

1. The telegraph clicks. The telegraph stops.
2. The operator listens. The operator waits.
3. The message begins. The message ends.
4. The operator hears. The crew hears.
5. The search begins. The search continues.
6. Men watch anxiously. Women watch anxiously.
7. Searchlights gleam. Searchlights flicker.
8. Helicopters leave. Boats leave.
9. The searchers return. The passengers return.
10. The people wait. The people rejoice.

Using Commas

You have learned that commas are used to set off words that interrupt a sentence. Sometimes you may begin a sentence with *yes, no,* or *well.* Other times you may begin or end a sentence with the name of a person who is spoken to directly.

Use a **comma** (,) to set off words such as *yes, no,* and *well* when they begin a sentence.

Yes, I read the newspaper this morning.

Use a **comma** (,) to set off the name of a person who is spoken to directly in a sentence.

Here is a letter for you, Lucia.
Tom, would you please answer the door?

Commas are used to separate the name of the day from the date, and the date from the year.

Use a **comma** (,) to separate the name of the day from the date and the date from the year.

Jack had a birthday party on Saturday, October 2, 1982.

Commas also take the place of pauses. Commas help your reader to understand exactly what you mean.

Use a **comma** (,) to separate each noun in a series of three or more nouns.

Chicken, peas, and potatoes cooked in the oven.

Use a **comma** (,) to separate each verb in a series of three or more verbs.

We washed, cooked, and ate the corn.

Talk About It

Read each sentence. Tell how you would use commas.

1. Mary Jane Ming Sam and Alice make movies.
2. Juan will sign fold and mail the letter.
3. No I didn't read the book.
4. Todd will return on Monday December 6 1982.

Skills Practice

Write each sentence. Use commas where necessary.

1. Adam Juan Roger and Carol deliver messages.
2. Karl where is the telephone book?
3. We received the telegram on Monday May 4 1981.
4. Yes Susan got a letter from Carol recently.
5. Reporters research write and edit their stories.
6. Ads stories news and pictures are found in newspapers.
7. No I didn't see the article on sailing.
8. I thought that you had written that story Doris.
9. It was printed on Thursday June 17 1982.
10. Our mail carrier must drive walk and climb stairs all day.

Writing Sentences

Write four sentences using commas.

1. Write a sentence which tells your four favorite foods.
2. Write a sentence which uses three or more verbs to tell how to do something.
3. Write a sentence which tells the name of the day and the date that you did something.
4. Write a sentence beginning with the word *yes*.

Sample Answer **1.** Adam, Juan, Roger, and Carol deliver messages.

Using Context Clues

Have you ever wanted to be a detective? You can be a word detective almost any time you read. You can often be a word detective even when you listen.

Sometimes you may not know the meaning of a word you read or hear. You could look the word up in the dictionary. But that is not always possible. There is another way to find out the meaning of a new word. You discover what a word means by looking for clues in the words and sentences near the new word.

- Read this pair of sentences. What is the meaning of the underlined word? What words give you a clue?

  I sent a <u>messenger</u> to the school.
  He carried a message to my teacher.

The second sentence tells you that someone carried a message to the teacher. Who carried the message? It must have been the messenger. Now you know that a messenger is someone who delivers a message.

Talk About It

Read each pair of sentences. Tell the meaning of the underlined word. Tell what words give you a clue to the meaning.

1. Ms. Johnson bought a new aquarium.
   Her old fish tank leaked.
2. George gave a sudden shriek.
   We all heard his loud cry.

Skills Practice

Read each pair of sentences. Write the meaning of the underlined word.

1. I had a terrible dream last night.
   The nightmare woke me up.
2. Mike said farewell to his old neighbors.
   He said hello to his new neighbors.
3. Mr. Baker's company manufactures radio parts.
   The company also makes TV sets.
4. Sally hummed a melody all day.
   That tune kept running through her head.
5. Gene saw a phantom in the old house.
   He now believes in ghosts.
6. Her boss gave Mary a higher salary.
   She deserved more money for her work.
7. Larry worked as a gaffer for that movie.
   He enjoys working on the lighting.

Sample Answer 1. terrible dream

Punctuating Conversations

When you talk with another person and share ideas, you are having a conversation. When you write a conversation, you follow certain rules.

Use **quotation marks** (" ") around the exact words that each speaker says.

Barry said, "I just finished writing a letter to our brother."

Use a **conversation word** such as *said, shouted,* or *whispered* to show how each person speaks.

Ann **replied**, "I have a letter for him also."

Use a **comma** (,) after the conversation word when the conversation word comes before the speaker's exact words.

Barry added, "I just have to address the envelope."

Put a **period** (.) before the last quotation mark at the end of the sentence when the speaker's words end the sentence.

Ann said, "I will walk to the post office with you."

Put a **comma** (,) before the last quotation mark when a conversation word ends the sentence.

"I am too tired to walk all the way," sighed Barry.

Indent the first word each time the speaker changes.
Capitalize the first word of each quotation.

→"Then we can drop the letter in the mailbox nearest to the house," Ann answered.

Talk About It

Read each sentence. Tell where commas and quotation marks belong.

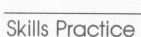

1. Ann said I collect stamps
2. I have a stamp from Canada Barry said
3. Ann answered I get stamps from my penpal
4. I do, too added Barry

Skills Practice

Write each sentence. Use correct punctuation and capitalization.

1. We will go to Spain in June Ann said
2. Barry replied you can meet your penpal
3. Ann said our parents know each other already
4. Your penpal is not a complete stranger Barry answered
5. Ann added I must practice my Spanish
6. I can help you Barry said
7. Ann answered my penpal speaks some English
8. Barry said my parents speak Spanish
9. Ann sighed I am having a hard time
10. I am a good teacher smiled Barry

Writing Sentences

Imagine Ann's meeting with her penpal Maria. Write a conversation for the two girls. The conversation should be four sentences.

1. Write two sentences in which the conversation word comes before the speaker's words.
2. Write two sentences in which the conversation words end the sentence.

Sample Answer 1. "We will go to Spain in June," Ann said.

Skills Review

Read each sentence. Write the predicate part. Underline the simple predicate.

1. Miguel types his work.
2. He types fast.
3. A reporter works hard.
4. I like his job.
5. My aunt writes ads.
6. She paints the pictures.
7. She draws with a pen.
8. I sketch with pencils.
9. I need erasers.
10. One woman finds mistakes.
11. She spells well.
12. She reads fast.
13. I saw the editor.
14. We worked together.

Combine the subject parts or the predicate parts of each sentence to form one sentence. Write the new sentence.

15. The reporter waited. The crowd waited.
16. The actor arrived. The actor waved.
17. The reporter talked. The actor talked.
18. The crowd listened. The crowd cheered.

Write each sentence. Use commas where necessary.

19. Plays skits and shows happen in our school.
20. The actors sing dance and walk on stage.
21. Rita will you come to our play?
22. Yes I plan to attend the first performance.
23. It will be held on Monday November 14 1983.
24. I will see you then Tina.

Read each pair of sentences. Write the meaning of the underlined word.

25. Dad was <u>speechless</u>.
    He couldn't say a word.

26. The movie <u>terrified</u> me.
Tom was scared, too.
27. I have an <u>urgent</u> message.
You must read it at once.
28. The garden is <u>fragrant</u>.
The flowers smell so sweet.

Write each sentence. Use correct punctuation and capitalization.

29. Jean said I just spoke with Uncle Henry
30. He is sending us some books Jean stated
31. Tom added I hope he visits us soon
32. Yes, it has been a long time added Mother
33. Father said perhaps he will come next month

Here are some compound subjects that you can understand in more than one way. See how many different kinds of things you can find in each sentence below by putting commas in different places.

Silk embroidered cotton cloth dolls and needles lay on the table. Ham sandwiches fruit punch corn muffins and nuts sat on the table, too.

Exploring Language

Using Test-Taking Skills

Tests can tell you what you know as well as what you need to study more. You can do better on tests by following a few easy rules.

1. Prepare for taking the test. Be sure to have all the materials you need. You may need pencils, pens, paper, and a ruler. Study the material which will be tested. Get a good night's sleep before the test.
2. Follow directions. Listen carefully if the directions are read to you. Read the directions carefully if they are written. Ask any questions you may have about the directions before you begin.
3. Do not rush. If the test is short enough, read through all the questions before you begin.
4. Mark your answers. Be sure to mark your answers neatly and in the correct manner. You will be told to mark your answers directly on the test paper, in a special answer row, or on a special answer sheet.

Look at the test below.

Choose the right word to complete each sentence. Fill in the circle for the right answer. Write only in the answer row.	**Name** __________ **Date** __________ **Grade** __________ **Answer Row**
1. Many people ____ to that song. **A.** dance **B.** dances **2.** Elena ____ her new boat. **A.** sails **B.** sail	**1.** A ○ B ○ **2.** A ○ B ○

Talk About It

Look at the test paper again.

1. Where would you write your name, the date, and grade?
2. Read the directions. How should you mark the answer?
3. How would you mark the correct answer to the first question? The second question?

Skills Practice

Read the test paper below. Look carefully to see if the person has followed directions.

Read each sentence carefully. Choose the answer that completes the sentence correctly. Fill in the circle for the correct answer in the answer column. Do not write on the test paper.	**Name** *May 6* **Date** *S Dean* **Grade** *4-B* **Answer Column**
1. Another word for begin is *start* **A.** end **B.** start **C.** go **D.** stop **2.** The correct plural for foot is ____. **A.** foots **B.** foote (**C.**) feet **D.** feets	**1.** A ○ B ● C ○ D ○ **2.** A ○ B ○ (C) ○ D ○

Write the answers to the following questions.

1. What is wrong with the name and date?
2. What mistake was made in answering the first question?
3. What mistake was made in answering the second question?

Speaking and Listening Skills

One of the first skills you learned was listening. You learned this skill when you were just a baby. You looked and listened to learn about the world around you.

You still learn many things by listening. You may listen to news on the radio. In school you must listen to directions and reports.

In many ways listening skills are like reading skills. When you listen to someone talk, you listen for the main idea. You also listen to details that tell about the main idea. You have worked hard to be a good reader. You must also work hard to be a good listener.

Here are some ways to become a good listener.

1. Look directly at the speaker.
2. Do not talk to others while you are listening.
3. Try to think only about what the speaker is saying.
4. Listen for the main idea. The speaker usually tells the subject at the beginning of the speech.
5. Try to remember at least two important details that the speaker gives.
6. When the speaker is finished, take notes. Write down the main idea and the details right away.
7. Ask questions about things you cannot remember or do not understand.

Sometimes you may be the speaker instead of the listener. You may have to give a talk or a report in your class or club. It is important to put your thoughts in order before you speak. Then you have to choose words that everyone will understand. You must also speak clearly.

Here are some rules to help you become a good speaker.

1. Plan what you want to say. Jot down your main points.
2. Practice your speech in front of someone before you give it for a group.
3. Look directly at your audience while you talk.
4. Speak slowly and say your words carefully.

Talk About It

Listen carefully as your teacher or classmate reads this paragraph. Name the main idea. Name the important details.

Satellites bring us messages from all over the universe. They bring us TV pictures from around the world. They let us telephone people anywhere in the world. Astronauts use satellites to talk to earth from outer space.

Skills Practice

1. Listen as your teacher or classmate reads this paragraph. Write a sentence telling the main idea. Write one or two sentences.

   Deaf people can talk in many ways. Some deaf people learn to use their voices. Most deaf people learn a special sign language. Special telephones let deaf people type their telephone talks.
2. Think about how you take care of something. Prepare a short talk to give to your classmates. (Jot down your main points.) You might tell the class how you take care of a pet, or a plant, or a special toy.

A Class Conversation

Thinking About Your Conversation

Your class is going to write a conversation together. The conversation will tell what Kim and Robert are saying in the pictures below. They are talking about delivering the newspapers.

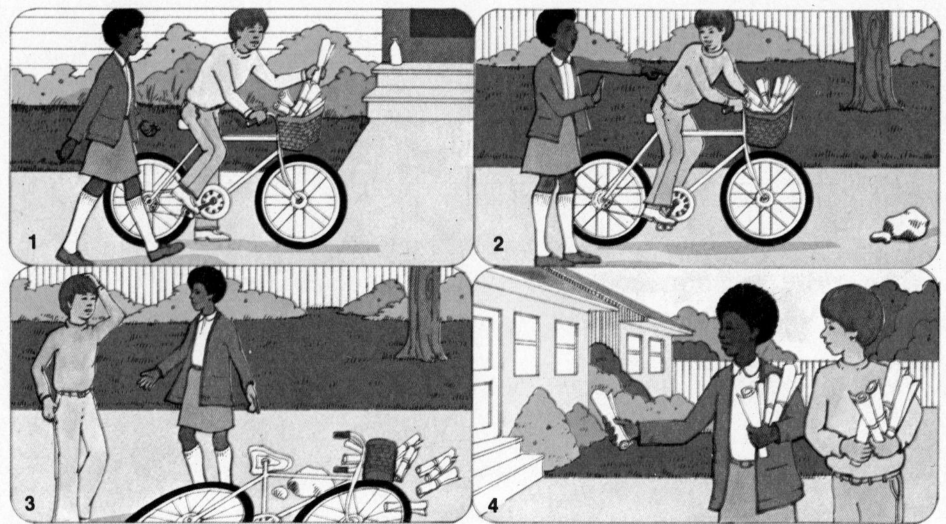

- Think about the rules for writing conversations.

1. Use *quotation marks* around the exact words that each speaker says.
2. Use *conversation words* such as *said, answered,* or *cried* to show how each person speaks.
3. Put a *comma* after each conversation word when the conversation word comes before the speaker's words.
4. Put a *period* before the last quotation mark at the end of the sentence when the speaker's words end the sentence.
5. Put a *comma* before the last quotation mark when a conversation word ends the sentence.
6. *Indent* the first word each time the speaker changes.
7. *Capitalize* the first word in each quotation.

Writing Your Conversation

Look at the pictures again. They will give you ideas for a conversation between Robert and Kim. Your teacher will write the conversation on the board.

1. Look at Box 1. The conversation between Robert and Kim might begin like this:

   Robert said, "My brother showed me how to deliver newspapers this way."

   Notice the conversation word that tells how Robert is speaking. Notice where quotation marks, a comma, and a period go in the sentence.

2. Now look at Box 2. Write what Kim might be saying to Robert.

3. Look at Box 3. Write what Robert might be saying to Kim.

4. Now look at Box 4. Write what Kim might be saying to Robert.

5. Read over the conversation on the board. Does it tell what Robert and Kim said to each other during their conversation? Has the conversation used quotation marks, commas, periods, and conversation words correctly? Is the first word indented each time the speaker changes?

Practicing a Conversation

Thinking About a Conversation

Now you will write a conversation between Mr. Nelson and Ruth. Ruth has brought in her television to be repaired. Review the rules for writing conversations on page 182.

Writing a Conversation

Look at the pictures above. Write the conversation between Mr. Nelson and Ruth. Remember to follow the conversation rules. The Word Bank may help you write your conversation.

Word Bank

- television
- broken
- repair
- screwdriver
- picture
- sound

1. Look at Box 1. The conversation between Mr. Nelson and Ruth might start like this:

   Ruth said, "My television set doesn't work, Mr. Nelson."

2. Now look at Box 2. Write a sentence that tells what Mr. Nelson said to Ruth.
3. Now look at Boxes 3 and 4. Write sentences telling what Ruth or Mr. Nelson said.

Edit Your Conversation

Read your conversation. Think about these questions.

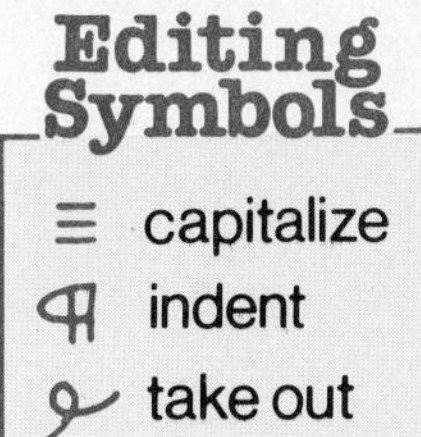

1. Did you put quotation marks around the exact words of each speaker?
2. Did you use a conversation word after the name of each speaker?
3. Did you put a comma after each conversation word when the conversation word comes before the speaker's words?
4. Did you put a period before the last quotation mark at the end of each sentence?
5. Did you put a comma before the last quotation mark when a conversation word ends the sentence?
6. Did you indent the first word each time the speaker changes?
7. Did you capitalize the first word of each quotation?

Correct your mistakes. If you need to, write your conversation again.

INDEPENDENT WRITING

A Persuasive Conversation

Prewriting Conversations add interest to the stories you write. You need practice writing clear conversations. Imagine you are having a conversation with two friends. You are trying to get your friends to read your favorite book. They don't seem interested in the book. What will you say to your friends to persuade them to read it? What will they say to you? Jot down notes about what you and your friends might say during the conversation.

Writing Write a conversation between you and two friends discussing your favorite book. Use your notes to help you.

Editing Use the check questions and the editing symbols above to edit your conversation.

Unit Review

Read each sentence. Look at the part in the box. Write **subject part** if it is a subject part. Write **predicate part** if it is a predicate part. *page 157*

1. Akiko | wrote a message.
2. A friend | got the message.
3. The boy | sent a card.
4. Luis | read the note.

Read each sentence. Write each subject part. Then draw a line under each simple subject. *pages 158–159*

5. A small girl wrote a note.
6. An old friend visited.
7. The shy boy read a book.
8. The dog barked loudly.

Write the subject part. Draw a line under the simple subjects. *pages 160–161*

9. Eva and her friend talk.
10. Connie and Martha listen.
11. Jim and Ed work together.
12. A cat and a pup drink water.

Write the form of the verb that belongs in the blank. *pages 162–163*

13. The boy and I ______. (whisper, whispers)
14. Brenda and Ted ____. (shouts, shout)
15. Amy and her brother ____ flags. (waves, wave)
16. You and I ____. (talk, talks)

Read each sentence. Write the predicate part. Draw a line under the simple predicate. *pages 166–167*

17. The children made a toy telephone.
18. They used paper cups and string.
19. The string stretched between the paper cups.
20. They talked into the paper cups.

Write each sentence. Use commas where they are needed. *pages 170–171*

21. Flags flashlights and signs carry sight messages.
22. Your speech will be next Joe.
23. Anita will be arriving on Monday August 15 1983.
24. Yes I have read today's newspaper.
25. This class will read write and spell today.
26. Juan please give each person a piece of paper.

Write each sentence. Use correct punctuation and capitalization. *pages 174–175*

27. joy said I put an ad in the newspaper to sell my bike
28. eva answered last year six people called about my ad
29. so far three people have called me joy added
30. eva said your bike will probably be sold by next week.

Now you are going to write a conversation. Imagine a telephone conversation between Jack and Jim. Jim wants to borrow Jack's favorite record. The conversation may begin like this: *pages 182–185*

"Hello, Jack," said Jim. "How are you?"
"I'm okay," answered Jack. "Why are you calling?"

31. **a.** Now write a sentence that tells why Jim is calling.
    b. Next write what Jack's answer to Jim might be.
    c. Last write two sentences in which the two boys say goodby.

A Play

This play tells about a contest between a girl and a computer. Read the play carefully. Be sure to read the directions in parentheses. They tell the players what to do.

THE COMPUTER GAME
CHARACTERS:
Gary Lopez, television game host
Joan Robinson
MT2, a computer
First Noisemaker
Second Noisemaker
Boy in audience
Girl in audience

SCENE: *A television studio.*

GARY LOPEZ: Good evening, ladies and gentlemen. Welcome to *The Computer Game.* Today another human player gets a chance to match wits with our very own computer—MT2!
(MT2 blinks its lights and the studio audience claps loudly.)

GARY LOPEZ: Today's player is Joan Robinson from the Oak Street School. Feeling smart, Joan?

JOAN: I think so.

GARY LOPEZ: I hope so! May I remind you no one has beat MT2 yet. Now, here's how we play the game. I'll ask a question. The first player to sound a noisemaker and give the correct answer scores one point. The first player to earn three points wins the game. Ready, players?

JOAN: Ready!

MT2 *(in a flat voice):* I am prepared to play.

GARY LOPEZ: First question. How much is 62,415 times 78,921?

FIRST NOISEMAKER: BLEEP!

MT2: The correct answer is 4,925,854,215.

GARY LOPEZ: Right! One point for the computer! *(The audience claps politely.)* Next question. Listen carefully. What date in history did the Pilgrims land at Plymouth Rock?

SECOND NOISEMAKER: BUZZ!

JOAN: 1620!

GARY LOPEZ: I'm sorry. That's not an exact enough answer.

FIRST NOISEMAKER: BLEEP!

MT2: The Pilgrims landed at Plymouth Rock on December 21 of the year 1620.

GARY LOPEZ: Right! Two points for the computer! If MT2 answers the next question correctly, it's all over, Joan!

BOY IN AUDIENCE: Come on, Joan!

GIRL IN AUDIENCE: You can beat that talking tin can!

GARY LOPEZ: Quiet, please. And here's the next question—

JOAN: Wait!

GARY LOPEZ: What's the matter?

JOAN: Could someone else ask the question, please?

GARY LOPEZ: What for?

JOAN: Maybe I'll have better luck with someone else.

GIRL *(coming up on stage)*: I'll ask it, Joan!

JOAN *(whispering to her)*: Put it in the form of a command. I think the computer's only programmed for questions.

GIRL *(looking at question):* Spell the word "chrysanthemum."

FIRST NOISEMAKER: BLEEP!

MT2: Chrysanthemum is spelled ... is spelled ...

GIRL: Yes?

MT2: I do not follow the question. Please repeat in the programmed form.

SECOND NOISEMAKER: BUZZ!

JOAN: Chrysanthemum. C-H-R-Y-S-A-N-T-H-E-M-U-M.

GIRL: Right! One point for Joan!

BOY: Hurrah!

MT2 *(slowing down)*: I am MT2, Computer ... I am MT2 ... I am MT ... MT ... M ... T ...

GARY LOPEZ: The computer's breaking down!

BOY: Then Joan's the winner!
(Suddenly MT2's lights begin flashing wildly. Smoke pours out of its top.)

GARY LOPEZ: Look what you've done. It's blown a fuse!

JOAN: Now that's what I call a poor loser!

Steven Otfinoski

Creative Activities

1. You and some other students can present this play in class. You may build a computer out of a cardboard box. Be sure to get any other objects needed for the play. Practice your play until all the players know their lines. Then present it in class.

2. **Creative Writing** Imagine you owned a computer or a robot that could do anything you wanted. Write a play that tells what you would do with the machine. You may write the play with a friend. Write what people say in the play. Also write directions in parentheses. When you have finished the play, you may present it to the class.

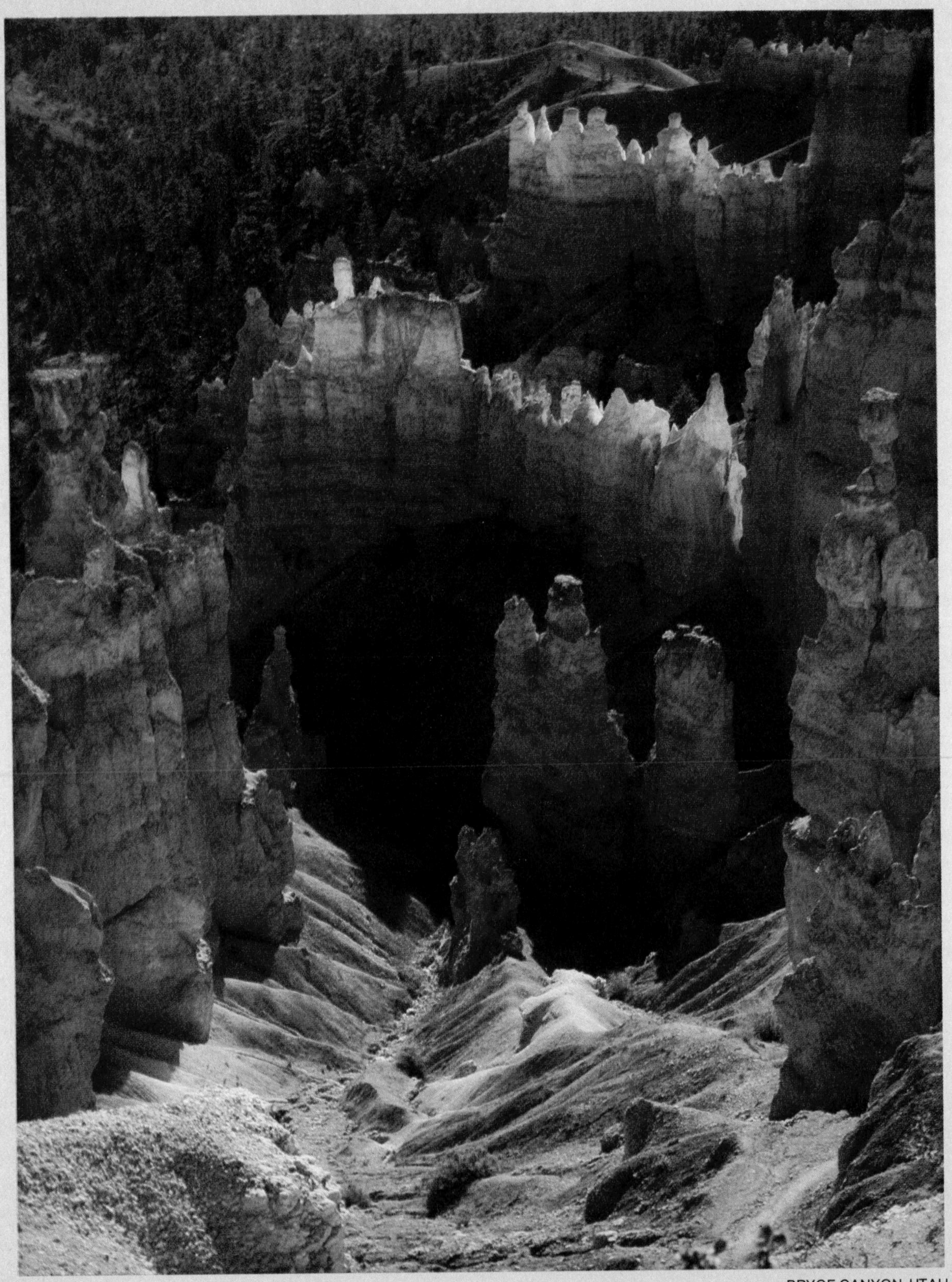

BRYCE CANYON, UTAH

Grammar and Related Language Skills

Adjectives
Adjectives That Compare
Using Adjectives
Making New Adjectives
Using Synonyms and Antonyms

Practical Communication

STUDY AND REFERENCE SKILLS
Using the Dictionary
COMPOSITION
Writing a One-Paragraph Report

Creative Expression

A Story

What material do you think forms the floor of this amazing canyon? People who study rock formations in canyons and other places are called geologists. Geologists take photographs and record their findings. If you were a geologist, what place would you like to explore? What writing skills would you need to write your report?

Adjectives

Imagine the world around you. What if everything were the same? All foods would taste alike. All flowers would smell alike. Luckily the world is full of different colors, sounds, smells, sizes, and shapes.

You can use words that describe exactly what things, people, and places are like. You use special words to describe nouns. Remember, a *noun* is a word that names a person, a place, or a thing.

- Find the nouns in this sentence. What word describes each noun?

Bright flags waved in the fresh air.

Flags and *air* are nouns.

The describing words *bright* and *fresh* are underlined. These describing words are called *adjectives*.

> An **adjective** is a word that describes a noun.

The sentence in the box would make sense if you took out the adjectives. But you would not know what kind of flags waved. You would not know that the air was fresh. Adjectives add more meaning to the nouns they describe.

Talk About It

Read each sentence. Which words are adjectives? What noun does each adjective describe?

1. The noisy crowd watched the wonderful show.
2. A fat clown climbed onto a tiny motorcycle.
3. A tiny woman rode on a golden pony.
4. Men and women paraded in sparkling costumes.

Skills Practice

Write each sentence. Draw a line under each adjective. Then draw two lines under the noun that the adjective describes.

1. A powerful lion showed sharp teeth.
2. The tall trainer called to the lion.
3. The huge lion jumped through a small hoop.
4. Beautiful horses trotted around a wide ring.
5. A brown horse wore a fancy hat.
6. A black horse danced.
7. The white horse wore a pretty feather.
8. Enormous elephants came next.
9. A little elephant ran behind the big elephants.
10. Funny dogs raced into the ring.

Writing Sentences

Imagine you are watching a pet parade.

1. Write two sentences about the pets using adjectives to describe them.
2. Write one sentence about the people in the crowd using adjectives to describe them.

Sample Answer 1. A powerful lion showed sharp teeth.

Adjectives That Compare

If you look around you, you can see many differences among people and things. A neighbor's dog may be the biggest dog you have ever seen. Or it may be smaller than your dog. You can describe one thing by comparing it with something else.

- Look at the sentences below.

Tony saw a small pig near the fence.
Rae saw a smaller pig than Tony saw.

In these sentences one pig has been described by comparing it with another pig. What happened to the word *small?* To compare one thing with another, you add *-er* to an adjective.

You can also describe one thing by comparing it with two or three other things. Or you might compare it with all the other things like it in the world.

- Look at the sentences below.

The Boyd Zoo has a tall bear.
The Paltz Zoo has a taller bear than the Boyd Zoo has.
The tallest bear of all is in another town.
The tallest bear in the world was on television.

The third bear has been described by comparing it with the two other bears. The last bear has been compared to all the other bears in the world. What happened to the word *tall* in the last two sentences? To compare several things, add *-est* to an adjective.

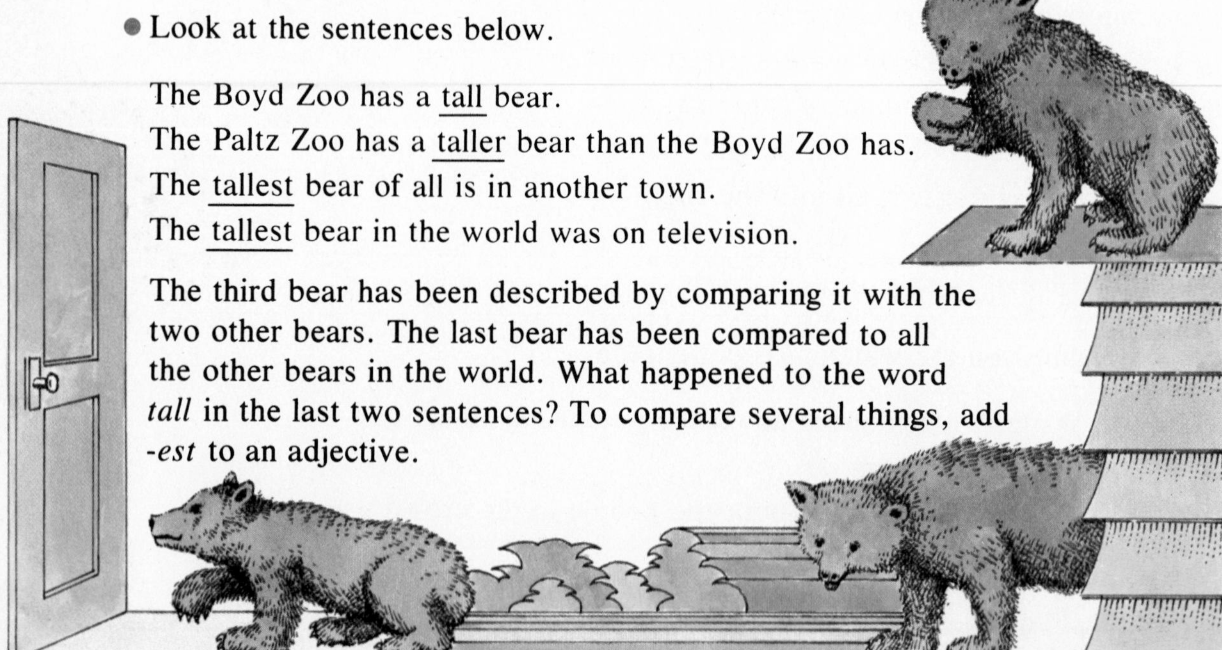

Talk About It

Complete each sentence. Choose the correct adjective to fit in each blank. Tell what nouns are being compared.

1. Amy has a smart dog.
   Roy has a ____ dog than Amy. (smarter, smartest)
2. I own a cute puppy.
   Kay owns a ____ puppy than I. (cuter, cutest)
3. Four large dogs stood outside the store.
   The ____ dog of all was gray. (larger, largest)
4. Luke found the ____ cat of all. (sweeter, sweetest)

Skills Practice

Write each sentence. Choose the correct adjective to complete each sentence.

1. Maria bought a small fish.
   Jill bought a ____ fish than Maria. (smaller, smallest)
2. Ron saw the ____ fish in the store. (smaller, smallest)
3. Jaime wanted the three green parrots.
   Pam got the ____ parrot of the three. (greener, greenest)
4. Roger found a strange pet.
   Tom found a ____ pet than Roger. (stranger, strangest)
5. Bill found the ____ pet of all. (stranger, strangest)
6. Tim needed the ____ leash of all. (longer, longest)

Writing Sentences

Imagine that you are watching ducks swim in a pond. Some are large, and some are small. Some are white, and some are gray. Write three sentences comparing the ducks.

Sample Answer 1. Jill bought a smaller fish than Maria.

More Adjectives That Compare

You have seen that you can describe a thing by comparing it to another thing. Then you add *-er* or *-est* to some adjectives.

- Read each sentence. What things are being compared? Which words are adjectives?

Jill worked in a small garden.
Dan worked in a smaller garden than Jill did.

Notice that the ending *-er* has been added to the adjective *small* to make the new adjective *smaller*.

- Now read these sentences. What things are being compared? Which words are the adjectives?

Julia found a pretty tulip.
Mrs. Romanos found a prettier tulip than Julia did.

Pretty is the adjective in the first sentence. Many adjectives end in *y*. Notice what happened to the spelling of pretty in the second sentence.

If an adjective ends with a consonant and **y**, change the **y** to **i** and add **-er** or **-est** to make the correct form of the adjective.

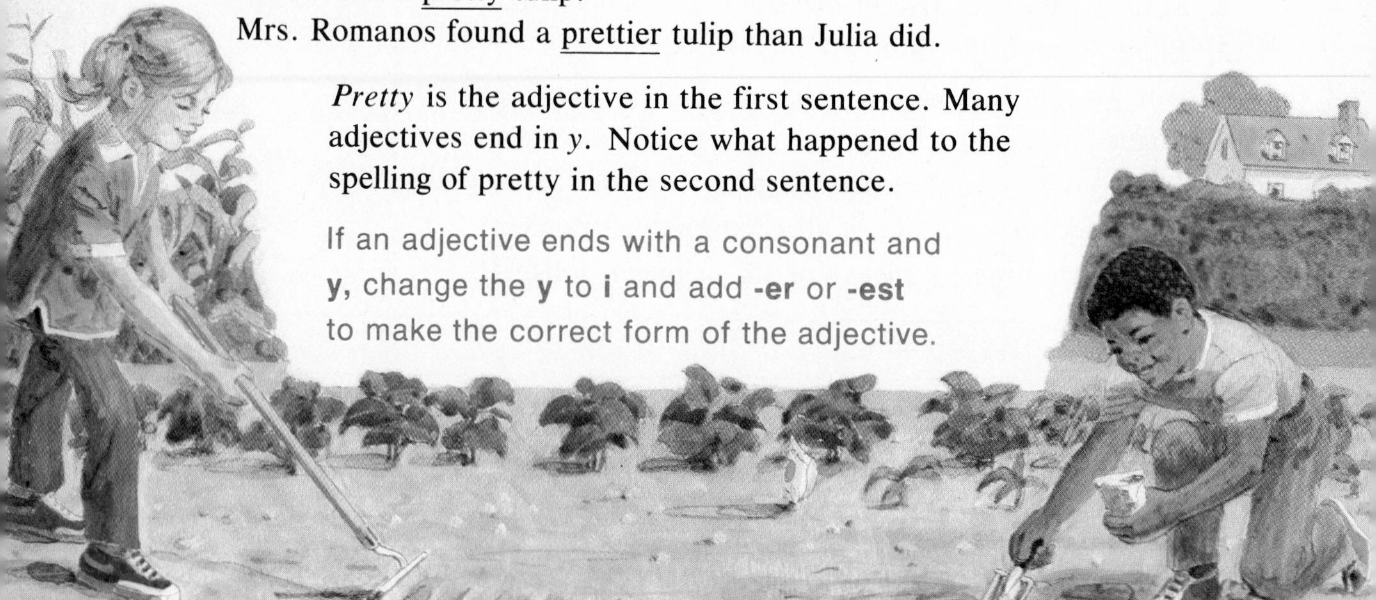

- Look at these sentences. Notice what happens to the word **hot** in the second sentence.

Jack worked on a <u>hot</u> day.
Mike worked on a <u>hotter</u> day than Jack did.

> If an adjective ends with a consonant, vowel, consonant, double the final consonant and add **-er** or **-est** to make the correct form of the adjective.

Talk About It

Read each sentence. Decide whether the adjective should end with **-er** or **-est.** Spell your answer.

1. I planted a big garden.
   Bill planted a ____ garden than I did. (big)
2. Mr. Bell grows the ____ vegetables in town. (tasty)
3. Marian held up the ____ pepper in the garden. (red)
4. Marian had a ____ pepper than I had. (hot)

Skills Practice

Read each sentence. Decide whether the adjective should end with **-er** or **-est.** Write the sentence.

1. Lin picked the ____ flower in our whole garden. (big)
2. The ____ flowers of all are growing near the gate. (tiny)
3. Jim raised a juicy melon.
   Ed raised a ____ melon than Jim did. (juicy)
4. We used a fat pumpkin on Halloween.
   Joy used a ____ pumpkin than we did. (fat)
5. Last summer was rainy.
   This summer was even ____ than last summer. (rainy)

Sample Answer 1. Lin picked the biggest flower in our whole garden.

Skills Review

Read each sentence. Write each adjective. Then write the noun that each adjective describes.

1. Delicious fruits grow in strange places.
2. Sweet blueberries grow near the old bridge.
3. Huge apple trees fill the big field.
4. Wild strawberries fill the sandy beaches.
5. Red flowers grow in the white sand.
6. A hungry bird nibbled a ripe blueberry.
7. Shiny eyes watched the empty pail.
8. A new visitor discovered the small bush.
9. Tom spoke with a gentle voice.
10. The angry bird gave a silent stare.
11. Liza moved to a new place.
12. The clever bird saved the tasty fruit.
13. The low bush gave good fruit, too.
14. Hao found the bigger fruit.

Choose the correct adjective to complete each sentence. Write the adjective.

15. Each spring two beavers come back to the deep pond.
    The ____ animal leads the way. (older, oldest)
16. The beavers built a new lodge this year.
    It is in ____ water than the other lodge. (deep, deeper)
17. A loud duck and a ____ frog share the pond.
    (louder, loudest)
18. The beavers cut down thirteen trees.
    Only the ____ tree fell into the water. (tall, tallest)
19. A beaver uses long teeth for the job.
    A beaver grows ____ teeth than a rabbit. (longer, longest)

20. A beaver eats the bark of a tree. A beaver eats a ___ dinner than a rabbit. (tougher, toughest)
21. The ducks and geese gulp down plants. The ___ plants of all float on top of the water. (tastier, tastiest)

Read each sentence. Decide whether the adjective should end with **-er** or **-est**. Write the adjective.

22. Of the many deer, we fed the ___ deer. (friendly)
23. Seven animals looked for some tasty food. The deer found the ___ meal of all. (tasty)
24. A squirrel made a mess. The mother squirrel made the ___ mess. (big)
25. One fat rabbit hid in the grass. An even ___ rabbit came and ate our food. (hungry)
26. Bonny walked along the rocky path. An even ___ path went up the hill. (rocky)
27. Bonny picked several flowers. She saw the ___ flower of all in the forest. (pretty)

If someone told you that you were a *silly* person, how would you feel? You probably would not be pleased. If someone told you that you were a *silly* person about one thousand years ago, you probably would not mind.

Some adjectives are very old. Many adjectives have not always had the meanings they have today. *Silly* used to mean *holy* or *blessed*. What does silly mean today?

Exploring Language

Using Adjectives

There are some short words that point out nouns in a special way. *A, an,* and *the* are three of these words.

The words *a* and *an* really mean *one*. You use the words *a* and *an* with singular nouns. A *singular noun* is a noun that names one person, place, or thing.

- Read each sentence. Notice when to use *a* and *an*.

Anita ate a blueberry.
Joe held an apple.
Sally picked an orange.
Pam wants a banana.

Use *a* with singular nouns that begin with a consonant. Use *an* with singular nouns that begin with a vowel.

- Now read these sentences. Notice how *the* changes the meaning.

Mable wants an orange.
Mable wants the orange.

In the first sentence you know that Mable wants an orange. And any orange will do. In the second sentence you know that she wants one special orange. No other orange will do.

You can use *the* with a singular noun to point out a special person or thing. You can use *the* with plural nouns, too. A *plural noun* is a noun that names more than one person, place, or thing.

- Look at these sentences. Notice the plural nouns.

An orange tree smells sweet.
The oranges grow quickly.
Pete took a banana.
The bananas are growing.

Number words are the most exact of these little words. Words like *one, two,* and *three* tell exactly how many people or things you mean.

- Read the sentences. How is the meaning of each sentence different?

The apple trees grow here. Three apple trees grow here.

Talk About It

Read each sentence. Complete each sentence by using **a** or **an** with singular nouns. For plural nouns, use **the** or number words from one to ten.

1. We have ____ oak trees in our yard now.
2. ____ apple tree grows in the backyard.
3. ____ apples always taste good.
4. ____ blueberry bush grows nearby.

Skills Practice

Write **a** or **an** with each of the words below.

1. insect	3. flower	5. elephant	7. animal
2. horse	4. orange	6. bear	8. cherry

Write each sentence. Complete each sentence by using **a** or **an** with singular nouns. For plural nouns use **the.**

9. Al had many uncles. ____ uncle of his brought wood.
10. Al made a present for his brother. He made ____ treehouse.
11. The house sits in ____ big tree.
12. ____ windows face a forest.
13. ____ owl lives in the tree.

Sample Answers **1.** an insect **9.** Al had many uncles. An uncle of his brought wood.

Making New Adjectives

You can make many words into adjectives. Just add the ending *-y* or *-ful*.

- Look at these sentences.

The salt spilled on the ground.
The pony ate the salty popcorn.

When you add *-y* to *salt,* it becomes an adjective. *Salty* means *full of salt*. The ending *-y* often means *having* or *full of.*

- Look at these sentences.

The boy has one hope. He wants to ride a horse.
The hopeful boy watches the horse.

When you add *-ful* to *hope,* the new word becomes an adjective. *Hopeful* means *full of hope*. The ending *-ful* often means *full of.*

- Now read these sentences. Notice how the spelling changes.

The sun shines on the field.
The horse trotted across the sunny field.

If a word ends with a consonant, vowel, consonant, double the last consonant and add *-y* to form the adjective.

- Read these sentences. Notice how the spelling changes.

Spines cover the plant.
The horse stepped on the spiny plant.

If a word ends in *e,* drop the *e* and add *-y* to form the adjective.

• Read each sentence. Notice how the spelling changes.

Pedro enjoys the beauty of a garden.
Pedro planted some beautiful flowers.

If a word ends with a consonant and *y*, change the *y* to *i* and add *-ful* to form the adjective.

Talk About It

How would you add a *-y* to each noun to make an adjective? Explain what spelling rule you would follow.

1. shine **2.** taste **3.** fog **4.** bag

Read each sentence. Add **-ful** to the word at the end of each sentence. Use the new adjective in the sentence.

5. A ____ bird ate the seeds. (color)
6. Eve fed the ____ bird some more seeds. (wonder)
7. Then the ____ bird flew away. (beauty)

Skills Practice

Write each sentence. Complete the sentence by adding **-ful** to the word at the end of the sentence.

1. The ____ cat chased a ball. (play)
2. The ____ girl threw the ball again. (cheer)
3. The cat curled up in a ____ corner. (peace)
4. Later a ____ man moved the chair. (power)

Add **-y** to each noun to make an adjective. Write the adjective.

5. paste	**7.** shade	**9.** fun	**11.** dirt
6. skin	**8.** noise	**10.** rain	**12.** wave

Sample Answers **1.** The playful cat chased a ball. **5.** pasty

Using Synonyms and Antonyms in Sentences

You know that adjectives are used to describe nouns. Some adjectives have nearly the same meaning. However, one word may be more interesting. One word may make your meaning clearer than another.

- Read the pair of sentences. Which words have nearly the same meaning?

The angry lion roared. The furious lion roared.

Angry and *furious* have nearly the same meaning. These words are *synonyms*.

A synonym is a word that has nearly the same meaning as another word.

Some adjectives have opposite meanings. Words that have opposite meanings are used to show how different things are.

- Which words in each sentence have opposite meanings?

Tim had a wet umbrella. Tim had a dry umbrella.

Wet and *dry* have opposite meanings. These words are *antonyms*.

An antonym is a word that means the opposite of another word.

You can change the meanings of some words by beginning the word with the prefix *un-*.

- Read each pair of words. See how the meaning changes when *un-* is added.

happy → unhappy usual → unusual friendly → unfriendly

Talk About It

Read each sentence. Tell the synonym for each underlined word.

1. My friend has a nice puppy. (friendly, unfriendly)
2. The loud thunder scared the animals. (silent, crashing)
3. The clever fox found food. (silly, sly)

Read each sentence. Tell the antonym for each underlined word.

4. The squirrel climbed onto a short branch. (leafy, long)
5. The kitten drank the cool milk. (warm, dry)
6. The old horse rested by the tree. (small, young)

Skills Practice

Read each sentence. Write the sentence using the synonym for each underlined word.

1. The large whale swam close to the boat. (enormous, old)
2. The whale made a big splash. (little, huge)
3. The scared passengers called for help. (unhappy, frightened)
4. The nice captain calmed the passengers. (kind, mean)
5. The captain spoke in a quiet voice. (deep, soft)
6. Then the strong whale swam away. (powerful, noisy)

Read each sentence. Write the sentence using the antonym for each underlined word.

7. Later we spotted a small shark. (young, large)
8. It was headed toward shallow water. (deep, cold)
9. Then a quiet seagull landed on a railing. (silly, noisy)
10. The nice bird stole a boy's lunch. (naughty, funny)
11. The unsurprised boy laughed. (happy, startled)
12. We spent a very boring day today. (exciting, tiring)

Sample Answer 1. The enormous whale swam close to the boat.

Skills Review

Write **a** or **an** with each of the words below.

1. egg
2. bee
3. orange
4. rose
5. tulip
6. animal
7. duck
8. uncle
9. worm
10. ear
11. oak
12. apple

Write each sentence. Complete each sentence by using **a** or **an** with singular nouns. For plural nouns use **the.**

13. ____ chipmunk lives nearby.
14. The animals live in ____ trees.
15. ____ fox lives there, too.
16. ____ robin rests in ____ nest.
17. ____ egg lies in the nest.
18. ____ children watch.

Read each sentence. Add **-ful** to the word at the end of the sentence. Write the word.

19. A ____ neighbor does many things. (help)
20. Sara played ____ music on the piano. (joy)
21. A ____ friend left the lunch at home. (forget)
22. ____ roses grow in the yard. (beauty)
23. Joe whistled a ____ song. (cheer)

Add **-y** to each word to make an adjective. Write the adjective.

24. fish
25. room
26. bone
27. shade
28. tin
29. rock
30. chop
31. ice
32. sun

Read each sentence. Write the synonym for each underlined word.

33. The prairie dog hid in the quiet desert. (silent, tough)
34. A snake wiggled through wet leaves. (crisp, damp)
35. Two butterflies rested on a thin petal. (slender, low)
36. A large rhinocerous waded. (scared, huge)

Read each sentence. Write the antonym for each underlined word.

37. The zebra moved its straight tail. (curved, fluffy)
38. A deer crossed the wide brook. (mean, narrow)
39. An eel floated in the cold water. (warm, plain)
40. Tigers wander in the short grass. (sweet, tall)

Exploring Language

You already know that words follow a certain order in sentences. Adjectives have a certain order, too. Most of us follow the right order of adjectives without ever thinking about it.

Do you say

brown twelve cows or **twelve brown cows?**
friendly two dogs or **two friendly dogs?**

Can you explain the rule for the order of adjectives?

Dictionary: Guide Words

When you read, you often discover words that are new to you. You can learn about these words in the dictionary. Remember that a dictionary is a book that has words in alphabetical order. It gives helpful information about words.

You can find words in a dictionary more quickly if you know which part to turn to. Think of dividing these words into a front part and a back part. You can find all the words beginning with *a* through *m* in the front part. You can find all the words beginning with *n* through *z* in the back part.

- Read each word. Would you find it in the front part or the back part of a dictionary?

action possible route huddle

There are two words at the top of almost every dictionary page. They are called *guide words*. They tell the first and last words on a dictionary page.

Guide words help you find words quickly. All the words on a dictionary page must come between the guide words. Look at the sample dictionary page on page 210. What are the guide words?

Talk About It

The guide words on a page are **wave/weep.** Which of these words would you find on this page?

1. warn	**3.** wax	**5.** weather	**7.** weigh
2. wave	**4.** weak	**6.** weed	**8.** whale

Skills Practice

Would you find each word in the front part or back part of a dictionary? Write the answer.

1. center **2.** offer **3.** dry **4.** trade

Read each word at the left. Does it come between the guide words in **a** or in **b**? Write the letter of the correct pair of words.

5. groom	**a. grieve/groan**	**7.** peer	**a. pea/pedal**
	b. grocer/ground		**b. peddle/peg**
6. litter	**a. lion/list**	**8.** dial	**a. detour/diary**
	b. listen/live		**b. dice/dim**

The guide words on a dictionary page are **player/poet.** Which of these words would you find on the page? Write the words.

9. plank	**11.** plod	**13.** plus	**15.** poetry
10. please	**12.** plow	**14.** poem	**16.** point

Sample Answers **1.** front part **5.** b

Dictionary: Words with Two Meanings

A dictionary tells you many things about words. One of the things it tells is the meaning of words.

Some words have two meanings. The dictionary gives both meanings of these words. You will find **1.** in front of the first meaning. You will find **2.** in front of the second meaning. Sometimes there is an example sentence to help show the meaning of the word.

Look at the word *mess* on the sample dictionary page. What is the second meaning of *mess*? Read the example sentence for this meaning.

meet / move

meet (mēt) **1.** To come together with someone. *I will meet you in the hall after class.* **2.** To join together. *This is the place where the river meets the ocean.*

mess (mes) **1.** A state of disorder. *My room is in a mess.* **2.** An amount of food. *We cooked a mess of fish.*

mind (mīnd) **1.** The part of the body where thought takes place. *José has a good mind and learns quickly.* **2.** To object to or care. *Do you mind if I borrow your book?*

miss (mis) **1.** To fail to do something. *Jennifer is late and will miss her train.* **2.** To feel sad when someone is away.

mold (mōld) **1.** To form or make something into a certain shape. *The artist molded the clay into the shape of a beautiful bird.* **2.** Something that grows on food when it is spoiled.

move (mo͞ov) **1.** To change position or place. *My family is going to move to the country.* **2.** To stir feelings. *The sad story moved him to tears.*

Talk About It

Use the sample dictionary page to answer each question.

1. What is the example sentence for the word *mold*?
2. Which meaning of *mold* does the sentence show?

Read each sentence. Use the sample dictionary page.
Tell which meaning of *miss* fits each sentence.

3. I miss my school friends during the summer.
4. I missed two questions on the test.

Skills Practice

Use the sample dictionary page to answer each question.
Write the answer.

1. What are the example sentences for the word mind?
2. Which meaning of mind does each sentence show?

Look at the underlined word in each sentence. Use the sample dictionary. Write **1.** if the word has the first meaning. Write **2.** if the word has the second meaning.

3. My bookcase is a mess.
4. We found mold on the old bread.
5. The words of the song moved Aunt Mae.
6. I had my mind on my homework.
7. We molded some unusual candles.
8. Will you help me move my bed?
9. Pine Street and Oak Street meet near my house.
10. My mother won't mind if I'm late.

Sample Answer 3. 1.

Reports

Thinking About Reports

Many times in school you are asked to write reports. A *report* tells facts and ideas about a topic.

A report can have any kind of paragraph. The report must have one main idea. The main idea sentence in the paragraph tells the main idea of the report. Each detail sentence tells more about the main idea.

- Read this report about growing tomatoes.

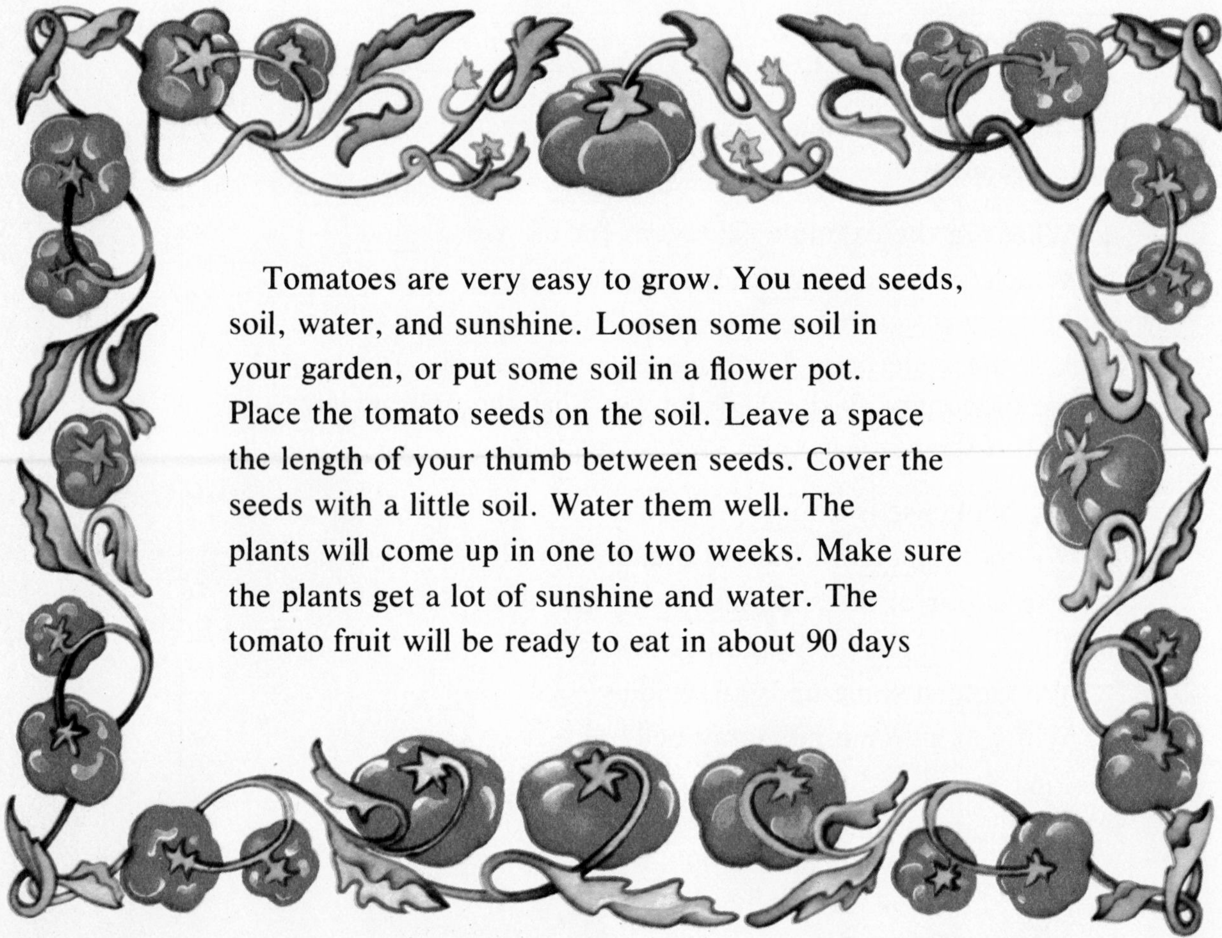

Tomatoes are very easy to grow. You need seeds, soil, water, and sunshine. Loosen some soil in your garden, or put some soil in a flower pot. Place the tomato seeds on the soil. Leave a space the length of your thumb between seeds. Cover the seeds with a little soil. Water them well. The plants will come up in one to two weeks. Make sure the plants get a lot of sunshine and water. The tomato fruit will be ready to eat in about 90 days

Talking About Reports

The paragraph in the report gave directions for growing tomatoes. Read the report again.

1. What is the main idea of the report?
2. What do you need to grow tomatoes?
3. How do you plant the seeds?
4. When will the fruit be ready to eat?

Writing a Report

Pretend you are writing a report on apples. Your main idea sentence is: *Apples can be served in different ways.* Read the sentences below. Choose the three detail sentences that belong in the report. Write the main idea sentence and the detail sentences you have chosen.

1. Apples can be cooked or eaten raw.
2. Apples are beautiful fruits.
3. People often bake apples in desserts.
4. Sometimes apples are made into applesauce.

Pretend you are writing another report on apples. Suppose your main idea sentence is: *Apples are good kinds of fruits to grow.* Read the sentences below. Choose the three detail sentences that belong in the report. Write the main idea sentence and the detail sentences you have chosen.

5. Red apples are prettier than yellow apples.
6. Apples can be kept for many months at a given temperature.
7. Apples can be shipped long distances without becoming spoiled.
8. You can grow apples in many kinds of climates.

A Class Report

Thinking About Reports

There are many places you might get information for a report. You may use encyclopedias or other library books. You may interview people or watch television. You can also get information from a survey.

In a survey you ask many people the same question. You write down the answer they give. Then you report on what you learned. You tell how many people gave the same answer.

Pretend your class wants to find out what kind of animal is the most popular pet. Your class took a survey to find out the answer. Your class asked all the students in the school what kind of pet they owned. After writing down the answers, the class put the information on a graph. Here is what the graph looks like.

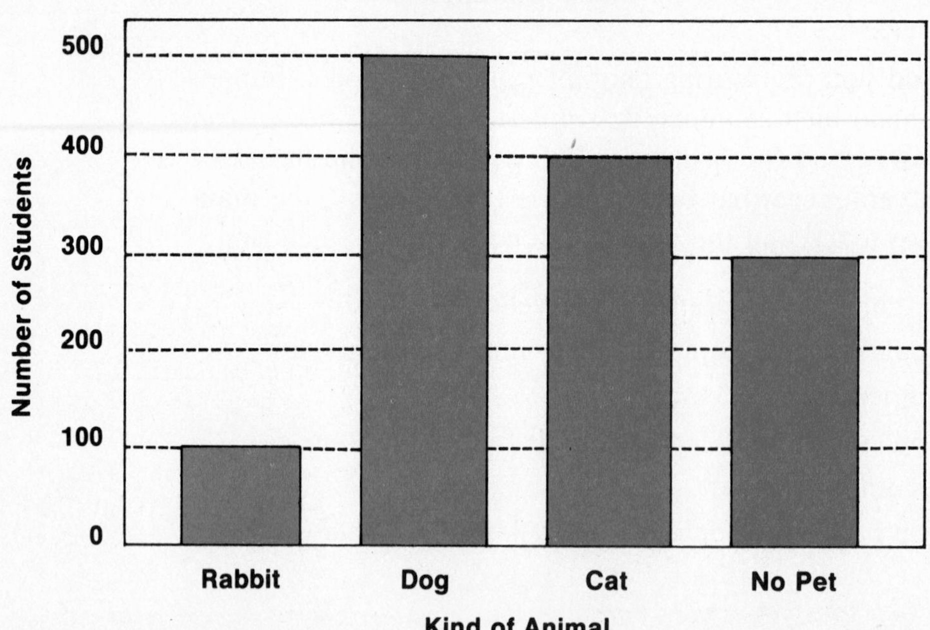

Now your class is going to write a paragraph together. The paragraph in your report will tell about the facts from your survey. The information on the graph will help you.

Writing a Report

Your teacher will write the sentences for the report on the board.

1. Your report will start with a main idea sentence. Your main idea sentence is: *In a recent survey, our class learned what kind of animal is the most popular pet.*
2. Think of a detail sentence that tells which animal is the most popular. In the sentence, tell how many students said they own that kind of animal.
3. Think of a sentence that tells about the next most popular animal.
4. Think of a detail sentence that tells about the least popular animal.
5. Think of a detail sentence that tells about students who said they do not own a pet.

Practicing a Report

Thinking About a Report

Now you will write a report. Suppose you wanted to write a report on the different ways energy from the sun can be used. You decide to interview a scientist who knows a lot about the subject. Here are the questions you asked and the answers you received during the interview.

Q: How can the sun be used to heat a home?

A: If you put a dark covering on your roof, the sunlight can travel into the house. It will heat a tank of water. The hot water helps to warm the house. Then you do not have to use expensive fuel.

Q: How can the sun's energy be used in the kitchen?

A: You can cook certain foods in a special oven. The oven receives the sun's rays. The food is cooked by the heat from the sun. I like to cook chicken this way.

Q: Will we always need to use gasoline for cars?

A: Scientists are trying to invent a car that runs on energy from the sun. Soon we may have cleaner air.

Word Bank

energy
oven
sunlight
heat
gasoline
cleaner

Writing a Report

1. Begin your report with this main idea sentence.
   The sun's energy can be used in many ways.
2. Decide which information from the interview is most important. Write three or four detail sentences. They should tell how the sun's energy can be used in homes, kitchens, and cars. The Word Bank may help you.
3. Read your report. Make sure your facts are correct.

Edit Your Report

Read your report again. Use these questions.

1. Does your report have a main idea sentence? Do the detail sentences tell more about the main idea?
2. Did you use only the most important information from the interview in your report?
3. Did you use precise adjectives?
4. Did you use capital letters and periods where they are needed?
5. Did you spell words correctly? Check the Word Bank.

Correct your mistakes. If you need to, write your report again.

Editing Symbols

≡ capitalize
¶ indent
take out
∧ add

INDEPENDENT WRITING

A Report

Prewriting Checkers and other board games can be lots of fun. Suppose you have been asked to write a report on favorite board games of fourth-grade students. First talk to at least ten students in your class and have them name their favorite board game. Choose the five games most often named. Conduct a survey with your class and find how many students like each of the five games. You may want to make a graph like the one on page 216 to organize and display your information.

Writing Write a report titled: *Favorite Board Games of Fourth-Grade Students*. Use the plan for writing your report on page 217. Start your report with a main idea sentence. Then use the survey to write detail sentences for your report.

Editing Use the check questions and editing symbols above to edit your report.

Unit Review

Read each sentence. Write each adjective. Then write the noun the adjective describes. *pages 194–195*

1. The brown lion lives in the green jungle.
2. Fierce tigers live there, too.
3. The big lion sleeps in the warm sun.
4. The lion took a long nap.
5. A funny monkey came up to the giant lion.

Choose the correct adjective to complete each sentence. Write the adjective. *pages 196–197*

6. Linda shouted in a loud voice.
   Juan shouted in a ____ voice. (louder, loudest)
7. Lu wanted the ____ cat of all. (softer, softest)
8. The rabbit took a long leap.
   Then the rabbit took a ____ leap. (longer, longest)
9. Barry had three carrots.
   He ate the ____ carrot. (smaller, smallest)

Read each sentence. Decide whether the adjective should end with **er** or **est.** Write the adjective. *pages 198–199*

10. Denise found a big bug.
    Mari found the ____ bug of all. (big)
11. The bug crawled to a pretty flower.
    A butterfly flew to a ____ flower. (pretty)
12. A red bug sat on a bean.
    An even ____ bug sat on a radish. (red)
13. Robert saw an ugly bug.
    Paul saw the ____ bug of all. (ugly)

Unit Review

Complete each sentence by using **a** or **an** with singular nouns. For plural nouns use **the.** Write the word. *pages 202–203*

14. Anna trains ____ animals.

15. ____ children watch.

16. We hear ____ animal roar.

17. ____ big bear dances.

Add **-ful** to each word to make an adjective. Write the word. *pages 204–205*

18. beauty **19.** help **20.** taste **21.** care

Add **-y** to each word to make an adjective. Write the word. *pages 204–205*

22. dirt **23.** shade **24.** shine **25.** sun

Read each sentence. Write the synonym for the underlined word. *pages 206–207*

26. A frog jumped out of the <u>dirty</u> water. (chilly, muddy)

27. The <u>frightened</u> rabbit hopped by. (tired, scared)

28. The animal walked across the <u>blazing</u> desert. (fiery, cold)

29. A bear crossed the <u>icy</u> stream. (freezing, flowing)

Read each sentence. Write the antonym for each underlined word. *pages 206–207*

30. A caterpillar crawled over the <u>smooth</u> path. (little, rough)

31. A bird flew to a <u>low</u> branch. (thin, high)

32. The moth landed on a <u>large</u> leaf. (small, young)

33. The ground in the woods was <u>dry</u>. (damp, cool)

Read the following sentences. They are for a report about the United States. The sentences are not in the right order. First find the main idea sentence. Next put the detail sentences in order. Write the report. *pages 214–219*

34. **a.** Later Alaska became the 49th state.
b. We began with the thirteen colonies in 1776.
c. Over the years the number of states grew to 48.
d. Our country has had a different number of states throughout history.
e. The 50th state in the country is Hawaii.

A Story

If a story has a good beginning, you want to read the middle and end. You want to find out what happens next. The beginning of a story tells about the problem in a story. The middle tells how the characters try to solve the problem. The end tells what happens to the characters.

In this story, Frog and Toad have a problem. They want to be as brave as the people in a story they have read. Frog and Toad find out that being brave is not easy.

DRAGONS and GIANTS

by Arnold Lobel

Frog and Toad
were reading a book together.
"The people in this book
are brave," said Toad.
"They fight dragons and giants,
and they are never afraid."

"I wonder if we are brave,"
said Frog.

Frog and Toad looked into a mirror.
"We look brave," said Frog.

"Yes, but are we?"
asked Toad.

Frog and Toad went outside.
"We can try to climb this mountain," said Frog. "That should tell us if we are brave."
Frog went leaping over rocks, and Toad came puffing up behind him.

They came to a dark cave.
A big snake came out of the cave.
"Hello lunch," said the snake when he saw Frog and Toad.
He opened his wide mouth.

Frog and Toad jumped away.
Toad was shaking.
"I am not afraid!" he cried.

They climbed higher,
and they heard a loud noise.
Many large stones
were rolling down the mountain.
"It's an avalanche!" cried Toad.

Frog and Toad jumped away.
Frog was trembling.
"I am not afraid!" he shouted.

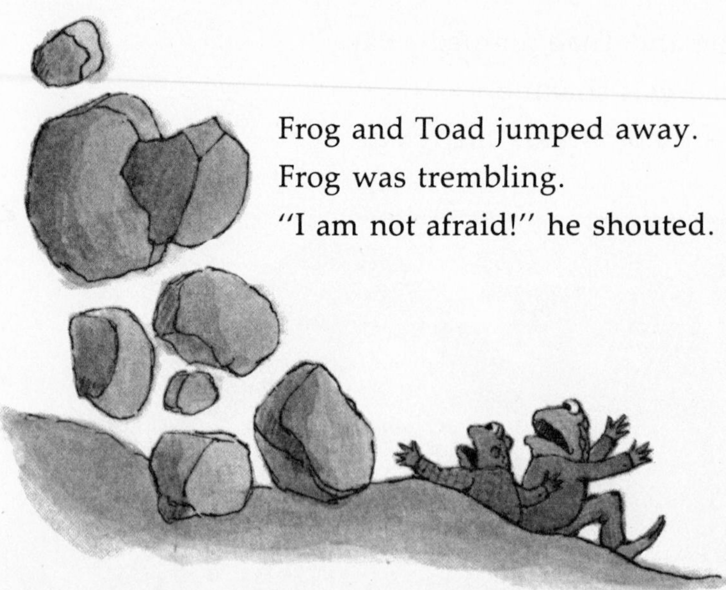

They came to the top
of the mountain.
The shadow of a hawk
fell over them.
Frog and Toad
jumped under a rock.
The hawk flew away.

"We are not afraid!"
screamed Frog and Toad
at the same time.
Then they ran down the mountain
very fast.
They ran past the place
where they saw the avalanche.
They ran past the place
where they saw the snake.
They ran all the way
to Toad's house.

"Frog, I am glad to have
a brave friend like you," said Toad.
He jumped into the bed
and pulled the covers
over his head.

"And I am happy to know
a brave person like you, Toad,"
said Frog.
He jumped into the closet
and shut the door.

Toad stayed in the bed,
and Frog stayed in the closet.

They stayed there
for a long time,
just feeling very brave together.

Creative Activities

1. Draw a map of Frog's and Toad's adventure. Start at the house and show their trip up the mountain. Show the places where they saw the snake, the avalanche, and the hawk. Then show how they got home.

2. **Creative Writing** Imagine that you were on the mountain with Frog and Toad. You saw the snake, the avalanche, and the hawk. Choose one of these and write a paragraph telling others about it. What did you see? What did you hear? How did you feel?

STAMP COLLECTOR

Grammar and Related Language Skills

Linking Verbs
Nouns and Adjectives After Linking Verbs
Linking Verbs in the Present Tense
Linking Verbs in the Past Tense
Adverbs

Practical Communication

STUDY AND REFERENCE SKILLS

Taking and Organizing Notes

COMPOSITION

Writing a Two-Paragraph Report

Creative Expression

A News Story

Do you collect stamps as a hobby? Stamp collectors save old and interesting stamps in special albums. Some stamps can be bought at the post office. Some stamp collectors trade or buy stamps from each other. Sometimes they write to stamp dealers for unusual stamps. What writing skills might a stamp collector need?

Linking Verbs

Every sentence has a verb. Some verbs name an action. Verbs like *skip, jump,* and *catch* name actions. Other verbs do not name an action, but they still help to make a statement.

> An **action verb** is a word that names an action.
>
> A **linking verb** is a verb that connects the subject part with a noun or adjective in the predicate part. It tells what the subject is or is like.

The verb *be* is a linking verb. The chart shows some of the forms of the verb *be*.

I	**am**	She He It	**is**	You We They	**are**

- Look at these two sentences.

Sandra builds model airplanes. Sandra is a builder.

The verb *builds* names an action. The verb *is* does not name an action. However, it still helps to make a statement. The verb *is* works as a linking verb.

Talk About It

Read each sentence. Name the verb and tell whether it is an **action verb** or a **linking verb.**

1. Some planes are wooden.
2. Sandra makes paper airplanes.
3. The planes fly.
4. One plane is old.
5. Sandra is careful.
6. Sandra cleans her tools.
7. She needs glue
8. Sandra paints the planes.
9. Her favorite plane is red.
10. Her friends help.
11. They cut paper.
12. The planes are small.

Skills Practice

Write each sentence and draw a line under the verb. If the verb names an action, write **action verb.** If the verb is a linking verb, write **linking verb.**

1. Sandra walks to the library.
2. The library is large.
3. Sandra reads books about airplanes.
4. The Wright Brothers flew in 1903.
5. Sandra made a model of the Wright Brothers' airplane.
6. That model is white.
7. I am a builder.
8. Sandra and I flew our airplanes in the park.
9. My plane is fast.
10. Her plane is faster.

Writing Sentences

Write four sentences about a hobby you have or would like to have. Use two action verbs and two linking verbs.

Sample Answer **1.** Sandra walks to the library. action verb

Nouns and Adjectives After Linking Verbs

A *linking verb* helps to make a statement without naming an action. Sometimes a linking verb is followed by a noun or an adjective. Remember,

> A **noun** is a word that names a person, a place, or a thing.
>
> An **adjective** is a word that describes a noun or a pronoun.

A linking verb *connects,* or links, the subject part with a noun or adjective in the predicate part.

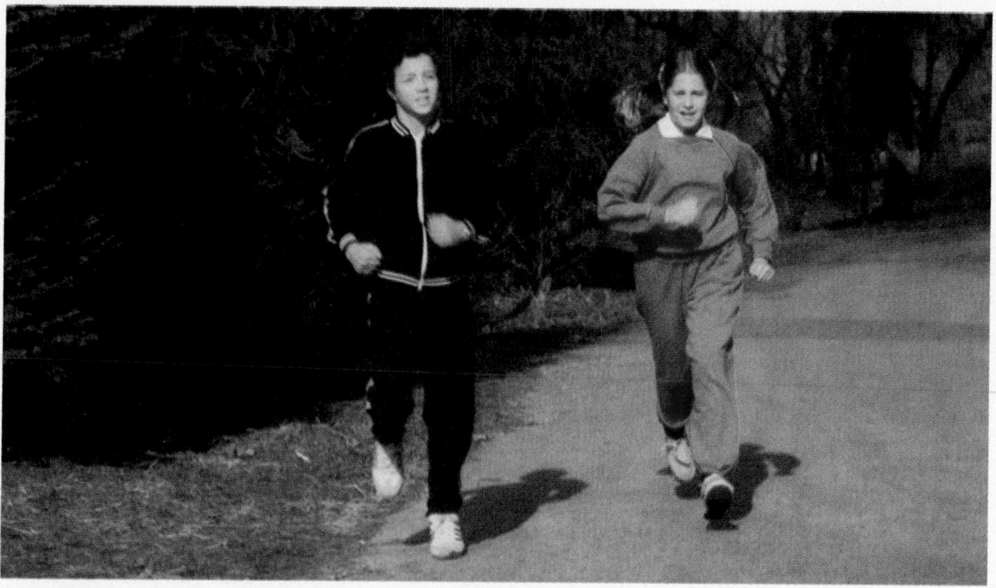

- Look at these sentences.

Ben is my friend. My friend is a runner.

In the first sentence the verb *is* connects the subject *Ben* with the noun *friend. Ben* and *friend* are the same person. In the second sentence the verb *is* connects the subject *friend* with the noun *runner. Friend* and *runner* are the same person.

- Now look at these sentences.

His legs are strong. His feet are sore.

In the first sentence the verb *are* connects the subject *legs* to the adjective *strong*. *Strong* describes *legs*. In the second sentence the verb *are* connects the subject *feet* to the adjective *sore*. *Sore* describes *feet*.

Talk About It

Tell whether a **noun** or an **adjective** follows each linking verb. Then tell to which word the noun or adjective is connected.

1. Ben is my classmate.
2. Debra is a runner.
3. My friends are quick.
4. Ben is happy.
5. His feet are sore.
6. Their hobby is fun.
7. The weather is warm.
8. The runners are healthy.
9. The judge is ready.
10. The judge is a runner.
11. The track is bumpy.
12. The stones are small.

Skills Practice

Write each sentence. Draw a line under the word that follows the linking verb. (Do not count words such as *a, an, the, his, her, my,* or *their.*) If the word is a noun, write **noun.** If the word is an adjective, write **adjective.**

1. The weather is fine.
2. The trees are beautiful.
3. Runners are strong.
4. Debra is my friend.
5. Her shoes are new.
6. Her shoes are blue.
7. Their track is the sidewalk.
8. They are healthy.
9. They are thirsty.
10. Water is his drink.
11. The water is cool.
12. Runners are workers.

Sample Answer 1. The weather is fine. adjective

Using Linking Verbs in the Present Tense

The *subject* of a sentence tells whom or what the sentence is about. The subject may be *singular.* Then it names one person, place, or thing. The subject may be *plural.* Then it names more than one person, place, or thing.

- Look at these sentences. Are the subjects singular or plural?

> I am a stamp hunter. This stamp is small.
> These stamps are large.

In the first sentence the subject *I* is singular. In the second sentence the subject *stamp* is singular. In the third sentence the subject *stamps* is plural.

- Look back at the sentences in the box. Can you find the linking verbs? They are *am, is,* and *are.* Remember, a *linking verb* is a verb that connects the subject part with a noun or adjective in the predicate part. It tells what the subject is or is like.

The linking verbs *am, is,* and *are* show present time. These linking verbs are in the present tense.

- Read the sentences that follow. Notice which linking verbs in the present tense are used with which subjects.

I am a stamp hunter.	She is a stamp hunter.	You are a stamp hunter.
	He is a stamp hunter.	We are stamp hunters.
	It is large.	They are stamp hunters.
	The stamp is large.	The girls are stamp hunters.

Use *am* for the present tense when the subject is *I*. Use *is* for the present tense when the subject is *she, he, it,* or a *singular noun*. Use *are* for the present tense when the subject is *you, we, they,* or a *plural noun*.

Talk About It

Look at the linking verbs at the end of each sentence. Tell which linking verb belongs in each sentence.

1. Stamps ____ my hobby. (are, am)
2. I ____ a stamp hunter. (is, am)
3. They ____ fun. (am, are)
4. My stamp book ____ heavy. (am, is)
5. It ____ full. (is, am)
6. We ____ happy. (are, is)

Skills Practice

Write each sentence. Use the correct form of the linking verb to complete each sentence.

1. My neighbor ____ a traveler. (is, are)
2. Her letters ____ useful. (is, are)
3. These stamps ____ Spanish. (are, am)
4. That stamp ____ old. (am, is)
5. That man ____ famous. (is, are)
6. He ____ a king. (are, is)
7. I ____ careful. (am, is)
8. That stamp ____ new. (are, is)
9. Those Spanish stamps ____ beautiful. (are, is)
10. I ____ happy with my stamp books. (am, is)
11. The stamp books ____ full. (is, are)
12. My neighbor ____ nice. (am, is)

Sample Answer 1. My neighbor is a traveler.

Contractions

Shortcuts help you get from place to place in less time. Language has shortcuts, too. One language shortcut is called a *contraction.* A contraction is formed when two words are shortened into one.

- Read each sentence.

You're builders. I'm the painter.

The word *you're* is a contraction of *you are*. The *a* was dropped from the word *are*. An apostrophe (') was put in its place. The word *I'm* is a contraction of *I am*. What was dropped from the word *am*? What took its place?

A **contraction** is a word made up of two words. The words are joined together to make one word by leaving out one or more letters.

Use an **apostrophe (')** in a contraction to show that one or more letters are missing.

CONTRACTION	SHORT FOR
I'm	I am
you're	you are
he's	he is
she's	she is
it's	it is
we're	we are
they're	they are

Some contractions sound the same as other words. Be careful when you use these words.

you're *You're* good builders. (*You are* good builders.)
your *Your* hobby is fun.

it's *It's* a nice dollhouse. (*It is* a nice dollhouse.)
its *Its* door is open.

they're *They're* hard workers. (*They are* hard workers.)
their *Their* dollhouse has five rooms.
there *There* is my dollhouse.

Talk About It

Read each sentence. Tell the contraction that can take the place of the underlined words.

1. It is complete at last.
2. We are ready for the inside.
3. She is the room planner.
4. They are all ready for work.
5. You are the chair makers.
6. I am happy.

Skills Practice

Write each sentence. Use the contraction that can take the place of the underlined words.

1. I am happy with this chair.
2. You are a clever worker.
3. We are all eager workers.
4. They are so shiny.
5. She is making a bed.
6. It is a gift for a friend.
7. She is a neighbor.
8. He is finished.
9. She is happy with her gift.
10. He is smiling.
11. They are laughing.
12. You are welcome.
13. We are glad you came.
14. She is busy with the dollhouse.
15. It is time to leave.
16. We are going home now.

Sample Answer 1. I'm happy with this chair.

Skills Review

Write the verb in each sentence. If the verb names an action, write **action verb** after the verb. If the verb is a linking verb, write **linking verb** after the verb.

1. Art is my hobby.
2. I paint with water colors.
3. My neighbor is a painter.
4. She is famous.
5. Her paintings are colorful.
6. She paints every day.
7. She makes clay pots.
8. She teaches me.
9. I am her pupil.
10. I learn quickly.

Read each sentence. Write the word that follows the linking verb. (Do not count words such as *a, an, the, his, her, my,* or *their*.) If the word is a noun, write **noun.** If the word is an adjective, write **adjective.**

11. This painting is large.
12. The lake is blue.
13. That circle is the sun.
14. The woman is my mother.
15. That kitten is Tiger.
16. Tiger is my pet.
17. Tiger is black.
18. This painting is pretty.

Read each sentence. Write the correct form of the linking verb to complete each sentence.

19. Shawn ____ my friend. (am, is)
20. Our hobbies ____ different. (is, are)
21. I ____ a builder. (am, are)
22. These castles ____ my buildings. (am, are)
23. The walls ____ toothpicks. (is, are)
24. This window ____ paper. (is, are)
25. Shawn ____ a ship builder. (is, are)
26. Ships ____ fun, too. (is, are)
27. This ship ____ complete now. (am, is)
28. That ship ____ fancy. (am, is)

Read each sentence. Write the contraction that can take the place of the underlined words.

29. I am very busy this week.
30. You are busy, too.
31. We are happy about the hobby fair.
32. It is a class hobby fair.
33. She is our class president.

Read this sentence.

Art is my hobby.

You can make some changes to the sentence above without changing its meaning. You can make the noun in the subject part change places with the noun in the predicate part.

Now read this sentence. Did the meaning change?

My hobby is art.

You can change the place of the nouns in some sentences that have linking verbs without changing the meaning.

Look what happens when you change the place of the nouns in a sentence with an action verb. Does the meaning change?

The man bit the dog.
The dog bit the man.

Think of other sentences with action verbs. Do the meanings change when you change the place of the nouns?

Exploring Language

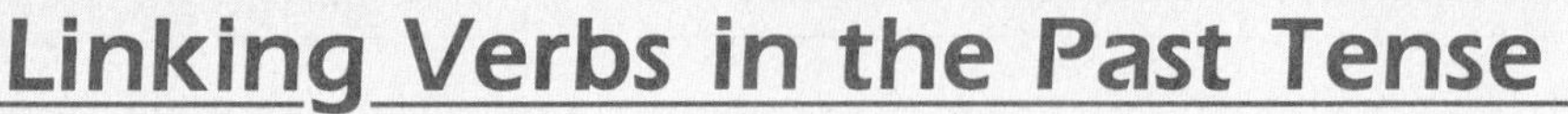

Linking Verbs in the Past Tense

Action verbs can name an action that already happened. These are action verbs in the past tense.

- Read each sentence below. Find the action verbs in the past tense.

  Joel hid baseball cards in his drawer.
  Joel collected many cards.

The underlined words are action verbs in the past tense.

Linking verbs can show past time, too. Remember, a *linking verb* is a verb that connects the subject part with a noun or adjective in the predicate part. The linking verbs *was* and *were* show past time.

- Read the sentences that follow. Find the past tense linking verbs.

The drawer was full.	A box was the answer.
Joel was sad.	They were fine in the box.
I was his friend.	

The past tense linking verbs *was* and *were* tell what a subject was or was like in the past.

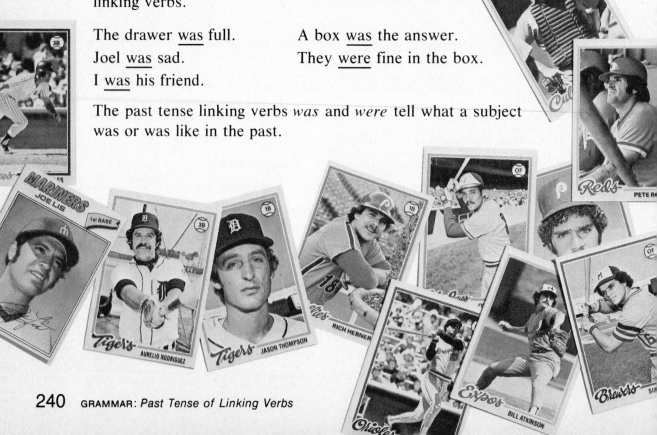

Talk About It

Read each sentence. Name the verb and tell whether it is a **linking verb** or an **action verb.**

1. Joel traded baseball cards.
2. He was thirteen years old.
3. He was too old for cards.
4. Joel gave the cards to Pam.
5. They were a gift.
6. It was her birthday.

Skills Practice

Write each sentence. Draw a line under the verb. If the verb names an action, write **action verb.** If the verb is a linking verb, write **linking verb.**

1. I traded baseball cards, too.
2. I read the cards.
3. They were interesting.
4. Old cards were our favorites.
5. Joel placed his cards here.
6. He was careful.
7. We bought football cards, too.
8. We tossed the cards.
9. My mother was helpful.
10. She gave me a book.
11. I learned facts about baseball.
12. I dreamed about baseball.
13. Our hobby was fun.
14. It was my joy.

Writing Sentences

Perhaps you have seen a baseball or a softball game. Perhaps you have even played these games. Write four sentences about being on a baseball or a softball team. Write two sentences using action verbs in the past tense. Write two sentences using linking verbs in the past tense.

Sample Answer 1. I traded baseball cards, too. action verb

Using Linking Verbs in the Past Tense

The linking verb in a sentence must work with the subject part. Some linking verbs show present time. The present tense linking verbs are *am, is,* and *are*.

Do you remember with which subjects those linking verbs agree? Use *am* when the subject is *I*. Use *is* when the subject is *she, he, it,* or a *singular noun*. Use *are* when the subject is *you, we, they,* or a *plural noun*.

Past tense linking verbs must agree with the subject part, too. Two linking verbs in the past tense are *was* and *were*.

- Read these sentences. Notice how the linking verbs *was* and *were* agree with the different subjects.

I was busy.	You were busy.
She was busy.	We were busy.
He was busy.	They were busy.
It was busy.	Two people were busy.
My neighbor was busy.	

Use *was* for the past tense when the subject is *I, she, he, it,* or a *singular noun*. Use *were* for the past tense when the subject is *you, we, they,* or a *plural noun*.

Talk About It

Read each sentence. Use the correct form of the linking verb at the end of the sentence.

1. An old chest ____ dusty. (was, were)
2. My neighbor ____ curious. (am, is, are)
3. The top ____ loose. (was, were)
4. We ____ careful. (was, were)

Skills Practice

Write each sentence. Use the correct form of the linking verb.

1. Our discovery ____ exciting. (was, were)
2. Old coins and stamps ____ our treasure. (was, were)
3. This penny ____ new. (am, is, are)
4. Dad ____ curious about the coin. (was, were)
5. It ____ an Indian head penny. (was, were)
6. My penny ____ unusual. (was, were)
7. The stamps ____ old, too. (was, were)
8. They ____ two-cent stamps. (was, were)
9. Stamps ____ my new hobby. (was, were)
10. I ____ happy with our discovery. (was, were)

Writing Sentences

Write three sentences about some kind of discovery you made. Use linking verbs in the past tense.

1. Name the discovery in the first sentence.
2. Next use an adjective to tell about the discovery.
3. Last tell how you felt about the discovery.

Sample Answer 1. Our discovery was exciting.

Adverbs

You use verbs to name an action. You also use words to describe these actions. These words tell more about the actions.

- Read this sentence.

The art teacher spoke loudly.

Loudly is an adverb. It describes the verb *spoke*. It tells us *how* the art teacher spoke.

An **adverb** is a word that describes an action.

- Look at these sentences.

Tracy painted carefully. Tom quickly drew a tree.

In the first sentence *carefully* describes the action verb *painted*. The word *carefully* tells *how* Tracy painted. In the second sentence *quickly* describes the action verb *drew*. The word *quickly* tells *how* Tom drew. *Carefully* and *quickly* are adverbs. They tell *how* the action is done.

Talk About It

What is the adverb in each sentence? What verb does it describe?

1. Doris calmly painted a picture.
2. The ship's bell rang loudly.
3. The waves broke slowly.
4. The children cheerfully played ball.
5. Some people sat lazily.
6. The hot sun shone brightly.

Skills Practice

Write each sentence. Underline the adverb in each sentence. Then write the verb it describes.

1. The art students quickly entered the room.
2. Eagerly they chose paints and paper.
3. The whole class drew carefully.
4. Some students talked quietly.
5. Pablo laughed softly.
6. Pam slowly painted a sea gull.
7. The colors blended beautifully.
8. The paints dried evenly.
9. Jack impatiently finished his painting.
10. The teacher smiled happily.

Sample Answer 1. The art students <u>quickly</u> entered the room. entered

More Adverbs

You know that an adverb is a word that describes an action verb. Some adverbs tell *how* an action is done. Other adverbs tell *when* an action is done.

- Read this sentence.

Yesterday the Magic Club practiced.

Yesterday is an adverb. It describes the verb *practiced*. It tells *when* the Magic Club practiced.

- Look at these sentences.

Lu arrived early. Tina came last.

In the first sentence *early* describes the action verb *arrived*. The word *early* tells *when* Lu arrived. In the second sentence *last* describes the action verb *came*. The word *last* tells *when* Tina came. *Early* and *last* are adverbs. They tell *when* the action is done.

Talk About It

What is the adverb in each sentence? What verb does it describe?

1. Today the Magic Club met.
2. Brian laughed often.
3. Marilyn arrived early.
4. Later Bev performed.
5. The Marshall twins left immediately.

Skills Practice

Write each sentence. Draw a line under the adverb in each sentence. Then draw two lines under the verb each adverb describes.

1. The show started tonight.
2. The members arrived early.
3. Suddenly Marilyn laughed.
4. Now Rita's mother watches.
5. Her father arrived promptly.
6. Yesterday Luisa practiced.
7. Then he bowed.
8. Rita came next.
9. Soon the show ended.
10. The curtain fell last.

Writing Sentences

Think about a magic show or some other show you might have seen. Write four sentences about it using adverbs. In the first two sentences, use adverbs telling *how* an action is done. In the next two sentences, use adverbs telling *when* an action is done.

Sample Answer **1.** The show started tonight.

Skills Review

Write the verb in each sentence. If the verb names an action, write **action verb** after the verb. If the verb is a linking verb, write **linking verb** after the verb.

1. Our hobby fair was fun.
2. That dollhouse was lovely.
3. The tiny lamps were cute.
4. I rocked the little rocking chair.
5. The model trains were my favorite.
6. The tracks wound around the mountains.
7. Bill and Maria were happy with their models.
8. They worked on them all week.
9. Maria's car was silver.

Read each sentence. Write the linking verb that belongs in each sentence.

10. The stamps ____ interesting. (was, were)
11. The round stamp ____ unusual. (was, were)
12. It ____ costly. (was, were)
13. My stamps ____ ordinary. (am, is, are)
14. One silver dollar ____ a hundred years old. (was, were)
15. I ____ curious about coins. (am, is, are)
16. The fair ____ very helpful to me. (was, were)
17. Mark ____ a painter. (am, is, are)
18. His paintings ____ good. (was, were)
19. Ben ____ a good cook. (am, is, are)
20. His muffins ____ delicious. (was, were)
21. His hobby ____ my favorite. (am, is, are)
22. Our hobby fair ____ bigger each year. (am, is, are)
23. It ____ a small fair at first. (was, were)

Write the adverb in each sentence. Then write the verb it describes.

24. The builders worked safely.
25. Their machines ran loudly.
26. Soon the other workers arrived.
27. The whistle blew early.
28. That man ate hungrily.
29. Slowly the delicious lunch disappeared.
30. A soft breeze always blew.
31. His friends often called.
32. Immediately Mr. Hill answered.
33. The whistle sounded noisily.

A long time ago, people speaking English used *are* or *were* with the subject pronoun *you* only for the plural. People used *art* and *wast* with the subject pronoun *thou*. *Thou* was the singular of *you*.

For example:

You are my friends. You were strangers.
Thou art my friend. Thou wast a stranger.

After a while most people stopped using *thou*. When they stopped using *thou*, they stopped using *art* and *wast*. They began to use *you are* and *you were* for both the singular and the plural.

Exploring Language

Reference Materials

The library is divided into several parts. One part has reference books. You have learned about one reference book, the dictionary. The encyclopedia, the atlas, and the almanac are other kinds of reference books.

An *encyclopedia* is a book or a set of books that give facts about many things. The subjects are arranged in alphabetical order. You can find information about almost every subject in an encyclopedia. There are many illustrations. The index tells in which book and on what page of the book you can find the facts you need.

An *atlas* is a book of maps. You can find maps of different countries in an atlas.

An *almanac* is a single book that gives you the latest facts and figures about many subjects. They give facts about important records, events, and people.

Newspapers, magazines, TV, and *radio* are reference materials that are not books.

Most *newspapers* are published every day. They give the latest information about news, sports, and weather all over the world.

Magazines usually have information about special subjects. Some magazines have sports news. Some magazines have science news. Other magazines have news about animals and outdoor life.

Many shows on *TV* and *radio* give general information or news of current events. News programs tell what is happening now. Some classes watch TV shows in school. These shows tell about special subjects.

Talk About It

Name the reference book you would use to find out about each of these.

1. The results of this year's election
2. The first automobile
3. How to pronounce the word *testimony*
4. A map of India
5. Yesterday's weather in London

Skills Practice

Name the best reference material you would use to find out about each of these. Write **encyclopedia, atlas, almanac, newspaper, magazine, TV and radio,** or **dictionary.**

1. The history of England
2. An article on sailing
3. Yesterday's bank robbery
4. The meaning of the word *primitive*
5. This year's sports records
6. News of the storm we are now having
7. How people live in Egypt
8. A map of Spain
9. The current mayor of Chicago
10. How to pronounce the word *glossary*

Sample Answer 1. encyclopedia

Taking Notes

When you prepare a report, you may read many books. You need to remember the important facts from each book. You can remember important facts by taking notes. When you *take notes,* you write all the important facts.

Max wants to write a report about where frogs live. He reads this paragraph. He takes notes as he reads. His notes should be the most important facts in the paragraph.

> Frogs live in many kinds of places. Most frogs live near wet areas. Some frogs live in trees. The spring peeper is a kind of frog that lives in a tree. Some frogs live underground, too.

Max can write his notes in sentences. He can write his notes in phrases, also. When he writes his notes in phrases, he writes only the important words.

Sentence Notes

1. Frogs live in different kinds of places.
2. Most frogs live near water.
3. Some frogs live in trees.
4. Other frogs live underground.

Phrase Notes

Kinds of places frogs live

1. Live near water
2. Live in trees
3. Live underground

Read the sentence notes and phrase notes again. All the notes tell the important facts in the paragraph.

Talk About It

Read this paragraph.

> Argentina is a country in South America. Argentina has many farms and ranches. It is famous for horse races. Race horses are very beautiful. Sheep are raised in Argentina, too.

You are writing a report about Argentina. Which of these sentence notes would you take?

1. Argentina is in South America.
2. There are many farms and ranches in Argentina.
3. Argentina is known for horse racing.
4. Race horses are pretty.
5. Argentina has sheep raising.

Skills Practice

Read this paragraph.

> There are many things to do in Hawaii. Hawaii is a state. You can go to Hawaii's beautiful beaches. You can see the sights. You can visit the different islands that make up Hawaii.

You are writing a report about what kinds of things you can do in Hawaii. Which of these phrase notes would you use? Write the notes.

1. Can do many things in Hawaii
2. Hawaii—a state
3. Go to the beaches
4. See the sights
5. Visit the islands
6. Honolulu, capital city

Writing an Outline

You often use books to find information for a report. After you take notes from the books, you must decide how all the notes fit together. You can write an outline. An outline is a way of putting your notes together in an order that makes sense.

Sue is working on a report about deer. This is the outline.

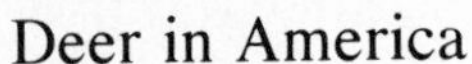

Deer in America

I. Kinds of Deer
   A. Mule deer
   B. White-tailed deer
II. Description of a Deer
   A. Antlers
   B. Legs and Hoofs

Look at Sue's outline.

1. Sue wrote a title for the outline. The title tells the main subject of her report.
2. She used Roman numerals to show her main ideas. This is what she wrote to show her first main idea.
   I. Kinds of Deer
3. Notice she put a period after each Roman numeral.
4. She used capital letters to show the details for each main idea. This is what she wrote to show the details for her first main idea.
   A. Mule deer
   B. White-tailed deer
5. Notice she put a period after each capital letter.
6. Notice that Sue used phrases in her outline. She could use sentences instead of phrases.

Talk About It

Read the outline about deer in America.

1. What is the main subject of the report?
2. What part of the outline tells this?
3. How would you write the first main idea?
4. How would you write the details for the first idea?
5. How would you write the second main idea?
6. How would you write the details for the second idea?

Skills Practice

Read this report.

Boats

There are many kinds of boats. One kind of boat is a motorboat. A rowboat is another kind of boat.

There are different ways of running a boat. Motorboats are run by motors. Oars are used to move rowboats.

Write an outline for this report. Use these steps.

1. Write the title of the outline.
2. Write this first main idea and detail.
   I. Kinds of Boats
      A. Motorboat
3. Write another detail for this first main idea.
4. Write the second main idea.
5. Write two details for this second idea.

A Two-Paragraph Report

Thinking About Paragraphs

You have written reports with one paragraph. However, most reports are longer than one paragraph. Some reports have two or more paragraphs. These paragraphs talk about the same main subject. Each paragraph tells about a different part of that subject. Each paragraph has its own main idea sentence and detail sentences.

A two-paragraph report can have different kinds of paragraphs. Each paragraph might give directions, tell facts, or describe.

For a two-paragraph report, you might find information in encyclopedias, graphs, tables, interviews, or surveys. You take notes on the information you find. Then you organize your notes into an outline. The outline tells you the order in which you will present the information in your report.

Alex wants to write a report on exercise. He took a survey to find out how many hours his classmates exercise each day after school. The graph on the left shows what he learned.

He also interviewed his classmates. He took notes. On the right is an outline of his notes.

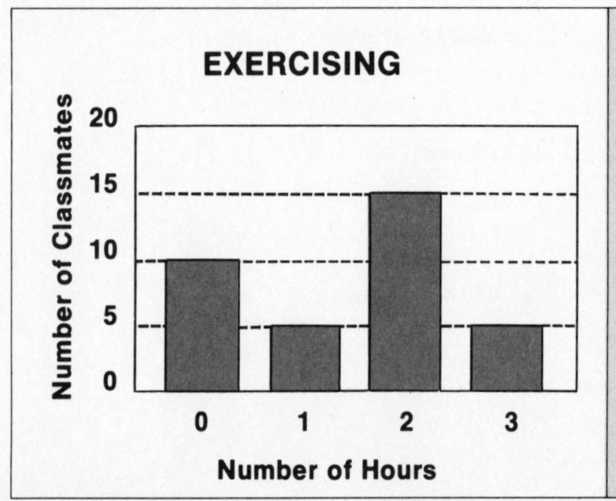

I. Kinds of Exercises
   A. Ride bikes
   B. Play ball
   C. Run
   D. Do exercise in a gym

Alex wrote this report. He used the information from the graph and the outline.

> I took a survey to find out how much my classmates exercise after school each day. Fifteen students told me they exercise two hours every day. Five students said they exercise for three hours. Another five students said they get one hour of exercise. And ten students reported that they do not exercise at all after school.
>
> My classmates do different kinds of exercises. Many of my classmates ride bikes. Some exercise by playing ball. Some like to run. A few students do exercise in a gym, too.

Talking About Paragraphs

Read both paragraphs of the report again.

1. What is the main subject of the whole report?
2. Find the main idea sentence in the first paragraph. What part of the main subject does it talk about?
3. Does the first paragraph give directions, tell facts, or describe?
4. Find the main idea sentence in the second paragraph. What part of the main subject does it talk about?
5. Does the second paragraph give directions, tell facts, or describe?

A Class Outline

Thinking About an Outline

There are several steps to writing a report. First you must find your information. As you find the information, you take notes. Then you make an outline from your notes. The outline shows how you plan to present the information.

Suppose you wanted to write a two-paragraph report on bicycles. You read an article about bicycles in an encyclopedia. You also interviewed an owner of a bicycle shop. Here is the information you got for your report.

Encyclopedia

There are three kinds of bicycles used today. The heaviest is the *standard.* It has large tires and a foot brake. The *middleweight* has a lighter frame and narrow tires. It has a gear shift and a foot brake. The *lightweight* has a diamond-shaped frame made of steel tubes. It has hand brakes and five or ten-speed gears.

Interview

1. I sell three kinds of bicycles in my store. The standard is used mostly by children.
2. The middleweight is used by many adults who ride for fun. I use a middleweight bike.
3. The lightweight bicycle is used by racers. Most of my friends use this kind of bike when they are in riding contests.

Now your class will make an outline from the information you have gathered. Remember to include only the most important information in the outline.

Writing an Outline

Your teacher will write the outline on the board. Use phrases in the outline.

1. The title of the report is "Bicycles." It is the main subject of the report. Write it at the top of the board.

2. Your first paragraph will describe the different kinds of bicycles. Use this phrase in your outline to show the main idea of the paragraph.
   I. Kinds of Bicycles

3. Look at the information you got from the encyclopedia. Give the three phrases that describe the three kinds of bicycles. Put the phrases next to the letters A, B, and C under Roman numeral I. This could be your first phrase.
   A. Standard

4. Now your outline should look like this.
   I. Kinds of Bicycles
      A. Standard

5. Your second paragraph will tell who uses bicycles. Use this phrase in your outline to show the main idea of the second paragraph.
   II. Users of Bicycles

6. Look at the information from the interview. Give three phrases that tell about people who use bicycles. Put the phrases next to the letters A, B, and C under Roman numeral II.

7. Write the outline on your paper. Save the outline.

Practicing a Two-Paragraph Report

Thinking About a Report

You and your class have made an outline for a two-paragraph report about bicycles. Now you will write the report. Your outline might look like this one.

Bicycles
I. Kinds of Bicycles
    A. Standard
    B. Middleweight
    C. Lightweight
II. Users of Bicycles
    A. Children
    B. Adults
    C. Racers

Writing a Report

1. The main subject of your report is bicycles. Write a title for the report.
2. Your first paragraph will be a paragraph that describes. Look at Roman numeral I in the outline. Choose one of these main idea sentences for the first paragraph.
   There are different kinds of bicycles.
   Bicycles come in different sizes and weights.
3. Write a detail sentence that tells about the information next to letter A under Roman numeral I. Then write a detail sentence that tells about letter B. Write a detail sentence that tells about letter C. The Word Bank may help you.
4. Your second paragraph will be a paragraph of facts. Look at Roman numeral II in the outline. Write a main idea sentence for this paragraph.
5. Write a detail sentence for each letter under Roman numeral II. You will have at least three detail sentences in this paragraph.

Word Bank

bicycle
standard
brake
middleweight
frame
gear
shift
lightweight

Edit Your Report

Read your report. Think about these questions.

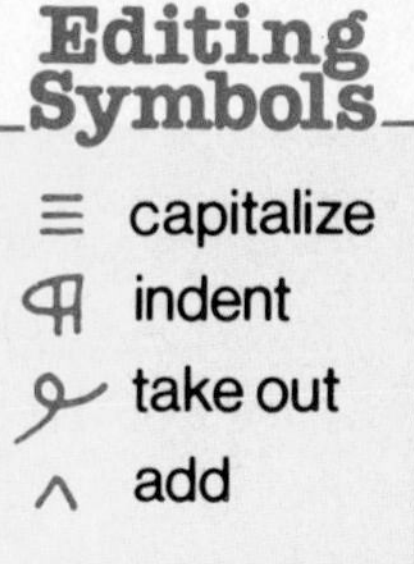

1. Does the whole report tell about one main subject?
2. Does each paragraph tell about a different part of the main subject? Does each paragraph have its own main idea sentence and detail sentences? Do all your sentences follow the order of the outline?
3. What linking verbs did you use in your report?
4. Did you indent the first word in each paragraph?
5. Did you use capital letters and periods where they were needed?
6. Did you spell all words correctly? Use the Word Bank.

Correct your mistakes. If you need to, write your report again.

INDEPENDENT WRITING

A Photo Essay Report

Prewriting A photo essay reports information using pictures and captions. Captions are sentences that describe or give facts about the pictures in the essay.

You are going to write a photo essay about your state. First make an outline. The main ideas for the outline might be I. General Facts, II. Farm Products, and III. Industries. Then find facts to complete the outline. One detail under General Facts might be A. State Bird. Next look for photographs and pictures, or draw pictures for each detail in the outline. Last jot down ideas for captions to describe each of your pictures.

Writing Write a photo essay report about your state. Use one page for each main idea of the outline. Arrange your photographs or pictures on each page. Write the sentence captions below them.

Editing Read your photo essay report again. Use the check questions and the editing symbols above to edit your report.

Unit Review

Write the verb in each sentence. If the verb names an action, write **action verb** after the verb. If the verb is a linking verb, write **linking verb** after the verb. *pages 230–231*

1. I am a gardener.
2. I plant the seeds.
3. He is my brother.
4. He is a gardener, too.
5. We pick the weeds.
6. Gardens are fun.

Read each sentence. Write the word that follows the linking verb. (Do not count words such as *a, an, the, his, her, my,* or *their*.) If the word is a noun, write **noun.** If the word is an adjective, write **adjective.** *pages 232–233*

7. Plants are my hobby.
8. I am a worker.
9. This soil is wet.
10. The sun is hot.
11. My brother is my helper.
12. That flower is a rose.

Write the correct form of the linking verb. *pages 234–235*

13. The sun ____ bright. (is, are)
14. The soil ____ warm. (are, is)
15. I ____ happy. (am, is)
16. The roses ____ nice. (is, are)

Write a contraction for the underlined words. *pages 236–237*

17. <u>They are</u> gardeners, too.
18. <u>We are</u> all hard workers.
19. <u>You are</u> a good gardener.
20. <u>I am</u> happy with my garden.
21. <u>He is</u> a cheerful person.
22. <u>It is</u> a beautiful garden.

Write the verb in each sentence. If the verb names an action, write **action verb** after the verb. If the verb is a linking verb, write **linking verb** after the verb. *pages 240–241*

23. The sun was hot today.
24. Sun hats were necessary.
25. We watered the plants.
26. My neighbor was a gardener.
27. He worked hard.
28. He picked three red roses.

Write the correct form of the linking verb. *pages 242–243*

29. The garden ____ beautiful this year. (was, were)
30. Tom and I ____ very busy. (was, were)
31. The vegetables ____ delicious. (was, were)
32. I ____ happy with our garden. (was, were)

Write the adverb in each sentence. Then write the verb it describes. *pages 244–247*

33. The weeds grew quickly.
34. We weeded often.
35. Yesterday we planted.
36. We worked cheerfully.
37. Then we rested.
38. I relaxed quietly.

Read these two main idea sentences for a two-paragraph report. Decide which main idea sentence will begin each paragraph. *pages 256–259*

39. **a.** We use different books in school.
b. I enjoy our reading book the most.

Read the six detail sentences below. Decide which detail sentences tell about each main idea sentence. Put the detail sentences in the right order. Write each paragraph with the main idea sentence and the detail sentences you have chosen. *pages 256–259*

40. **a.** The action in each story is exciting.
b. One book is used for arithmetic.
c. Another book has stories for us to read.
d. The characters are interesting, too.
e. The pictures help show the action.
f. A third book teaches us about science.

A News Story

You read for many reasons. Sometimes you read stories, plays, and poems for fun. You also read to learn new things about the world. You read true stories in newspapers and magazines. They give facts about other people and places.

A news story is written in a special way. The first paragraph always gives the main idea of the story. It is called the lead paragraph. The *lead paragraph* usually tells *who, what, when,* and sometimes *where* and *why.* The other paragraphs in the story give details about these five "W" questions.

Most news stories have a headline. A *headline* is like a title in a story. Headlines are written to catch your interest. If the headline is really interesting, you will probably read the whole news story.

This story is about "junk food." Read the lead paragraph carefully. Can you find answers to the five "W" questions? Look at the *Words to Think About.* They may help you understand the way these words are used in this news story.

Words to Think About

proposal, new idea
restriction, limit

prohibit, stop
decline, fall

eliminate, do away with
consumption, eating

School Meals Get Priority Over "Junk"

She claimed many students do not eat healthy lunches. They fill up on snack foods instead.

Washington (AP) The Agriculture Department wants a new law passed regarding "junk food" in schools. The law would stop schools from selling items such as candy, gum, and soft drinks until all meals have been served each day. Now many students can buy these foods during lunch and sometimes before.

The Assistant Secretary of the Department explained the reason for the law. She claimed many students do not eat healthy lunches. They fill up on snack foods instead.

Under the proposed law, certain foods could not be sold in schools until the last meal

Junk Food

Healthy Food

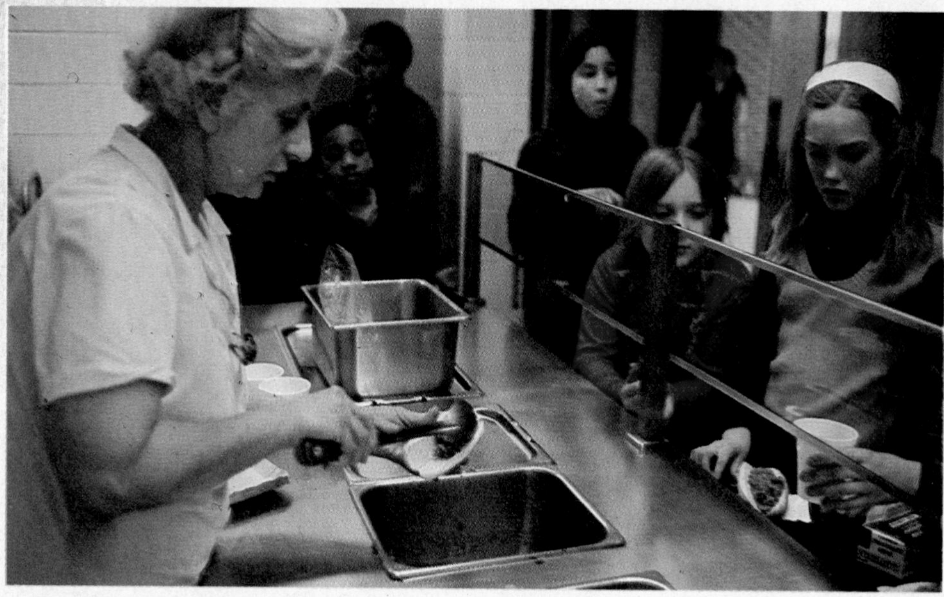

has been served each day. The foods include candy, soda drinks, chewing gum, and some frozen desserts. The frozen desserts are flavored ice bars and sherbets. Ice cream, however, could be sold with lunch. The law would also allow the sale of cookies, potato chips, peanuts, fruit, and milk at lunch time.

Walter Reed is against the new law. He represents the strong National Automatic Merchandising Association. Mr. Reed says snack foods do not replace cafeteria meals. He quoted a survey showing that vending machines sold an average of 3.5 candy bars and 3 soft drinks to each student per month.

The Agriculture Department hopes the law will stop the sale of sweets that are not part of regular school menus. The Department is in charge of all food programs for children including school breakfasts and lunches. About 25 million pupils are served daily under the school lunch program.

Creative Activities

1. **Creative Writing** News stories are written about events that are happening right now. Pretend you are a reporter for the school newspaper. Follow these steps and write your own news story.

   a. Choose an idea. Think about what is going on in your school. Here are some ideas. You may think of better ones.

   A play given by the fourth grade
   New playground equipment
   Opening of the school store

   b. Think about your lead paragraph. Try to answer the questions, who, what, when, where, and why.

   c. Write your news story.

   d. Think about a headline. Remember it has to catch the interest of your readers. Write your headline.

   e. Add a picture to your news story if you like.

2. Many news stories are given on the evening news on television. Your class can plan a television news program. Choose the news stories you want to read. You might even tape-record them to see how they sound. Present your news program. You could even include some commercials.

SKIER

Grammar and Related Language Skills

Review of Sentences
Compound Subjects
Compound Sentences
Building Compound Sentences
Using Commas

Practical Communication

STUDY AND REFERENCE SKILLS
Fact and Opinion

COMPOSITION
Writing a Persuasive Paragraph

Creative Expression

Fables

If you could have ski equipment, how would you know which kind to buy? A person who helps you select an item in a store is a salesperson. A salesperson in a sporting goods store must know about many types of sports equipment. What speaking and listening skills would a salesperson need? What speaking skills would help you explain your needs to a salesperson?

Reviewing Sentences

You have learned that a *sentence* is a group of words that state a complete idea. There are four kinds of sentences. Each kind states a complete idea in a different way.

A **declarative sentence** is a sentence that tells something.

Jane's class entered a baseball contest.

An **interrogative sentence** is a sentence that asks something.

How many students will play?

An **exclamatory sentence** is a sentence that shows excitement or strong feelings.

How exciting it will be!

An **imperative sentence** is a sentence that tells or asks someone to do something.

Come to all the practices.

You have also learned to use signals to make your meaning clear. You use signals to show where sentences begin. You use signals to show where sentences end.

Use a **capital letter** to begin the first word of every sentence.

Use a **period** (.) at the end of a declarative or an imperative sentence.

Use a **question mark** (?) at the end of an interrogative sentence.

Use an **exclamation mark** (!) at the end of an exclamatory sentence.

Talk About It

Read each sentence. Tell if it is a declarative sentence, an interrogative sentence, an exclamatory sentence, or an imperative sentence.

1. Saturday arrives at last.
2. How excited the children are!
3. Does Joe have a good seat?
4. Sit next to Mae.
5. Who will take the pictures?
6. The class smiles happily.

Tell how each sentence should begin and end. Tell what kind of sentence each sentence is.

7. who bats first
8. how bright the sun is
9. the sky is blue
10. watch the players warm up
11. what a beautiful day it is
12. the game begins

Skills Practice

Read each sentence. Decide which kind of sentence each one is. Write **declarative, interrogative, exclamatory,** or **imperative.**

1. The first batter swings hard.
2. How noisily the crowd cheers!
3. Will the player catch the ball?
4. The ball hits the fence with a bang.
5. Throw the ball to the person on third base.

Write each sentence so that it begins and ends correctly.

6. light rain starts to fall in the park
7. does the baseball game end now
8. stop the game for a short while
9. the rain shower stops after ten minutes
10. what a scare the children had

Sample Answers 1. declarative **6.** Light rain starts to fall in the park.

Reviewing Subject Parts

You have learned that a *sentence* is a group of words that state a complete idea. Each sentence has two parts. The *subject part* names whom or what the sentence is about. The *predicate part* tells what action the subject part does.

- Look at the subject part of this sentence. The subject part is in a blue box.

My best friend plays basketball.

Notice that the subject part has three words. The word *friend* is the main word of the subject part. It is what is being talked about.

The **simple subject** is the main word in the subject part.

- Read these sentences. What is the simple subject in each?

Players work together.

Our players work together.

Our basketball players work together.

The simple subject is the word *players*. *Players* is the main word of the subject part.

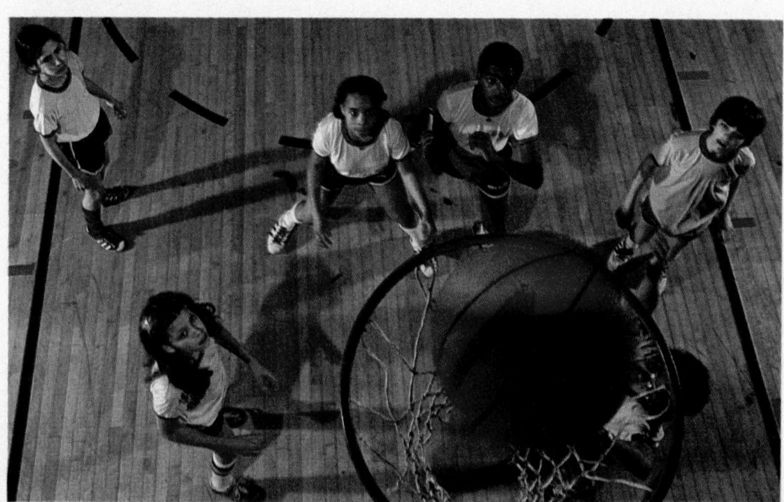

Talk About It

Read each sentence. What is the subject part of each sentence? What is the simple subject?

1. Our school has a basketball team.
2. The team plays after school.
3. Most players come from the sixth grade.
4. Some girls play on the team, too.
5. Many children watch the basketball games.
6. My friends go to most of them.

Skills Practice

Write the subject part of each sentence. Draw a line under the simple subject.

1. Our team played an exciting game.
2. The two teams played very hard.
3. My friend added eight points for our team.
4. My whole class went to the game.
5. Rita passed the ball quickly to Miyo.
6. One play brought many cheers.
7. Nora bounced the ball close to the basket.
8. The basketball swished through the net.
9. Our players smiled happily.
10. The other team received the ball.

Writing Sentences

Think of a time when you or someone you know played in a school baseball, basketball, or soccer game. Write four sentences to tell about the game. Use one of these simple subjects in the subject part of each sentence.

team   players   crowd   ball

Sample Answer **1.** Our team

Reviewing Predicate Parts

Each subject part of a sentence has a main word. You call this word the simple subject of a sentence. The predicate part of a sentence tells what action the subject does. You can probably tell that the predicate part of a sentence has a main word, too.

- Look at the predicate part of this sentence. The predicate part is in a red box.

Roger kicked the ball.

Notice that the predicate part has three words. The word *kicked* is the main word of the predicate part. *Kicked* is the verb that names the action.

> The **simple predicate** is the main word in the predicate part.

- Read these sentences. What is the simple predicate in each sentence?

The ball fell.

The ball fell quickly.

The ball fell over the fence.

Fell is the simple predicate in each sentence. It is the main word in the predicate part.

Talk About It

Read each sentence. What is the predicate part? What is the simple predicate?

1. All my friends play kickball after school.
2. The players practice on the kickball field.
3. My teacher watches sometimes.
4. He pitched for my team once.
5. Mr. Thomas pitches very well.
6. He throws the ball very fast.
7. He watches the batter.
8. The batter misses it every time.

Skills Practice

Write the predicate part of each sentence. Draw a line under the simple predicate.

1. Our team captain kicked the ball hard.
2. He ran very fast.
3. José won a track medal last year.
4. We voted Meg the captain of the other team.
5. She ran with José at the track meet.
6. I play in the outfield.
7. I caught a ball yesterday.
8. It surprised the other team.
9. Outfielders practice often.
10. Maria caught the ball for our team.
11. The crowd cheered for Maria.
12. Maria won the award for best sport in our class.

Sample Answer 1. kicked the ball hard

Compound Subjects

Many of the sentences you use have only one simple subject in the subject part. Sometimes sentences have two or more simple subjects in the subject part. A subject part that has two or more simple subjects is called a *compound subject*.

A **compound subject** has two or more simple subjects that have the same predicate. The subjects are joined by *and*.

- Read these sentences.

The boys and girls | pitch hay.

The horses and ponies | watch hungrily.

The riders and trainers | talk excitedly.

The subject part of each sentence is in a blue box. The two simple subjects in each sentence are underlined. The word *and* joins the simple subjects in a compound subject.

Sometimes you can make two sentences into one sentence. You join the simple subjects to make a compound subject.

Remember, a compound subject has more than one subject. The verb in the sentence must agree with the subject.

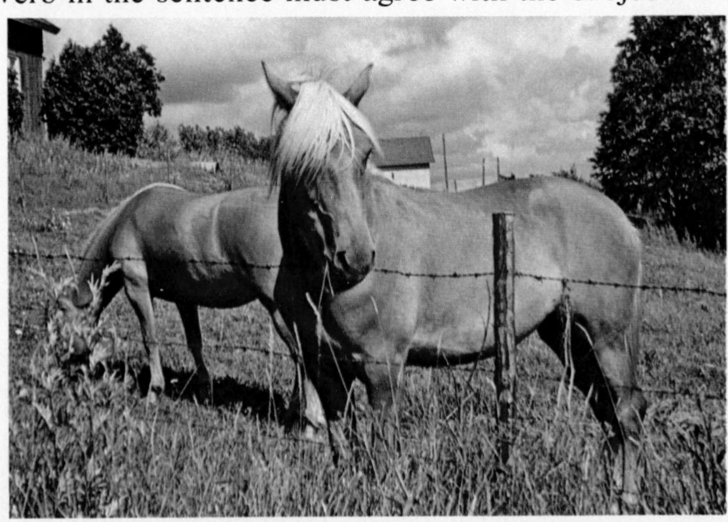

Here is an example.

Pete likes horses. I like horses.
Pete and I like horses.

Talk About It

What is the subject part? Name the simple subjects.

1. Mr. Stern and Mrs. Lansky tell about the horse show.
2. The girls and boys shine their boots.
3. Parents and friends watch the riders.
4. The horses and the riders perform well.

Skills Practice

Write the subject part. Underline the simple subjects.

1. Parents and trainers arrive early.
2. Racers and jumpers practice before the show.
3. My friends and I ride horses on a ranch.
4. The riders and horses race through the fields.
5. Angelo and Nadia walk to the brook.
6. The water and rocks glow in the sun.
7. Parents and children enjoy the day.

Writing Sentences

Imagine receiving a horse for your birthday. Here are some sentences telling about that day. Make each pair of sentences into one sentence with a compound subject.

1. Mother smiled at us. Father smiled at us.
2. My brother whispered. My sister whispered.
3. My family knew a secret. My friends knew a secret.

Sample Answer 1. Parents and trainers

Levels of Usage

Sometimes you wear jeans. Sometimes you dress up in special clothes. You wear different clothes at different times. For special situations you wear special clothes.

Using language is a lot like wearing clothes. You use language differently at different times. *Yeah, O.K., yes,* and *very well* mean nearly the same thing. But you choose the words to fit the situation. In everyday situations you use everyday words. In special situations you use special words.

Writing is a special situation. When you write, your reader cannot see you. You must use language carefully. Then you will be understood.

The adult in the picture is puzzled. Is the child enjoying the garden or is he digging up the flowers? The adult can't tell. Talking to an adult is a special situation. The child could have chosen different words to make his meaning clear.

If you write, "My sister's cool," it might mean that she needs a sweater. It also might mean that you enjoy her company. If you write, "My sister feels cool," or "My sister's fun to be with," your meaning would be clear to a reader.

Talk About It

Each sentence describes a situation. Choose the phrase or sentence that is appropriate to the situation.

1. Your mother's boss gives you a rare stamp.
   a. Gee, it's nifty. Thanks a heap. **b.** Thank you very much.
2. Your younger sister draws a picture for you.
   a. Thanks a lot. **b.** I am pleased to receive this, my dear.

Act out each situation using appropriate language.

3. You want a job mowing your neighbor's grass. You go to the neighbor and tell why you should be hired.
4. You want to wash cars in your neighborhood. Offer your services to several of your neighbors.

Skills Practice

Choose the phrase or sentence you would use in each situation.

1. You write a note inviting a friend to your house.
   a. Hope to see you. **b.** I hope you will join us.
2. You write a letter to an aunt in another city.
   a. Please write me a letter. **b.** Drop me a line.
3. You write a note thanking the librarian who helped your class.
   a. Thanks for everything. **b.** Thank you for all your help.
4. You write a note to friends of your parents who ask you to visit.
   a. Thank you for asking me. **b.** Thanks a bunch.

Writing Sentences

Write a sentence you would use in each of these situations.

1. Your friend said something you did not understand.
2. You notice an unusual paperweight on the principal's desk.

Skills Review

Read each sentence. Decide which kind of sentence each one is. Write **declarative, interrogative, exclamatory,** or **imperative.**

1. Does the class enjoy picnics in the park?
2. What a good time the children are having!
3. The softball game starts first.
4. Watch the captains choose players.
5. Who will pitch for our team?
6. A good pitcher helps a team.

Write each sentence so that it begins and ends correctly.

7. you really catch well
8. who pitches next
9. go get a new ball
10. where is the old ball
11. eddie hit it into the woods
12. what a good hit Eddie had

Write the subject part of each sentence. Draw a line under the simple subject.

13. Hungry children end the game soon.
14. Both teams hurry to the picnic tables.
15. One captain brings the ball.
16. The other captain brings the bats.
17. A curious squirrel watches from a tree.
18. The players clean the area after lunch.
19. Some children prepare for a hike.
20. Beth finds some horseshoes in the bus.
21. A basketball game interests some children.
22. The children play basketball.
23. The players find a basket on a wall.
24. The basketball misses the basket.

Write the predicate part of each sentence. Draw a line under the simple predicate.

25. Five children gather the horseshoes.
26. They find some clear flat ground.
27. Lenny's horseshoe sails through the air.
28. Dust clouds rise from the ground.
29. Kate aims the horseshoe carefully.
30. Kate's horseshoe hits the nail.
31. All the players shake Kate's hand.

Write the subject part. Underline the simple subjects.

32. The girls and boys meet for races.
33. The teachers and parents mark off the field.
34. Jess and I like the three-legged races.
35. The runners and judges prepare for the race.
36. The lemonade and ice cream taste good after the race.

Exploring Language

Some words do many different jobs. You find these words in different parts of a sentence. You must look carefully to see what job these words do. Sometimes the meaning of a word changes when the word changes jobs.

Read each pair of sentences. Notice how the underlined word changes in meaning.

The boys duck under the fence.

The duck swims on the pond.

The birds fly away fast.
He hit a fly ball.

Compound Sentences

You often use several sentences to state your ideas. Sometimes the ideas in two sentences go together. Then you can join the two ideas with the word *and*.

- Look at these sentences.

Maria plays basketball. Clara plays soccer.
Maria plays basketball, and Clara plays soccer.

The first sentence is *Maria plays basketball.* The second sentence is *Clara plays soccer.* The two sentences are joined by the word *and* in the third sentence. The third sentence is a *compound sentence.*

A **compound sentence** contains two sentences joined by **and.**

- Now read these sentences.

I told Matt about my boat trip.
He laughed.
I told Matt about my boat trip, and he laughed.

Notice that the word *and* joins the two sentences. Pay special attention to the comma before the word *and.*

Use a **comma** (,) before **and** when it joins two sentences.

Talk About It

Read each sentence. Which sentences are compound sentences?

1. We rowed down the North River last summer.
2. The trip started nicely, and we sang songs.
3. A fish swam nearby, and I fed it.
4. An eagle flew overhead, and we took its picture.
5. Lunchtime arrived, and we stopped along the bank.
6. We needed the short rest.

Skills Practice

Read each sentence. Write **compound** if the sentence is compound. Write **not compound** if the sentence is not compound.

1. The sun shined brightly, and the wind blew gently.
2. We hurried to the boats.
3. The river forked, and we rowed to the left.
4. Our trouble began soon.
5. We paddled in the low water, and our boats hit the bottom.
6. We saw rocks, and we bumped into them.
7. We heard the wind, and we watched the sun sink.
8. Insects bit us, and we wanted a drink of water.
9. I dreamed about a cool swim.
10. We rowed very hard, and we wanted help.
11. The water filled the boats, and we were still far from camp.
12. We stepped into the water.
13. Sam pushed our boat, and I pulled it.
14. Rangers arrived at last, and we received help.
15. Our adventure ended happily.

Sample Answer 1. compound

Building Compound Sentences

You join sentences together to show that the ideas they state are related. Joining sentences together helps you tell your ideas in a clearer way.

- Read these sentences. Notice how the ideas go together.

  Mae plays basketball. She belongs to the track team.
  Mae plays basketball, and she belongs to the track team.

  The track team has many members. They all work hard.
  The track team has many members, and they all work hard.

Remember,

> Use a **comma** (,) before **and** when it joins two sentences.

- Look at this sentence. What is wrong with it?

  Mae plays basketball, and she belongs to the track team, and it has many members, and they all work hard.

This sentence contains more than two complete ideas. It is confusing. Do not join more than two complete ideas in a compound sentence.

- Now look at these two compound sentences. They are easy to understand.

  Mae plays basketball, and she belongs to the track team.
  It has many members, and they all work hard.

Talk About It

Read each pair of sentences. Tell how to make each pair of sentences into one compound sentence.

1. Our town has a track meet each spring. We all go.
2. Carlos won two blue ribbons. Ben won a red ribbon.
3. Mae won a ribbon. She hung it in her room.

Add another complete idea to each sentence to make a compound sentence. Tell your sentence.

4. Ruth runs very fast, and ____.
5. I am proud of our team, and ___.
6. Our coach helps us, and ____.

Skills Practice

Make each pair of sentences into one compound sentence. Write the compound sentence.

1. I often race with my friends. We check our speed.
2. Don likes the high jump. I like the long jump.
3. The track meet begins soon. I practice running.
4. I practice every day. My sister often helps me.
5. I run in two races. I do the long jump.

Writing Sentences

Add another complete idea to each group of words below. Write each new compound sentence.

1. The races come first, and ____.
2. The tug of war comes last, and ____.
3. We have a picnic after the track meet, and ____.

Sample Answer 1. I often race with my friends, and we check our speed.

Parts of Speech

Each kind of word does a special job in a sentence. You have learned about these kinds of words: *nouns, pronouns, verbs, adjectives,* and *adverbs*. These words are all called *parts of speech*.

A **noun** is a word that names a person, a place, or a thing.

A **pronoun** is a word that takes the place of one or more nouns.

- Read these sentences.

Jay found the lost animal. He found it near the tree.

Jay is a noun. *He* is a pronoun.

You know about two kinds of verbs. An *action verb* shows action. The other kind of verb is called a *linking verb*.

An **action verb** is a word that names an action.

A **linking verb** is a word that connects the subject part with a noun or adjective in the predicate part. It tells what the subject *is* or *is like*.

- Read each sentence.

Jay is a hunter. He hunts for sick animals.

The linking verb *is* connects the subject part *Jay* to the noun *hunter* in the predicate part. The verb *hunts* is an action verb.

An **adjective** is a word that describes a noun or a pronoun.

An **adverb** is a word that describes an action.

- Read these sentences.

The little dog barked. It barked loudly.

The word *little* is the adjective in the first sentence. *Little* describes the noun *dog*. *Loudly* is the adverb in the second sentence. It describes the action verb *barked*.

Talk About It

Read each sentence. Tell whether each underlined word is a **noun,** a **pronoun,** a **verb,** an **adjective,** or an **adverb.**

1. Visitors drive to the park.
2. Beautiful birds come here.
3. Many people visit the park.
4. Rangers teach Jay about animals.
5. He learns quickly.
6. He is a good student.

Skills Practice

Read each sentence. Write the underlined words in each. Write whether each word is a **noun,** a **pronoun,** a **verb,** an **adjective,** or an **adverb.**

1. Anna helps the rangers sometimes.
2. Seabirds were in trouble.
3. She saw the birds.
4. A terrible accident happened.
5. A ship spilled oil.
6. Thick oil covered the water.
7. It washed onto the shore.
8. Sticky oil was everywhere.
9. The helpers worked quickly.
10. They cleaned oily feathers.

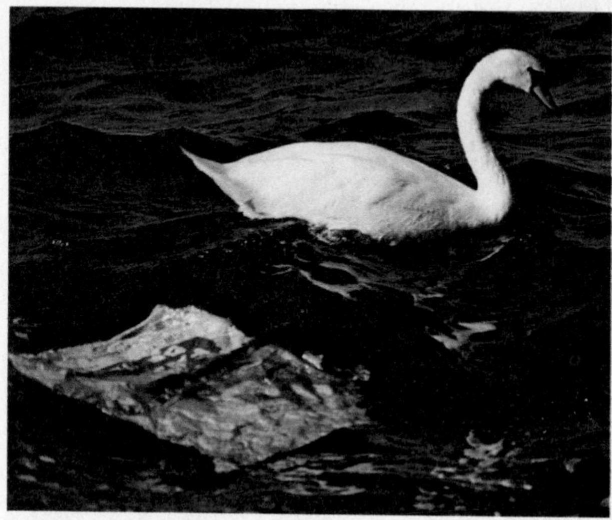

Sample Answer 1. Anna, noun; helps, verb; sometimes, adverb

Using Commas

Commas are used to set off words that interrupt a sentence.

Some sentences begin or end with the name of a person spoken to directly.

> Use a **comma** (,) to set off words such as *yes, no,* and *well* when they begin a sentence.

Yes, Jackie Robinson is in the Baseball Hall of Fame.

> Use a **comma** (,) to set off the name of a person who is spoken to directly in a sentence.

Phil, have you been to Cooperstown?
Is the Baseball Hall of Fame there, Lisa?

Commas also take the place of pauses. Then you use commas to separate a group of similar items.

> Use a **comma** (,) to separate each noun in a series of three or more nouns.

Coaches, players, and fans waited.

> Use a **comma** (,) to separate each verb in a series of three or more verbs.

Then they cheered, clapped, and whistled.

A comma is used to separate the name of the day from the date, and the date from the year.

> Use a **comma** (,) to separate the name of the day from the date, and the date from the year.

I visited Cooperstown on Monday, November 8, 1982.

Commas are used to separate conversation words from the exact words of a speaker.

Use a **comma** (,) after conversation words that come before the speaker's exact words.

Lou said, "I saw Babe Ruth's bat at Cooperstown."

Use a **comma** (,) before the last quotation mark when the conversation word comes after the speaker's exact words.

"That sounds exciting," said Marcy.

Talk About It

Tell where you would put commas in each sentence.

1. Peg said "I like baseball games."
2. Let's go to Cooperstown this year Mark.
3. You can see famous bats gloves and balls there.
4. We visited there on Wednesday June 17 1982.

Skills Practice

Write each sentence. Put commas where they are necessary.

1. Babe Ruth batted caught and pitched the ball well.
2. Yes he hit 714 homeruns.
3. No one hit more homeruns until Monday April 8 1974.
4. Peg did Hank Aaron break Babe Ruth's record?
5. "Tell me more about baseball" Tim said.
6. I like basketball football and hockey more than baseball.

Sample Answer 1. Babe Ruth batted, caught, and pitched the ball well.

Skills Review

Read each sentence. Write **compound** if the sentence is compound. Write **not compound** if the sentence is not compound.

1. My parents bowl on Saturday, and we go along.
2. The whole family gets up early.
3. My parents prepare breakfast, and we make the beds.
4. My sister carries one ball, and I carry the other.
5. The bowling ball feels heavy.
6. Many people bowl, and we wait for our turn.
7. Mom starts, and Dad goes next.
8. Mom's ball goes straight, and it hits many pins.
9. Dad falls down, and he tries again.
10. Dad hits the pins well, and he smiles broadly.
11. The family cheers at Dad's success.
12. Dad laughs at us, and he bowls again.
13. My parents decide to go home, and my sister wants to stay.
14. We talk, and she decides to leave with us.
15. The whole family rides the bus home.
16. My parents talk, and we watch the people on the streets.
17. The bus stops, and we get off.
18. The family enjoys bowling on Saturday.

Make each pair of sentences into one compound sentence. Write the compound sentence.

19. Pete has a sailboat. He sails on the lake.
20. His boat needed repairs. He fixed it.
21. Pete often takes me for a sail. I help.
22. Pete sails well. I learn from him.
23. I helped Pete. He thanked me.

Read each sentence. Write the underlined word. Write whether each word is a **noun**, a **pronoun**, a **verb**, an **adjective**, or an **adverb**.

24. The skaters came to our school today.
25. I watched the racers.
26. They raced on the ice.
27. The skaters wore shiny skates.
28. They started the race.
29. The judge watched the skaters carefully.
30. A happy skater won the race.
31. The judge happily gave a prize to the winner.

Write each sentence. Put commas where they are necessary.

32. Jim are you going to the next game?
33. Yes I think my family wants to attend the game too.
34. When is it Stacy?
35. The game is on Tuesday October 5 1982.
36. Meg Todd and Sharon are on the team.
37. They jog swim and lift weights every day.
38. "Let's get enough tickets today" said Stacy.

Careers

Would you like to be the owner of a hobby shop? You could help people learn about hobbies. How could you learn about hobbies? You could read about them in books and magazines. You could write letters to people who know about these hobbies. Reading and writing are important skills for the owner of a hobby shop.

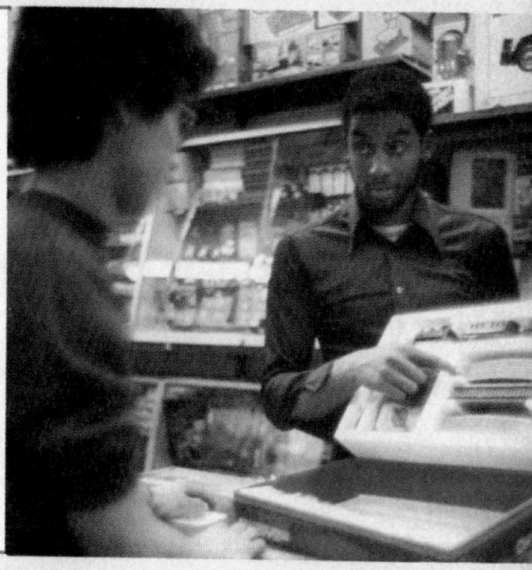

Fact and Opinion

Many books give interesting information. Encyclopedias and other reference books give facts. *Facts* state information that is true. Facts can also be checked. Some books give opinions. *Opinions* tell what someone thinks or feels.

- Look at these pages. Which page gives facts? Which page gives opinions?

Pilots must have special training before they fly airplanes.
A
Pilots are lucky. They can fly almost anywhere they want to go.
C-542
B

Page **A** gives facts. You can check to see if the information is true. Page **B** gives an opinion. It tells how the author feels about pilots.

When you watch TV or read a newspaper, you see many advertisements. An *advertisement* tells you about things you can buy. Sometimes an advertisement is called an ad for short.

Grape-O Juice tastes great.
It has vitamin C.
Grape-O is the best juice.
It is freshly canned.

Read the ad about *Grape-O Juice*. Two of the sentences give *opinions*. *Grape-O Juice tastes great* and *Grape-O is the best juice* are opinions. Two of the sentences give *facts*. *It has vitamin C* and *It is freshly canned* are facts. You can check this information to see if it is true.

Talk About It

Read each sentence. Does it state a fact or an opinion?

1. News reporters have interesting jobs.
2. Some reporters interview famous people.
3. Sports writers go to games.
4. They are very lucky.

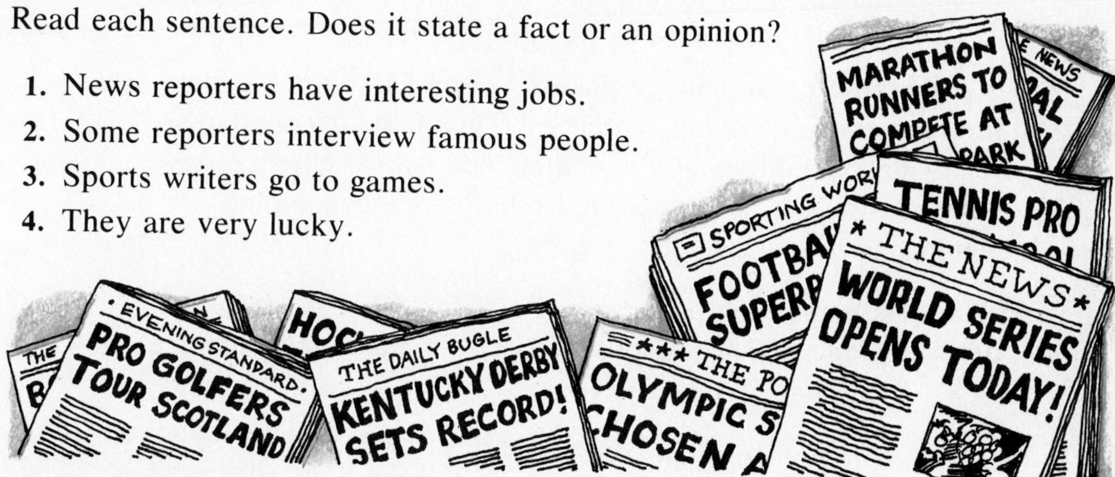

Skills Practice

Read each sentence. Write **F** if the sentence states a fact. Write **O** if the sentence gives an opinion.

1. Football is very exciting.
2. Football players wear helmets during a game.
3. *Sluggo* helmets are made from heavy plastic.
4. *Sluggo* helmets are the best helmets to wear.
5. Basketball is the best sport.
6. Basketball players wear uniforms.
7. Green and white uniforms are the best.
8. Baseball players have the nicest uniforms.
9. Baseball is a team sport.
10. The catcher wears a special baseball glove.

Sample Answer 1. O

A Persuasive Paragraph of Reasons

Talking About a Paragraph of Reasons

You have learned how to write different kinds of paragraphs. Some paragraphs tell a story. Some paragraphs tell facts. Other paragraphs describe people, places, or things. Still other paragraphs explain how to do something.

Suppose you want to persuade someone to agree with you. Then you write a persuasive paragraph.

Like other paragraphs, a persuasive paragraph has a main idea sentence and detail sentences. The main idea sentence tells your opinion about something. The detail sentences give good reasons for your opinion. Sometimes a concluding sentence emphasizes your opinion.

- Read this persuasive paragraph. Look for the reasons in the detail sentences. The reasons support the main idea sentence.

Our school playground needs new equipment. There have been a dozen more accidents this year because a lot of the equipment is too old and worn out. Some of the metal on the slide is rusted and jagged. Last week a boy was cut while playing on it. The wooden see-saw has splintered. There are only two swing seats left for the whole school. Finally the basketball hoop has come loose from the backboard. We would like to have safer and more modern playground equipment.

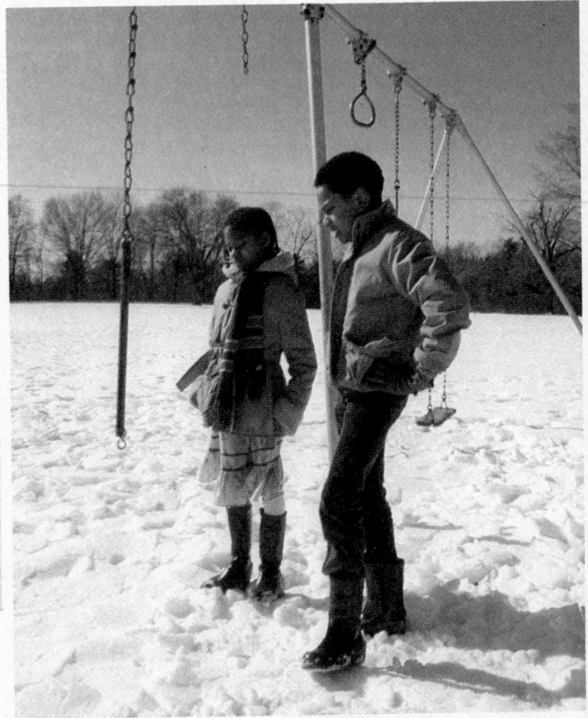

Talking About Persuasive Paragraphs

1. What opinion is stated in the main idea sentence?
2. How many reasons does the paragraph give to support the main idea sentence? How could the P.T.A members find out if the reasons are good ones?
3. Which detail sentence do you think is the strongest? Why? Where does it come in the paragraph?
4. What does the last sentence tell?
5. Can you think of any other reasons why a school would want or need new playground equipment? Can you think of any reasons not to get new equipment?

Writing a Persuasive Paragraph

Below are six sentences from a persuasive paragraph. Change the order of the sentences so that the paragraph begins with a main idea sentence. Arrange the detail sentences in an order that makes sense. Then write the whole paragraph on your paper. Remember to indent the first sentence.

1. We sometimes got our things mixed up.
2. We have just enough space in our room for two more tables.
3. When we were finished, we couldn't display all the projects.
4. Our classroom needs more work tables.
5. We have too many students at each table.
6. While working on our science projects last week, we kept getting in each other's way.

A Class Paragraph

Thinking About a Paragraph

Your class is going to write a persuasive paragraph together. Think about all the advertisements that you see on television or read in magazines and newspapers. Think about how they persuade people to buy something or to attend an event.

Imagine that the P.T.A. and the students of your school want to have an arts and crafts fair in order to raise money for the new playground equipment. Each class is responsible for making items to sell. The fourth grade class has also been given the task of writing an advertisement. The ad will appear in the local newspaper.

When you write a paragraph, you begin with a main idea sentence. Your detail sentences should include several reasons why the people in your own town should attend. At the end of your paragraph, list the necessary facts that people need to know to come to the fair. Remember that you want to persuade people to come. Give good reasons.

Come to the

ARTS AND CRAFTS FAIR

Time: 9:00 A.M. to 5:00 P.M.

Place: Main Street School
Main Street

Date: October 8, 1984

Arts, crafts, plants
and baked goods for sale

Writing a Paragraph

Look at the pictures on the other page. They will give you ideas for your sentences. Your teacher will write the sentences on the board.

1. Choose one of the sentences below for the main idea sentence of your advertisement.
   Come to the Fair.
   The Main Street School will have an Arts and Crafts Fair.
2. Write a detail sentence that tells why your school is having a fair.
3. Write two more detail sentences that tell what people will enjoy when they come. You might include a description of some of the articles and baked goods for sale.
4. Look at the poster again. Write two more sentences that tell when and where the fair will take place.
5. Choose one of the sentences below to end your advertisement.
   We know you will have a good time at the fair.
   Please support Main Street School, and come to the fair.

Practicing a Persuasive Paragraph

Thinking About Your Paragraph

There will be many times when you will want to persuade someone to agree with your point of view. Sometimes you may say what you think and give reasons for your beliefs. At other times you may write your ideas in a paragraph.

Look at the picture below. Imagine that it is an empty lot in your neighborhood. You and all your friends play there after school. You have worked very hard to keep the lot neat. Last week it was announced that the lot is going to be turned into a parking lot. You and your friends have decided to write to the City Council.

Writing Your Paragraph

1. Begin your paragraph with a main idea sentence that states what you feel about the situation. Do you agree with the decision?
2. Continue your paragraph with detail sentences that give reasons why the lot should not be turned into a parking lot. Be sure to use reasons explaining how the lot is now used and why you and your friends use it.
3. Try to end your paragraph with a sentence that summarizes your point of view.

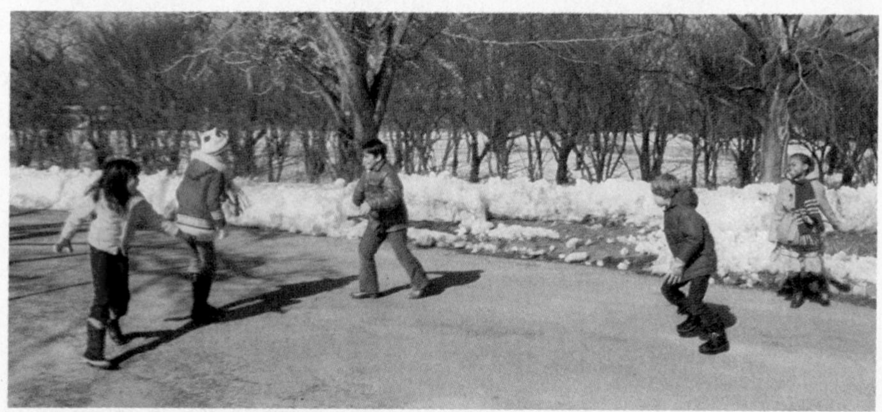

Edit Your Paragraph

Read your paragraph again. Use the questions below.

1. Does your paragraph begin with a main idea that clearly states your point of view?
2. Do your detail sentences give reasons to support your point of view?
3. Does each sentence have a subject part and a predicate part?
4. Did you indent the first word in your paragraph?
5. Are capital letters and periods used correctly?
6. Did you spell all words correctly?

Correct your mistakes. If you need to, write your paragraph again.

Editing Symbols

≡ capitalize
¶ indent
ᒧ take out
^ add

INDEPENDENT WRITING

A Persuasive Paragraph

Prewriting Think of several different situations where you might want to persuade your parents to let you do something. It could be anything such as permitting you to get a new pet, increasing your allowance, or making your bedtime an hour later. Decide on your topic. Then make notes that include your reasons. Be sure your reasons are good.

Writing Write a persuasive paragraph using your notes. If you need help in writing, you can follow the plan on page

Editing Use the check questions and editing symbols above to edit your paragraph.

Unit Review

Write each sentence so that it begins and ends correctly. *pages 270–271*

1. do you enjoy sports
2. irene rides horses
3. dan plays tennis
4. how well he plays
5. what does Jill do
6. she swims on a team
7. how quickly she swims
8. do you want to swim

Write the subject part of each sentence. Draw a line under each simple subject. *pages 272–273*

9. The bike belongs to Jim.
10. A new club opens.
11. The club takes bike trips.
12. The riders pedal fast.

Write the predicate part of each sentence. Draw a line under the simple predicate. *pages 274–275*

13. The riders prepared well.
14. Jim entered the race.
15. Jim went ahead.
16. Jim won the race.

Write the subject part. Underline the simple subjects. *pages 276–277*

17. Tom and I ran quickly.
18. Mom and Sue followed us.
19. Dad and Jim laughed at us.
20. Parents and children had fun.

Read each sentence. Write **compound** if the sentence is compound. Write **not compound** if the sentence is not compound. *pages 282–283*

21. I enjoy swimming, and I swim all summer.
22. My brother comes to the pool with Bob and me.
23. I like swimming, and he likes diving.
24. We had lots of fun last summer at the beach.

Write each pair of sentences as one compound sentence. *pages 284–285*

25. My friends swim in the pool. They play water games.
26. Sometimes we play tag. Sometimes we play water polo.
27. One day Sam ran after Linn. Linn fell into the pool.
28. Sam brought a towel. Linn dried herself.

Unit Review

Read each sentence. Write the underlined word. Write whether each word is a **noun,** a **pronoun,** a **verb,** an **adjective,** or an **adverb.** *pages 286–287*

29. My class runs around the field.
30. The new teacher runs with us.
31. He coaches the children.
32. The children practice often.
33. They work hard every afternoon.

Write each sentence. Put commas where they are necessary. *pages 288–289*

34. Juan runs jumps and swims very well.
35. Basketball tennis and skating are my favorite sports.
36. Susan won her first race on Tuesday December 1 1981.
37. Do you know how to play hockey George?
38. Yes I have been on a team for three years.
39. Sid said "I have two tickets to the hockey game."
40. "Let's go to dinner before the game" said George.

You are going to write a persuasive paragraph.

41. Write this sentence as your main idea sentence:
Babe Ruth was a great home-run hitter.
42. Read the six sentences below. Choose the four sentences that support the main idea sentence. Write the main idea sentence and the detail sentences you have chosen.
pages 294–299

a. He hit 60 home runs in just one season.
b. Ruth hit 714 home runs during his lifetime.
c. Once he hit a home run after pointing to the outfield.
d. He wore the number 3.
e. Ruth often visited children in the hospital.
f. Many of his home-run balls traveled very far.

Fables

Fables are stories that teach a lesson. These fables were told thousands of years ago by a man named Aesop. People still read fables today because they teach such good lessons. As you read these stories, think about what lesson is in each one.

THE SEVEN STICKS

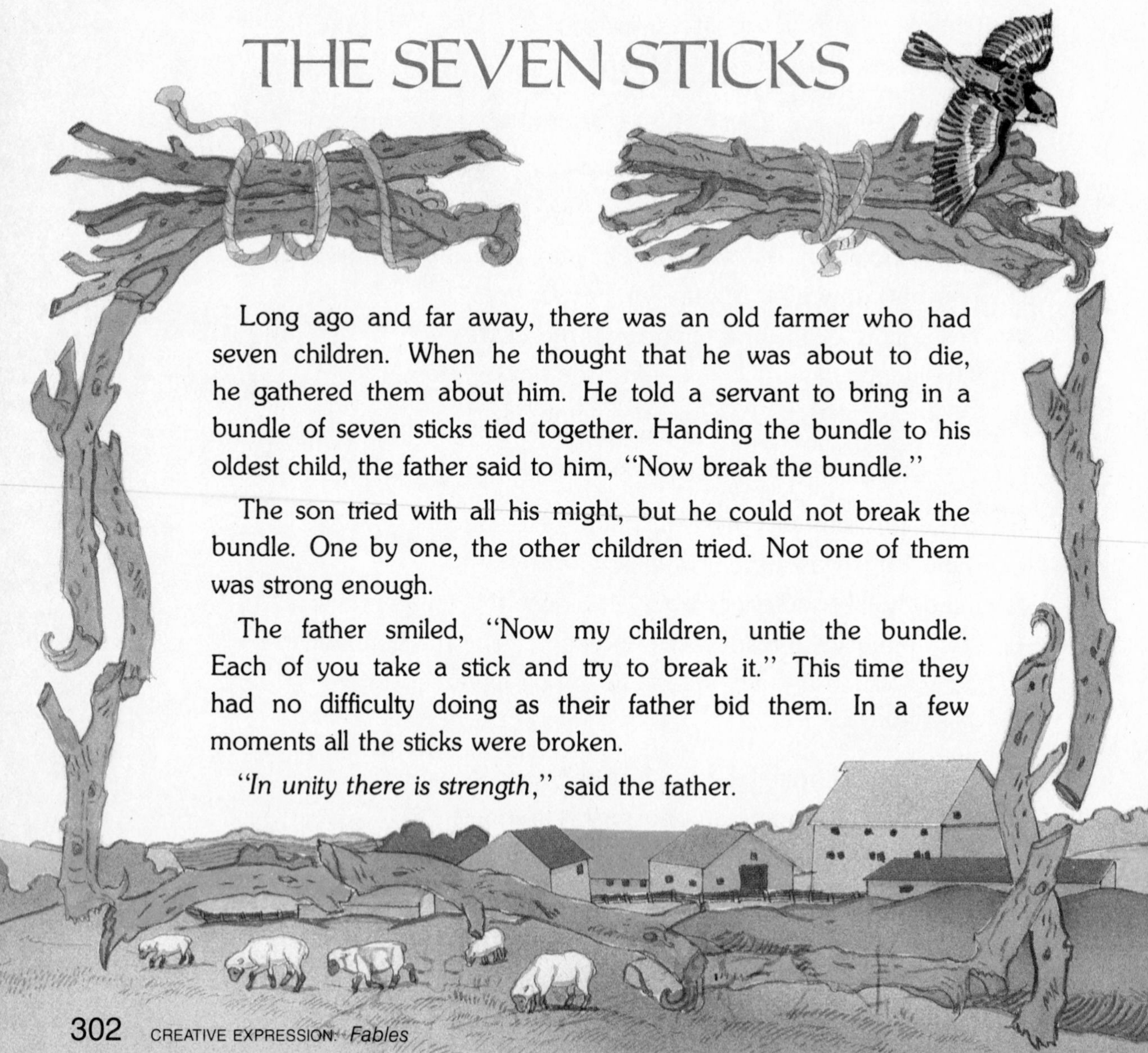

Long ago and far away, there was an old farmer who had seven children. When he thought that he was about to die, he gathered them about him. He told a servant to bring in a bundle of seven sticks tied together. Handing the bundle to his oldest child, the father said to him, "Now break the bundle."

The son tried with all his might, but he could not break the bundle. One by one, the other children tried. Not one of them was strong enough.

The father smiled, "Now my children, untie the bundle. Each of you take a stick and try to break it." This time they had no difficulty doing as their father bid them. In a few moments all the sticks were broken.

"*In unity there is strength*," said the father.

THE CROW AND THE PITCHER

Once upon a time a thirsty crow came upon a pitcher, half full of water. With the greatest of joy, she stuck in her beak, for she was almost dead of thirst. But her beak was short and the water was very low in the pitcher. Try as she might, she could not reach a drop.

Just as she thought she would have to give up, she had a bright idea. She took a pebble in her beak and dropped it into the pitcher. Then she picked up another pebble and dropped it in, too. Another and another and another pebble went into the pitcher. Little by little, the water began to rise. At last, it was close enough for the crow to drink. She dipped her beak and drank till she was full.

"Where there's a will, there's a way," said she.

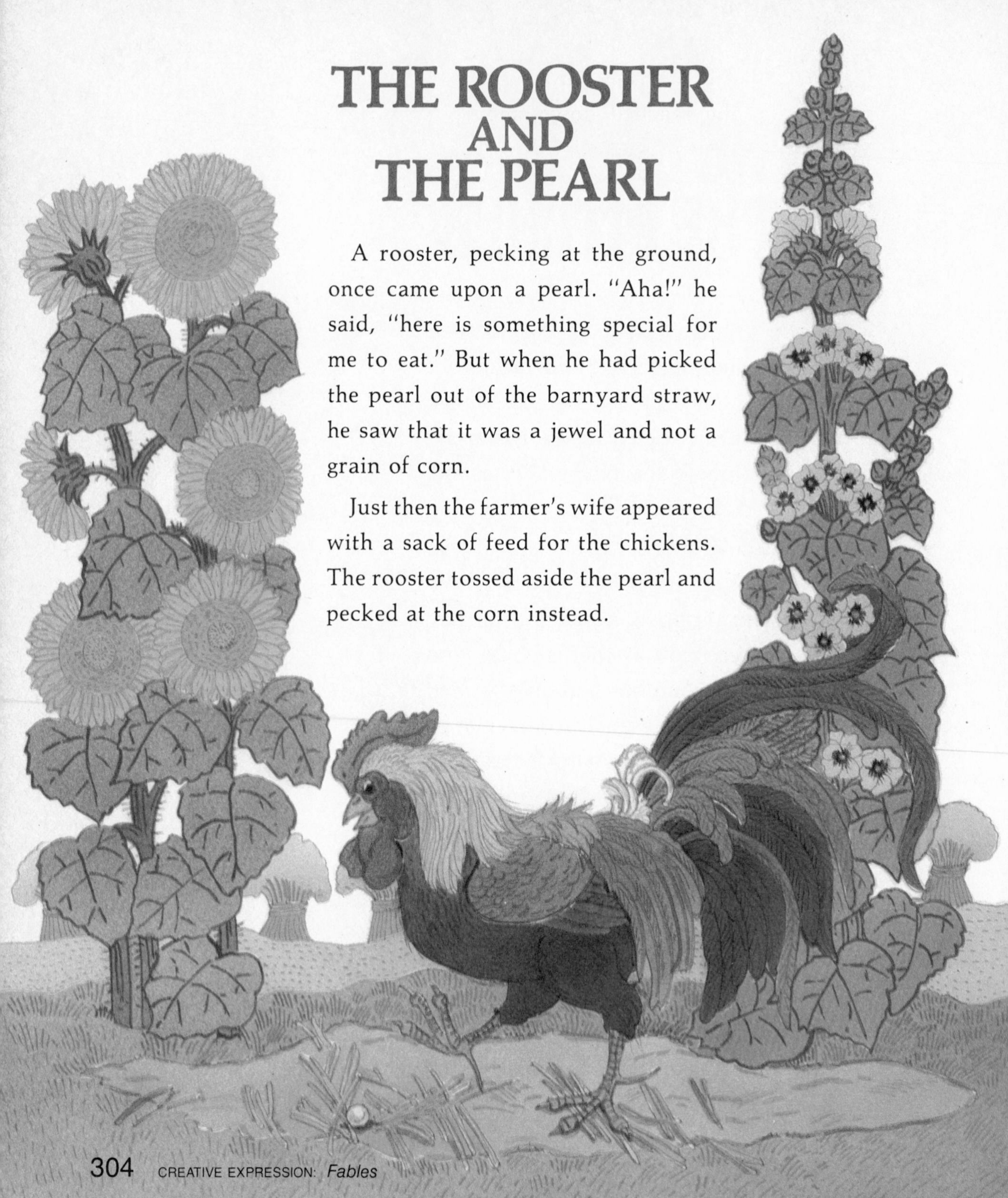

THE ROOSTER AND THE PEARL

A rooster, pecking at the ground, once came upon a pearl. "Aha!" he said, "here is something special for me to eat." But when he had picked the pearl out of the barnyard straw, he saw that it was a jewel and not a grain of corn.

Just then the farmer's wife appeared with a sack of feed for the chickens. The rooster tossed aside the pearl and pecked at the corn instead.

The farmer's wife saw the pearl. She reached down and snatched it up with delight.

"Well," said the rooster, "that pearl may be a treasure to her. But since I cannot eat it, it's of no use to me. I would rather have a small bit of food than a large sack of pearls."

The rooster watched the woman hurry away with her treasure. He pecked happily at his corn.

"To each his own," he said.

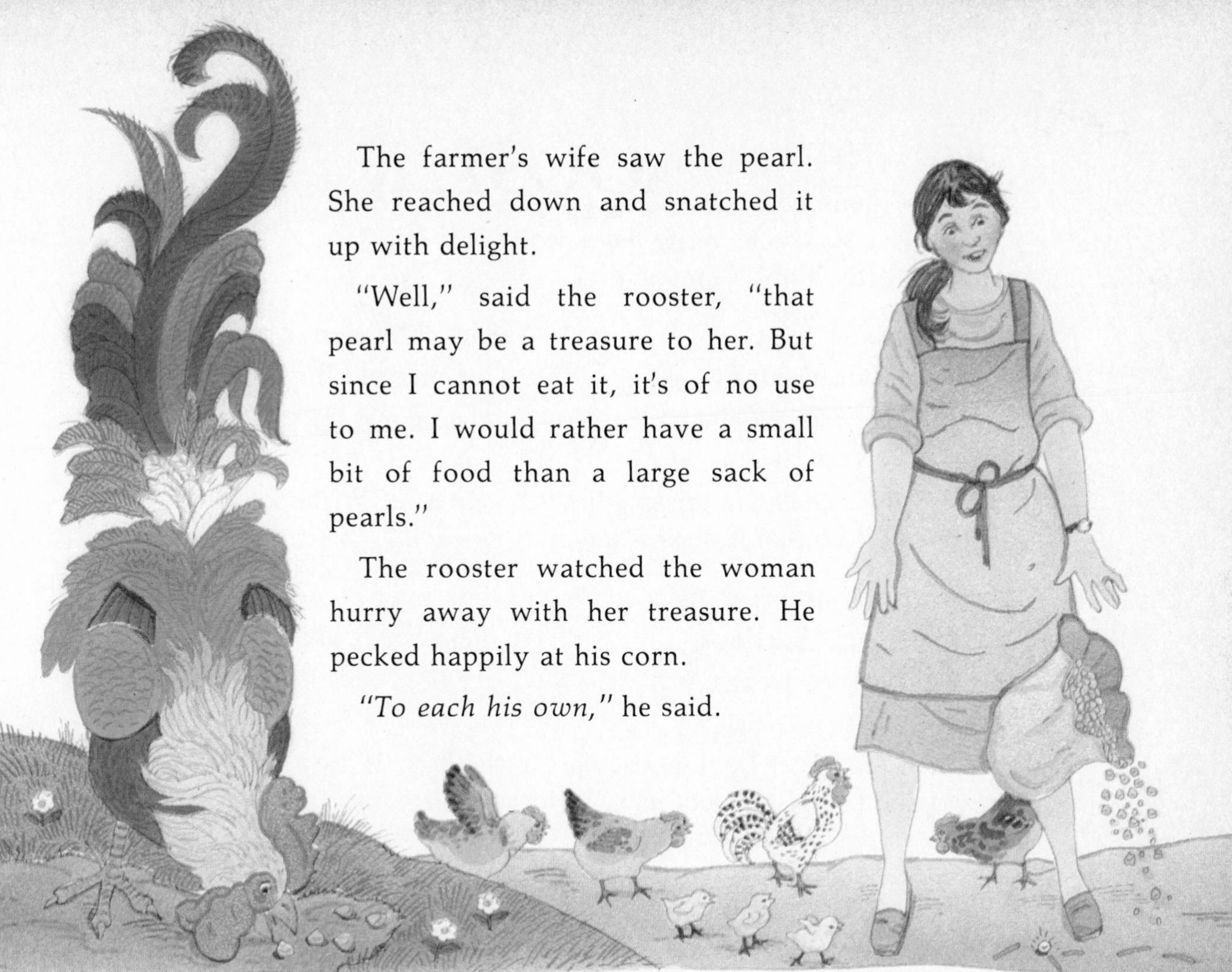

Creative Activities

1. Your class can do *The Seven Sticks* as a play. First you will need to find seven sticks. Then you must tie them together. You can take turns playing the father and his seven children.

2. **Creative Writing** In the fable about the rooster, the rooster likes corn more than he likes the pearl. The farmer's wife likes the pearl more than she likes the corn. Everyone likes different things. Make a list of five things you like to do most. Use complete sentences. Compare your list with the list of one of your friends.

Read each group of words. Write **sentence** if the group of words is a sentence. Write **not a sentence** if the group of words is not a sentence. *pages 2–3*

1. A very loud noise.
2. People looked outside.
3. The huge airplane landed.
4. Left the plane in a hurry.
5. Joe enjoyed the trip.
6. The people on the plane.

Some special signals are missing in each sentence. Write each sentence so that it begins and ends correctly. *pages 6–7*

7. space travelers wear space suits
8. how strange they look
9. did they come from Earth
10. look over here
11. these rocks are red
12. are the rocks heavy

Read each sentence. Look at the part in the box. Write **subject part** if it is a subject part. Write **predicate part** if it is a predicate part. *pages 10–11*

13. Lucía [visited Cape Kennedy last year.]
14. [Rona] saw a new rocket.
15. [The family] sat inside the rocket.
16. The large rocket [made a funny noise.]
17. [A scientist] explained how the rocket worked.
18. Rona [sat in a comfortable seat.]

Write each sentence. Use commas where they are necessary. *pages 14–15*

19. Carl when is Mike arriving?
20. He will get here on Thursday November 11 1982.
21. Well we are all anxious to see him.
22. Yes it has been a long time Jack.

End-of-Year Review

Read each sentence. At the end of the sentence is a singular noun. Write the plural form of the noun. *pages 40–42*

23. He puts two ____ in. (foot)
24. The ____ sit down. (woman)
25. She tells ____. (story)
26. The ____ squeak. (mouse)
27. They have tiny ____. (tooth)
28. We need ____ to see. (glass)

Write each sentence correctly. Use capital letters where they belong. *pages 46–49*

29. We visited susan in alaska.
30. He crossed the atlantic ocean.
31. Mei went to lake erie.
32. Her sister saw kent, ohio.
33. That trip was in may.
34. She will visit canada next.

At the end of each sentence is a singular or plural noun. Write each sentence using the correct possessive form. *pages 50–51*

35. The ____ feet hurt. (women)
36. We heard the ____ song. (child)
37. The ____ eyes glow. (owls)
38. The ____ tails curled. (pigs)
39. My ____ pig is pink. (friend)
40. One ____ name is Tiny. (pig)

Write the verb in each sentence. Then write whether the verb is in the **past, present,** or **future** tense. *pages 78–79*

41. Snow fell yesterday.
42. Sally builds a snow fort.
43. Tom will have cold toes.
44. The children laugh loudly.
45. Sleds moved across the snow.
46. They will meet again soon.

Read each sentence. Write the correct form of the verb in the present tense. *pages 80–82, 93*

47. A ship ____ by us. (hurry)
48. Rita ____ the river. (watch)
49. Polly ____ dinner. (make)
50. She ____ fish. (fry)
51. Dinner ____ good. (taste)
52. Dan ____ the fish. (catch)

Write the correct form of the verb in the past tense. *pages 86–87, 92–93*

53. We ____ at the boats. (stare)
54. A sailor ____ a rope. (grab)
55. He ____ a tune. (hum)
56. Wind ____ the sails. (fill)
57. The sailor ____. (hurry)
58. The ship ____. (circle)

Write the correct form of the main verb. *pages 88–91*

59. The day has ____. (end)
60. John has ____ the zoo. (see)
61. Alice has ____ home. (ride)
62. The bears have ____ in. (go)
63. We have ____ cards. (write)
64. Polly has ____ a rock. (find)

Read each pair of sentences. Write the pronoun that takes the place of the underlined word or words. *pages 116–119*

65. Nancy works in the city. ____ walks to her job.
66. The children go to school. ____ travel by bus.
67. A car passes by. ____ stops at the corner.
68. A man gets out. ____ wears a green shirt.

Read each pair of sentences. Write the form of the verb in the present tense that agrees with the pronoun. *pages 120–121*

69. Juan is a detective. He ____ robbers. (catch)
70. Trudy is an artist. She ____ pictures. (paint)
71. Lynn has two helpers. They ____ paint. (mix)
72. My parents are teachers. They ____ in a grade school. (teach)

Write the possessive pronoun for each blank space. *pages 126–127*

73. Tom and Ed have a farm. ____ farm has chickens.
74. I live on a farm. A river runs by ____ house.
75. Elisa is in school. ____ class studies birds.
76. My class likes animals. ____ teacher has horses.

Read each sentence. Write the correct pronoun in place of the underlined words. *pages 128–129*

77. John saw <u>Jan and me</u>.
John saw ____.

78. I can't find <u>the book</u>.
Kathleen found ____.

79. Jose called <u>Maria</u>.
Jose called ____.

80. I answered <u>Mom and Dad</u>.
I answered ____.

Read each sentence. Write each subject part. Then draw a line under each simple subject. *pages 158–159*

81. My best friend plays music.

82. A good musician works hard.

83. The whole club practices.

84. My old piano sounds fine.

85. My piano teacher lives here.

86. His favorite song is "Birds."

Write the subject part. Underline the simple subjects. *pages 160–161*

87. A man and a boy read.

88. The girls and boys talk.

89. Sue and Tom sing songs.

90. Paper and red pens are here.

91. Mr. Díaz and I write letters.

92. My letters and cards have come.

Read each sentence. Write the form of the verb that belongs in the blank. *pages 162–163*

93. Vera and Ramon ____ the paper. (read, reads)

94. They and I ____ about the news. (talk, talks)

95. My neighbors and brothers ____ television. (watch, watches)

96. Pam and Sara ____ their grandmother. (call, calls)

Read each sentence. Write the predicate part. Underline the simple predicate. *pages 166–167*

97. Leroy enters the building.

98. He rides in the elevator.

99. It moves quickly.

100. People walk on and off.

101. A bell rings softly.

102. The door opens quietly.

Write each sentence. Use commas where they are necessary. *pages 170–171*

103. Iris Terry Olga and Betty performed in a play.
104. Yes we all enjoyed the show.
105. You did a beautiful job Iris.
106. We will arrive on Tuesday June 2 1981.

Write each sentence. Use correct punctuation and capitalization. *pages 174–175*

107. Mom said Finish your homework, Carol
108. I have only one more problem replied Carol
109. We will have dinner early Mother added
110. Carol said I am very hungry

Read each sentence. Write each adjective. Then write the noun that the adjective describes. *pages 194–195*

111. The strong workers built a new house.
112. A big man carried a large window.
113. A curious neighbor watched the busy workers.
114. The noisy children played in the green grass.
115. A little dog ran behind the large boxes.
116. A tall woman painted the front door.

Write the correct form of the adjective in ( ) using **-er** or **-est**. *pages 198–199*

117. The two sisters played tag. The ____ sister won. (young)
118. My brother is very happy. He is the ____ person of all. (happy)
119. We have two cats. The ____ cat is mine. (big)
120. My father is very tall. He is the ____ man I know. (tall)

Write the correct form of the verb to complete each sentence. *pages 234–235*

121. Books ____ here. (is, are)
122. They ____ colorful. (is, are)
123. I ____ a student. (is, am)
124. The box ____ here. (is, are)
125. A fly ____ in there. (am, is)
126. I ____ a dancer. (is, am)

Write the contraction for each pair of words. *pages 236–237*

127. they are
128. it is
129. I am
130. she is
131. we are
132. you are

Write the linking verb that belongs in each sentence. *pages 242–243*

133. The books ____ interesting. (was, were)
134. My story ____ exciting. (was, were)
135. It ____ about a large bear. (was, were)
136. The other animals ____ frightened. (was, were)

Write the adverb in each sentence. Then write the verb it describes. *pages 244–247*

137. The buzzer rang loudly.
138. The door quickly opened.
139. Then Polly entered.
140. Tom came early.
141. He laughed softly.
142. Susan called last.

Write **compound** if the sentence is compound. Write **not compound** if the sentence is not compound. *pages 282–283*

143. Sam runs, and Sue swims.
144. Peter plays ball, and I fly kites.
145. My family enjoys these sports.
146. Peter ran to catch a ball.
147. She pitched, and I caught.
148. The game ended in a tie.

Write each pair of sentences as a compound sentence. *pages 284–285*

149. Andy plays basketball. He scores may points.
150. I saw Andy. He waved to me.
151. Mona arrived. She drove us to the game.

Write each underlined word. Write whether each word is a **noun**, a **pronoun**, a **verb**, an **adjective**, or an **adverb.** *pages 286–287*

152. The dancers <u>kicked</u> their <u>legs</u> high.
153. <u>They</u> danced for many <u>hours</u>.
154. A <u>big</u> band played <u>loudly</u>.
155. <u>We</u> sat on <u>blankets</u> on the grass.

Handbook Contents

Handbook

I. Grammar and Usage

Sentences

DEFINITION

A **sentence** is a group of words that state a complete idea. page 2 MORE PRACTICE, page 331

We took a trip last summer.

Mom visited many friends.

PARTS OF SENTENCES

The **subject part** of a sentence names whom or what the sentence is about. page 10 MORE PRACTICE, pages 332, 339, 345

A group of boys played together. John sat on a swing.

The **simple subject** is the main word in the subject part. Page 158 MORE PRACTICE, page 339

Two strange firemen visited the house.

A crowd watched the fire engine.

A **compound subject** has two or more simple subjects that have the same predicate. The subjects are joined by **and.** pages 160, 276 MORE PRACTICE, pages 339, 345

The cat and mouse looked at each other.

Alligators and crocodiles live in the water.

The **predicate part** of a sentence tells what action the subject part does. page 10 MORE PRACTICE, pages 332, 339, 345

Tom pitched the ball.

Flora ran from second base.

The **simple predicate** is the main word or group of words in the predicate part. page 166 MORE PRACTICE, page 340

The scouts walked through the forest.

The leader praised the hikers.

KINDS OF SENTENCES

A **declarative sentence** is a sentence that makes a statement or tells something. page 4 MORE PRACTICE, pages 331, 345

The children cleaned the garage.

Dad moved the car.

An **interrogative sentence** is a sentence that asks something. page 4 MORE PRACTICE, pages 331, 345

Which team wears the red jackets?

When does the game start?

An **imperative sentence** is a sentence that tells or asks someone to do something. page 4 MORE PRACTICE, pages 331, 345

Watch this game.

Walk down the steps carefully.

An **exclamatory sentence** is a sentence that shows excitement or strong feeling. page 4 MORE PRACTICE, pages 331, 345

How the crowd cheers!

What a game the team played!

A **simple sentence** is a sentence that has one subject part and one predicate part. pages 2-3 MORE PRACTICE, page 331

The cat | ran with me. The dog | barked all day.

A **compound sentence** contains two simple sentences joined by **and.** page 282 MORE PRACTICE, page 346

The lightning flashed, and the thunder roared.

The squirrels climbed the tree, and the birds flew away.

Parts of Speech

NOUN

A **noun** is a word that names a person, a place, or a thing. page 36 MORE PRACTICE, page 332

The rooster sat in the barn. The hens waited for food.

A **singular noun** is a noun that names one person, place, or thing. page 38 MORE PRACTICE, page 333

My sister read a book. My big brother built a kite.

A **plural noun** is a noun that names more than one person, place, or thing. page 38 MORE PRACTICE, page 333

The dogs slept in the sun. Tall trees grew along the hills.

A **compound noun** is a noun that is formed from two smaller words. page 43 MORE PRACTICE, page 333

The windmill creaked. The airplane flew in the sky.

A **common noun** is a noun that names any person, place, or thing. page 46 MORE PRACTICE, page 333

The boy fished in the lake.

The girl rowed the boat.

A **proper noun** is a noun that names a special person, place, or thing. page 46 MORE PRACTICE, pages 333, 334

The Smiths visited Ohio.

They drove to Arizona.

A **possessive noun** is a noun that names who or what has something. page 50 MORE PRACTICE, page 334

Alice's skate fell apart.

Pedro fixed the girl's skate.

Use the words **a** and **an** with singular nouns. Use **a** with singular nouns that begin with a consonant. Use **an** with singular nouns that begin with a vowel. page 202 MORE PRACTICE, page 342

An apple fell from a tree.

Joe ate a pear for lunch.

Use the word **the** with singular or plural nouns to point out a special person or thing. page 202 MORE PRACTICE, page 342

The girls acted in the play.

PRONOUN

A **pronoun** is a word that takes the place of one or more nouns. page 116 MORE PRACTICE, pages 337, 338

Jack dusted the apartment.

Then he washed the windows.

The children stopped at a shop.

They bought some post cards.

A **possessive pronoun** is a pronoun that names who or what has something. page 126 MORE PRACTICE, page 338

Jane bought a new watch.

Her new watch keeps good time.

Carl works at the cement plant.

His job pays well.

A **pronoun** in the predicate part of a sentence must agree with the noun it replaces. page 128 MORE PRACTICE, page 338

John calls Mr. Jones.

John calls him.

Sue sees Jack and me.

Sue sees us.

VERB

An **action verb** is a word that names an action. It may contain more than one word. page 76 MORE PRACTICE, page 335

The wood burned in the stove.

We piled logs outside.

The **present tense** of a verb names an action that happens now. page 78 MORE PRACTICE, page 335

The man helps the boys.

They buy food for the picnic.

The **past tense** of a verb names an action that already happened. page 78 MORE PRACTICE, page 336

The elephant raised its trunk.

Monkeys leaped about.

The **future tense** of a verb names an action that will take place in the future. page 79 MORE PRACTICE, page 335

Our class will visit the zoo.

We will write reports.

A **helping verb** is a verb that helps the main verb to name an action. pages 79-88 MORE PRACTICE, page 336

They have crossed the street.

Tami has waited at the corner.

A **linking verb** is a verb that connects the subject part with a noun or adjective in the predicate part. It tells what the subject is or is like. page 230 MORE PRACTICE, page 343

Carl is a skater.

The children are happy.

Add **-s** to most verbs to make them agree with a singular noun. page 80 MORE PRACTICE, page 335

James feeds a toad

The toad jumps around.

Add **-es** to a verb that ends in **s, ss, x, ch, z,** or **sh** to make it agree with a singular noun. page 82 MORE PRACTICE, page 335

Susan wishes for a trip to Japan.

Ray watches shows about Asia.

Change the **y** to **i** and add **-es** to a verb that ends in a consonant and **y** to make it agree with a singular noun. page 93
The child fries eggs. MORE PRACTICE, page 336
A man dries the dish.

The chart below shows how to form the past tense and the past with *have* or *has* of some verbs. pages 90-91 MORE PRACTICE, page 336

Verb	Past	Past with Have or Has
begin	began	have or has begun
bring	brought	have or has brought
come	came	have or has come
do	did	have or has done
draw	drew	have or has drawn
drive	drove	have or has driven
eat	ate	have or has eaten
fall	fell	have or has fallen
find	found	have or has found
fly	flew	have or has flown
go	went	have or has gone
make	made	have or has made
ride	rode	have or has ridden
run	ran	have or has run
say	said	have or has said
see	saw	have or has seen
speak	spoke	have or has spoken
teach	taught	have or has taught
throw	threw	have or has thrown
write	wrote	have or has written

Do not use **-s** or **-es** to form the present tense of a verb when the subject is a plural noun or *I, you, we,* or *they.* page 120 MORE PRACTICE, page 337

They wish for good weather.

We hike in the woods.

Use **-s** or **-es** to form the present tense of a verb when the subject is a singular noun or *it, he,* or *she.* page 120 MORE PRACTICE, page 337

She hands the dishes to Peter.

He washes the plates.

ADJECTIVE

An **adjective** is a word that describes a noun or a pronoun. pages 194, 232 MORE PRACTICE, page 341

The happy people came home. The travelers were sleepy.

Add **-er** to an adjective to compare one thing with another. page 196 MORE PRACTICE, page 341

The Miller's driveway is longer than the Stein's.

The house is smaller than the barn.

Add **-est** to an adjective to compare several things. page 196 MORE PRACTICE, page 341

Jane was the tallest person in the room.

The greenest grass is in the third field.

ADVERB

An **adverb** is a word that describes an action. pages 244-246 MORE PRACTICE, page 344

They arrived late. The moon shone brightly.

Then we went to dinner. Later we drove home.

II. Mechanics

Capitalization

Use a **capital letter** to begin the first words of every sentence. page 6 MORE PRACTICE, pages 331, 345

A sword was stuck in a stone. The young boy pulled at the sword.

Begin each important word in a proper noun with a **capital letter.** page 47 MORE PRACTICE, page 334

They named the baby Marie. The student attended Drew College.

Begin a title with a **capital letter.** End most titles with a period. page 48 MORE PRACTICE, page 334

John's father sent Dr. Brown a check.

The check went to Mr. Brown instead.

Begin each shortened word with a **capital letter.** End each shortened word with a period. page 48 MORE PRACTICE, page 334

Third Ave. Oak St. Wilson Ave. Broad St.

Punctuation

Use a **period** (.) at the end of a declarative or an imperative sentence. page 6 MORE PRACTICE, pages 331, 345

The moon circles the earth every twenty-eight days.

Use a **question mark** (?) at the end of an interrogative sentence. page 6 MORE PRACTICE, pages 331, 345

When did the thieves break in?

Use an **exclamation mark (!)** at the end of an exclamatory sentence. page 6 MORE PRACTICE, pages 331, 345

What a day this has been! How high the kite flies!

Use a **comma** (,) to set off words such as **yes, no,** and **well** when they begin a sentence. page 14 MORE PRACTICE, pages 332, 340, 346

Yes, I read that book. Well, I will write the report tonight.

Use a **comma** (,) to set off the name of a person who is spoken to directly in a sentence. page 14 MORE PRACTICE, pages 332, 340, 346

David, please write a letter to me.

The telephone is ringing, Janie.

Use a **comma** (,) to separate the name of the day from the date, and the date from the year. page 14 MORE PRACTICE, pages 332, 340, 346

My sister bought the radio on Tuesday, May 9, 1978.

Use a **comma** (,) to separate each noun in a series of three or more nouns. page 170 MORE PRACTICE, pages 340, 346

Beets, radishes, and carrots are root crops.

I put tomatoes, beans, onions, and cheese in the salad.

Use a **comma** (,) to separate each verb in a series of three or more verbs. page 170 MORE PRACTICE, pages 340, 346

Anita weeded, mowed, and raked the lawn.

We plant, grow, pick, and eat our own vegetables.

Use a **comma** (,) before **and** when it joins two sentences. page 276 MORE PRACTICE, page 346

Mr. Lewis opened the door, and the children ran out.

Mrs. Lewis swept the porch, and James raked leaves.

Add an **apostrophe** and **-s** (**'s**) to form the possessive of most singular nouns. page 50 MORE PRACTICE, page 334

The broom's handle broke into two pieces.

Mother washed Martha's apron.

Add an **apostrophe** (') to form the possessive of plural nouns that end with **s.** page 50 MORE PRACTICE, page 334

Jack cleaned the animals' cages.

The trainer trimmed the horses' tails.

Add an **apostrophe** and **-s** (**'s**) to form the possessive of plural nouns that do not end with **s.** page 51 MORE PRACTICE, page 334

The group talked about women's rights.

The children's nurse attended the party.

Use an **apostrophe** (') in a contraction to show that one or more letters are missing. page 236 MORE PRACTICE, page 344

She's very fond of apples. You're allowed one wish.

Handbook

Capitalization and Punctuation in Conversations

Use **quotation marks** (" ") around the exact words that each speaker says. page 174 MORE PRACTICE, page 340

Jennifer shouted, "Please wait for Jody and me to catch up to you."

Use a **conversation word** such as said, shouted, or whispered to show how each person speaks. page 174 MORE PRACTICE, page 340

Marilyn answered, "I have to meet my brother in five minutes."

Use a **comma** (,) after the conversation word when the conversation word comes before the speaker's exact words. page 174 MORE PRACTICE, page 340

Jody asked, "Where do you have to meet your brother?"

Put a **period** (.) before the last quotation mark at the end of a sentence when the speaker's words end the sentence. page 174 MORE PRACTICE, page 340

Marilyn said, "I have to meet him in front of the hardware store."

Use a **comma** (,) before the last quotation mark when the conversation word comes after the speaker's exact words. page 174 MORE PRACTICE, page 340

"We have to go to the grocery store," added Jennifer.

Indent the first word each time the speaker changes. page 174
Capitalize the first word of each quotation. MORE PRACTICE, page 340

→ "We would like to walk along with you to the store," said Jody.

→ "Let's go then," said Marilyn.

III. Spelling

Spelling Nouns

If a singular noun ends with **s, ss, x, ch, z,** or **sh**, add **-es** to form the plural. page 40 MORE PRACTICE, page 333

princess box bush
princesses boxes bushes

If a singular noun ends with a consonant and **y**, change the **y** to **i** and add **-es** to form the plural. page 42 MORE PRACTICE, page 333

company library party
companies libraries parties

Spelling Verbs

Add **-s** to most verbs to make them agree with a singular noun. page 80 MORE PRACTICE, page 335

sit pour wait
sits pours waits

If a verb ends in **s, ss, x, ch, z,** or **sh,** add **-es** to the verb to make the correct form of the present tense. pages 82, 120 MORE PRACTICE, page 335

pass fix rush
passes fixes rushes

Add **-ed** to most verbs to form the past tense. page 86 MORE PRACTICE, page 336

paint clean walk
painted cleaned walked

If a verb ends in **e,** drop the **e** and add **-ed** to form the past tense. page 86 MORE PRACTICE, page 336

live move wave
lived moved waved

If a verb ends with consonant, vowel, consonant, double the last consonant and add **-ed** to make the past tense. Verbs that end in **w, x,** or **y** are exceptions to this rule. page 92 MORE PRACTICE, page 336

pet	nap	plan
petted	napped	planned

If a verb ends in a consonant and **y,** change the **y** to **i** and add **-es** to make the correct form of the present tense. page 93 MORE PRACTICE, page 336

study	dry	try
studies	dries	tries

If a verb ends in a consonant and **y,** change the **y to i** and add **-ed** to form the past tense. page 93 MORE PRACTICE, page 336

study	dry	try
studied	dried	tried

Spelling Adjectives

If an adjective ends with a consonant and **y,** change the **y** to **i** and add **-er** or **-est** to make the correct form of the adjective. page 198 MORE PRACTICE, page 341

lovely	pretty	tasty
lovelier	prettier	tastier
loveliest	prettiest	tastiest

If an adjective ends with a consonant, vowel, consonant, double the final consonant and add **-er** or **-est** to make the correct form of the adjective. Adjectives that end in **w, x,** or **y** are exceptions to this rule. page 199 MORE PRACTICE, page 341

big	hot	fat
bigger	hotter	fatter
biggest	hottest	fattest

If a word ends with a consonant, vowel, consonant, double the last consonant and add **-y** to form the adjective. Words that end in **w, x,** or **y** are exceptions to this rule. page 204 MORE PRACTICE, page 342

sun	mud	fog
sunny	muddy	foggy

If a word ends in **e,** drop the **e** and add **-y** to form the adjective. page 204 MORE PRACTICE, page 342

scare	wave	noise
scary	wavy	noisy

If a word ends with a consonant and **y,** change the **y** to **i** and add **-ful** to form the adjective. page 205 MORE PRACTICE, page 342

fancy	beauty	plenty
fanciful	beautiful	plentiful

Handbook

IV. Vocabulary

An **abbreviation** is the short form of a word. page 48 MORE PRACTICE, page 334

Dr. Mr. Mrs.

If you use the title **instead of** the name, you spell it out. You only use the short form **with** the person's name. page 48 MORE PRACTICE, page 334

The doctor and her husband smiled at the guests.

Dr. and Mr. Brown entered the room.

A **prefix** is a letter or group of letters added to the beginning of a word. page 83 MORE PRACTICE, page 335

Father unlocked the door of the house.

The children repacked the bags.

A **suffix** is one or more letters added to the end of a word. page 52 MORE PRACTICE, page 334

June's father works as an actor.

Sally's father is a teacher.

A **synonym** is a word that has nearly the same meaning as another word. page 206 MORE PRACTICE, page 342

Alfred's pal injured an arm.

Alfred's friend injured an arm.

Alfred knew the right first aid methods.

Alfred knew the correct first aid methods.

An **antonym** is a word that means the opposite of another word. page 206 MORE PRACTICE, page 343

The jacket was too tight. The shoes felt heavy.

The jacket was too loose. The shoes felt light.

A **contraction** is a word made up of two words. The words are joined together to make one word by leaving out one or more letters. page 236 MORE PRACTICE, page 344

He's the best baker in town. We're lucky to know him.

V. Special Forms

Friendly Letter

Use this form to write a friendly letter. page 102

76 Newtown Avenue ← heading
Atlanta, Georgia 30304
October 17, 19— ← date

Dear Kate, ← greeting

Yesterday I sold food at our Girl Scout picnic. People bought 250 tuna fish sandwiches. They also bought 150 peanut butter sandwiches. I sold 200 plates of salad. People bought 400 glasses of milk. ← body

Your friend, ← closing
Roberta ← name

Use this form to address an envelope. page 103

Roberta Shaw
19 Mill Street
Atlanta, Georgia 30098

Kate Wilson
683 Ledge Road
Indianapolis, Indiana 46228

←Return Address

←Address

Invitation

Use this form to write an invitation. page 136

Name: Mr. Nelson's class

Place: 10 Park Lane, Room 227

Date: April 14, 19—

Time: 11:30

Phone number: 568-0993

Handbook

Book Report

Use this form to help you write a book report. page 142

Name____________________

My Book Report

Title____________________

Author ____________________

1. Write your name, the book's title, and the author.
2. Write a main idea sentence that tells about the most important character in the book.
3. Write four or five detail sentences that describe what the character thinks, says, or does in the story.

Here is a sample of how you might write your book report.

Rocket to the Moon
by Mona Riley

This book is about a brave woman named Linda Smith. She thinks about traveling to the moon some day. She tells her friends about her idea. Ms. Smith bravely rides in a rocket ship. She fights with people who try to blow up the moon.

Handbook

Outline

Use this form to arrange ideas into an outline. page 254

Deer in America

I. Kinds of Deer

A. Mule Deer

B. White-tailed deer

II. Description of Deer

A. Antlers

B. Legs and Hoofs

Use these steps to write the outline.

1. Write the title for the outline. The title tells the main subject of the report.
2. Use Roman numerals to show the main ideas. This is the first main idea.

   I. Kinds of Deer.
3. Notice a period after each Roman numeral.
4. Use capital letters to show the details for each main idea. This shows the details for the first main idea.

   A. Mule deer
   B. White-tailed deer
5. Notice a period after each capital letter.
6. Notice that phrases are used in the outline. Sentences could be used instead of phrases.

Handbook

Learning About Sentences, pages 2–3

Read each group of words. Write **sentence** if the group of words is a sentence. Write **not a sentence** if the group of words is not a sentence.

1. The rocket takes off.
2. The rocket with explorers.
3. The explorers climb in.
4. The motors start.
5. Engineers with tools.
6. Motors with many parts.

Four Kinds of Sentences, pages 4–5

Read each sentence. Decide which kind of sentence each one is. Write **declarative, interrogative, exclamatory**, or **imperative.**

1. The pilot watches the highway.
2. The pilot makes traffic reports on the radio.
3. Listen to the traffic reports.
4. What a lot of cars stand still!
5. How many cars there are!
6. Did that big truck run out of gas?

Capitalizing and Punctuating Sentences, pages 6–7

Some signals are missing in each sentence. Write each sentence so that it begins and ends in the right way.

1. Jennifer wrote a story
2. did Louis fly to Mars
3. how did Louis start the motor
4. how cold Louis felt
5. then Louis flew to a blue star
6. how the heat burned Louis

More Practice

Subject and Predicate Parts, pages 10–11

Look at the part in the box. Write **subject part** if it is a subject part. Write **predicate part** if it is a predicate part.

1. The scientist told the class about stars.
2. The class listened to the speech.
3. Tony asked about the sun.
4. The sun shines during the day.
5. Scientists view the sun through telescopes.

Commas, pages 14–15

Write each sentence. Use commas where they are necessary.

1. Janet when are you going on vacation?
2. We leave on Wednesday December 1 1982.
3. Will you be gone long Mr. Lewis?
4. Well we plan to stay for two weeks.
5. Are you going Mrs. Lewis?
6. Yes we are all traveling together.

Learning About Nouns, pages 36–37

Write each sentence. Underline each noun.

1. Clouds shade a mountain.
2. A trail runs by a stream.
3. The wind blows trees.
4. A deer runs in the woods.
5. Mice live in the grass.
6. Tents stand in a field.

Singular and Plural Nouns, pages 38–42

Write each sentence. Underline each noun. Write **singular** beside each singular noun. Write **plural** beside each plural noun.

1. Girls walk on the trail.
2. Berries grow on trees.
3. Leaves fall on the road.
4. Susan makes a fire.
5. Cooks stir with a spoon.
6. The hungry friends eat.

Write each sentence. Use the plural form of the noun in ( ).

7. The ____ wash the fruit. (child)
8. Jamie opens the ____. (box)
9. The boys chase ____. (fly)
10. ____ light the ovens. (man)
11. Father bought the ____. (grocery)
12. The children fed the ____. (goose)

Compound Nouns, page 43

Write the meaning of each compound word.

1. sunlight
2. pancake
3. footprint
4. keyhole
5. newspaper
6. airplane

Common and Proper Nouns, pages 46–47

Think of a proper noun for each common noun. Write the proper noun.

1. girl
2. city
3. river
4. pet
5. boy
6. city

More Practice

Capitalizing Proper Nouns, pages 48–49

Write each sentence correctly. Use capital letters where they belong.

1. May drives to burt camp.
2. Hikers walk to pear river.
3. Bob visits green park.
4. The dog jumps on rick.
5. Boys meet at silver pond.
6. Girls skate at pine lake.

Write each address correctly.

7. mr Tony Jones
   413 mern st
8. ms Beverly Sweet
   212 third ave
9. dr Laura Peterson
   9216 weitz ave
10. mrs Elena Moreno
    310 park st

Possessive Nouns, pages 50–51

At the end of each sentence is a singular or plural noun. Write each sentence using the correct possessive form.

1. The ____ lights shine. (shop)
2. ____ works hang on the walls. (Artists)
3. Chris looks at the ____ paintings. (women)
4. The ____ guide likes his job. (visitors)
5. That ____ work sits at the doorway. (painter)
6. The ____ statue has the longest title. (king)

Making New Words, pages 53–54

Add the **-er** or **-or** suffix to form a new word. Write the word. Then write the meaning of each new word.

1. dance
2. act
3. write
4. conduct
5. catch
6. visit

Verbs, pages 76–77

Write each sentence. Underline each verb.

1. Mr. Fox writes books about other countries.
2. Ms. West visits a different country each year.
3. Some people wear unusual clothes.
4. Mrs. Case meets many people from other places.
5. The people speak different languages.

Verb Tenses, pages 78–79

Write the verb in each sentence. Write whether the verb is in the **past, present,** or **future** tense.

1. Joan passed a little inn on the mountain.
2. The owner of the inn fixes a broken lock.
3. Terry catches fish in the morning.
4. Jorge will wash the dishes after lunch.
5. Joan will travel farther tomorrow.

Using the Present Tense, pages 80–82

Write each sentence with the correct verb.

1. Many cities ____ beautiful hotels. (has, have)
2. Tony usually ____ through small towns. (walk, walks)
3. The children ____ about the towns. (ask, asks)
4. A street cleaner ____ the dirty streets. (wash, washes)
5. A large bus ____ the excited children. (pass, passes)

Making New Words, page 83

Write the meaning of each verb.

1. uncover
2. refreeze
3. reclean
4. unload
5. unzip
6. repaint

More Practice

Verbs in the Past Tense, pages 86–87, 90–91

Write each sentence. Use the correct form of each verb in the past tense.

1. Last year Alice ____ to the space museum. (travel)
2. Alice ____ at all the sights. (smile)
3. Some visitors ____ around the buildings. (walk)
4. The spaceship ____ many visitors. (excite)
5. Steve ____ the trip in January. (begin)
6. First Steve ____ on an airplane. (go)
7. The passengers ____ clouds all around them. (see)
8. The airplane ____ to a stop. (come)

The Past with Have or Has, pages 88–91

Write each sentence. Use the correct form of the main verb.

1. Mark has ____ on many lakes. (sail)
2. Margaret has ____ the lakes on a map. (locate)
3. Many people have ____ letters to Mark. (mail)
4. The sailors have ____ to Canada this summer. (travel)
5. Mark has ____ to his family about Canada. (write)
6. The children have ____ in canoes. (ride)

Spelling Verbs, pages 92–93

Write the past tense of each verb.

1. hug
2. hum
3. step
4. grin
5. pin
6. plan

Write each sentence two times. First use the verb in the present tense. Then use the verb in the past tense.

7. Sue ____ to a bus. (hurry)
8. Al ____ about traffic. (worry)
9. Tom ____ the sink. (empty)
10. Jo ____ the fish. (fry)

Pronouns, pages 116–117

Write each pair of sentences. Underline the pronoun from the second sentence of each pair.

1. Many people write stories. I write stories, too.
2. Some people write for grownups. We write for children.
3. Dave draws pictures. He draws pictures for stories.
4. Joan writes stories. She uses Dave's pictures.
5. Dave draws the pictures. Then she writes the story.
6. Joan and Dave work happily. They write good books.

Using Pronouns, pages 118–119

Write each pair of sentences. Use the pronoun that takes the place of the underlined word or words.

1. Pablo and Esther work on a ranch. ____ rope cows.
2. Pablo rides a horse. ____ rides very well.
3. Sometimes Esther helps. ____ rides horses, too.
4. Pablo and I rope cows. ____ bring the cows home.
5. The horse runs a lot. ____ works hard.
6. That horse belongs to me. ____ take care of it.

Pronouns with Verbs, pages 120–121

Write each pair of sentences. Use the form of the verb in the present tense that agrees with the pronoun.

1. Ruth and Barney make toys.
   They ____ together. (work)
2. Ruth makes puppets.
   She ____ the puppets. (dress)
3. Barney paints the puppets.
   He ____ the puppets, too. (fix)
4. Barney often makes toy planes.
   He ____ the wings first. (build)
5. Barney runs after the planes.
   He ____ them in the air. (catch)
6. Ruth likes to see the planes.
   She ____ Barney fly them. (watch)

More Practice

More About Using Pronouns, pages 122–123

Write the second sentence of each pair. Use the correct word to fill in the blank space.

1. Ed fed his cat.
   ____ ate happily. (He, The cat)
2. Mei wrote a letter to Sue.
   ____ got the letter. (She, Sue)
3. The dogs ate many bones.
   ____ tasted good. (They, The bones)
4. Ed and Al own stores.
   ____ sell hats. (They, Ed and Al)

Possessive Pronouns, pages 126–127

Write each pair of sentences. Use the correct possessive pronoun to fill in each blank space.

1. Carl's store sells books. ____ store sells gifts, too.
2. Jean works in a library. ____ library has old books.
3. Jean repairs old books. She mends ____ covers, too.
4. Ann and I buy books. ____ books cost a lot.

Using Pronouns After Action Verbs, pages 128–129

Write the second sentence. Use the correct pronoun in place of the underlined words.

1. Maria and Luis see <u>Juan</u>.
   Maria and Luis see ____.
2. Sue lost her <u>book</u>.
   Tom found ____.
3. Mr. Jones calls <u>the boys</u>.
   Mr. Jones calls ____.
4. Jan writes <u>Mom and me</u>.
   Jan writes ____.

Words Often Confused, pages 130–131

Write each sentence. Use the correct word for each blank space.

1. One day I went ____ my uncle's house. (to, too, two)
2. ____ two hours away from my house. (Its, It's)
3. My uncle gave his cats ____ food. (there, their)
4. The ____ cats are both yellow. (to, two, too)

Sentence Messages, pages 156–157

Read each sentence. Look at the part in the box. Write **subject part** if it is a subject part. Write **predicate part** if it is a predicate part.

1. Jody Wiggins | broke her leg.
2. Her classmates | visited her.
3. A large white cast | stayed around her leg.
4. The whole class | signed her cast.
5. The students | wrote funny things.
6. One boy | drew a silly picture.

Simple Subjects, pages 158–159

Write each sentence. Draw a line under the subject part. Draw a second line under the simple subject.

1. Many people watch TV.
2. Some people enjoy the news.
3. My sister looks at cartoons.
4. My parents go to movies.
5. Nature programs show facts.
6. The children watch the shows.

Compound Subjects, pages 160–161

Write each sentence. Draw a line under the subject part. Draw a second line under the simple subjects.

1. Cher and Fernando put a message in a bottle.
2. Waves and wind rolled the bottle to shore.
3. A boy and a girl found the bottle on the beach.
4. A woman and a dog ran up to them.
5. Sand and water got into the bottle.
6. Frank and Helen write another message.

More Practice

Subjects and Verbs, pages 162–163

Write each sentence. Use the correct form of the verb.

1. Snow and rain ____ on the wires. (falls, fall)
2. Lines and wires ____. (breaks, break)
3. Sisters and brothers ____. (reads, read)
4. Teachers and students ____. (talks, talk)

Simple Predicates, pages 166–167

Write each sentence. Draw a line under the predicate part. Draw a second line under the simple predicate. Write the predicate part. Underline the simple predicate.

1. Joe delivered newspapers.
2. The class read the paper.
3. Dorothy saved her copy.
4. Mr. Wilson gave one to me.
5. Cary rolled paper logs.
6. Bob made paper snowballs.

Using Commas, pages 170–171

Write each sentence. Use commas where necessary.

1. Letters notes and postcards record messages.
2. Karen washed dried and stacked the dishes.
3. Yes I heard the radio news report.
4. Paul will you please close the door?
5. Rafael arrived on Tuesday May 6 1980.

Punctuating Conversations, pages 174–175

Write each sentence. Use correct punctuation and capitalization.

1. Linda said we just got back from the movies
2. Dad replied tell me about the film
3. we saw a space adventure answered Dave
4. it was very interesting and exciting said Linda
5. Dave added you and Mom would really enjoy it

Adjectives, pages 194–195

Write each sentence. Draw a line under each adjective. Then draw two lines under the noun that each adjective describes.

1. The class visited the huge zoo.
2. The children watched a playful monkey.
3. The tricky monkey hung on a long rope.
4. Lee saw a tall giraffe.
5. The giant giraffe was looking over the old fence.

Adjectives That Compare, pages 196–197

Choose the correct adjective to complete each sentence. Write the sentence.

1. A tall tree grows upon the hillside.
   A ____ tree grows along the river. (taller, tallest)
2. The ____ tree on the farm grows here. (taller, tallest)
3. A thick branch is filled with holes.
   A ____ branch is covered with moss. (thicker, thickest)
4. The ____ branch of all has dead leaves. (thick, thickest)

More Adjectives That Compare, pages 198–199

Decide whether the adjective should end with **-er** or **-est.** Write the second sentence with the correct adjective.

1. Catherine saw two squirrels.
   The ____ squirrel of the two scooted around the tree. (tiny)
2. Yoko sat on the big rock.
   John ran to the ____ rock of all. (big)
3. Felix spotted several rocks.
   He saw the ____ rock in the woods. (shiny)
4. Tom and Sue walked the two dogs.
   The ____ dog barked at a cat. (small)

More Practice

Using Adjectives, pages 202–203

Read each sentence. Complete each sentence by using **a** or **an** with singular nouns. For plural nouns use **the** or number words from one to ten. Write each sentence.

1. ____ tiny flowers grew by the stream.
2. ____ small boy picked ____ tiny flower.
3. ____ boy put ____ flower in ____ basket.
4. ____ boy gave ____ basket to ____ friend.
5. The friend gave the boy ____ apple.
6. ____ children looked for more flowers.

Making New Adjectives, pages 204–205

Write each sentence. Add **-ful** to the word at the end of the sentence.

1. Many farmers own ____ horses. (beauty)
2. A ____ farmer got a horse for a good price. (cheer)
3. The ____ farmer told his wife. (thank)

Add **-y** to each word to make an adjective. Write the adjective.

4. smoke   5. tin   6. rock   7. chop

Using Synonyms and Antonyms in Sentences, pages 206–207

Write each sentence using the synonym for each underlined word.

1. A <u>small</u> ant climbed up the side of the wall. (huge, tiny)
2. My brother found a <u>bright</u> coin in the grass. (shiny, dull)
3. The <u>silly</u> little puppy jumped up and down. (sleepy, funny)
4. The <u>happy</u> child smiled at her parents. (cheerful, noisy)

Write each sentence using the antonym for each underlined word.

5. Dad carried the <u>light</u> box to the car. (small, heavy)
6. The puppy rolled in the <u>dry</u> grass. (wet, hard)
7. It is difficult to walk in <u>loose</u> boots. (worn, tight)
8. We used a <u>dull</u> knife to cut the cheese. (sharp, new)

Linking Verbs, pages 230–231

Write the verb in each sentence. If the verb names an action, write **action verb** after the verb. If the verb is a linking verb, write **linking verb** after the verb.

1. Jim is a fisherman.
2. We are friends.
3. Alice sails boats.
4. I hunt for shells.
5. Jim catches fish.
6. We are happy.

Nouns and Adjectives After Linking Verbs, pages 232–233

Read each sentence. Write the word that follows the linking verb. (Do not count words such as *a, an, the, his, her, my,* or *their*.) If the word is a noun, write **noun.** If the word is an adjective, write **adjective.**

1. The shore is nice.
2. The fish are big.
3. The boat is a sloop.
4. The fishing pole is strong.
5. This fish is a bass.
6. The gulls are white.

Using Linking Verbs in the Present Tense, pages 234–235

Write the sentence. Use the correct form of the linking verb.

1. My friend ____ a good fisher. (is, am)
2. Her rods ____ her treasures. (is, are)
3. She ____ a collector of shells. (is, are)
4. I ____ glad about her shells. (am, is)

More Practice

Contractions, pages 236–237

Write each sentence. Use a contraction for the underlined words.

1. It is time for lunch.
2. I am too busy.
3. They are very sandy.
4. You are a great fisher.

Linking Verbs in the Past Tense, pages 240–241

Write the verb. If the verb names an action, write **action verb.** If the verb is a linking verb, write **linking verb.**

1. Ms. Chen collected shells.
2. She went to the beach.
3. Ms. Chen hunted for shells.
4. The shells were treasures.
5. She was happy.
6. She walked on the beach slowly.

Using Linking Verbs in the Past Tense, pages 242–243

Write each sentence. Use the correct linking verb.

1. Kim ____ at the beach. (was, were)
2. The sand ____ hot. (was, were)
3. The shells ____ all over the beach. (was, were)
4. The waves ____ noisy. (was, were)
5. The people ____ loud. (was, were)
6. Kim ____ tired. (was, were)

Adverbs, pages 244–247

Write each sentence. Draw a line under the adverb in each sentence. Then draw two lines under the verb it describes.

1. Suddenly the morning sun rose.
2. Several small animals scampered softly.
3. Then some more campers arrived.
4. We awakened early.
5. Pam and Elaine quickly cooked breakfast.
6. We ate hungrily.

Reviewing Sentences, pages 270–271

Write each sentence so that it begins and ends correctly. Then tell what kind of sentence each sentence is.

1. our family goes fishing
2. does your family go, too
3. how I like fishing
4. do you want to come
5. we will wake up early
6. john and I make lunch
7. bring the peanut butter
8. when do we leave
9. get in the back seat
10. what fun we will have

Reviewing Subject Parts, pages 272–273

Write the subject part of each sentence. Draw a line under the simple subject.

1. My father bought a new boat.
2. The new boat works very well.
3. My sister wants a new boat.
4. Her friends like to fish.
5. My mother sails, too.
6. Her red boat is tiny.

Reviewing Predicate Parts, pages 274–275

Write the predicate part of each sentence. Draw a line under the simple predicate.

1. Our family goes fishing.
2. We catch many big fish.
3. Our fishing trip ends nicely.
4. We ride the ocean waves.
5. Our captain waves to us.
6. We watch the boat sail off.

Compound Subjects, pages 276–277

Write the subject part. Underline the simple subjects.

1. My sister and I enjoy fishing and tennis.
2. Fishing and tennis keep us very busy after school.
3. Our friends and families enjoy these two sports, too.
4. Our mother and father play tennis every day.

More Practice

Compound Sentences, pages 282–283

Write each sentence. Write **compound** if the sentence is compound. Write **not compound** if the sentence is not compound.

1. Our class plays tennis, and our teacher coaches us.
2. She enjoys tennis very much.
3. She plays very well.
4. Yesterday I played Liza, and she beat me.

Building Compound Sentences, pages 284–285

Make each pair of sentences into one compound sentence. Write the compound sentence.

1. I hit a fast ball. She sent it right back.
2. She hit a ball over my head. I missed it.
3. I placed a ball in the corner. She got it.
4. She returned the ball. It hit the net.

Parts of Speech, pages 286–287

Write each underlined word. Write whether each word is a **noun,** a **pronoun,** a **verb,** an **adjective,** or an **adverb.**

1. My <u>mother</u> <u>was</u> at a tennis <u>game</u>.
2. <u>She</u> <u>saw</u> two <u>good</u> players.
3. The <u>tall</u> <u>player</u> <u>hit</u> the ball.
4. The <u>ball</u> <u>dropped</u> <u>suddenly</u>.

Using Commas, pages 288–289

Write each sentence. Use commas where they are necessary.

1. Mrs. Hall asked "Greg will you help me next week?"
2. "Yes I will be there early on Saturday" Greg said.
3. Greg Jody and Allison helped Mrs. Hall.
4. They mowed raked and weeded all day.
5. Mrs. Hall gave them tickets for the circus on Saturday October 5 1985.

Workbook

Workbook

Learning About Sentences pages 2-3

A **sentence** is a group of words that state a complete idea.

Sentence: The students toured a space museum.

Not a sentence: The students.

Read each group of words. Write each group of words that is a sentence. If a group of words is not a sentence, write **not a sentence.**

1. A satellite for television.
2. Soared into the air.
3. People watched the rocket.
4. A satellite circled earth.
5. Signals from TV stations.
6. People far away.

Four Kinds of Sentences pages 4-5

A **declarative sentence** is a sentence that tells something.

The rocket needed fuel in its tanks.

An **interrogative sentence** is a sentence that asks something.

When will the fuel tanks be filled?

An **exclamatory sentence** is a sentence that shows strong feelings.

What a dangerous job those workers have!

An **imperative sentence** is a sentence that tells or asks someone to do something.

Look at the worker on the fuel truck.

Write each sentence. Next to each, write whether it is **declarative**, **interrogative**, **exclamatory**, or **imperative**.

1. A space craft carries passengers
2. Look at the photographs.
3. Watch this film of the craft.
4. The craft uses a rocket booster.
5. How is that craft launched?
6. Can the craft fly alone?
7. The crew works hard.
8. What a difficult job they have!

Workbook

Capitalizing and Punctuating Sentences pages 6-7

Use a **capital letter** to begin the first word of every sentence.

Use a **period (.)** at the end of a declarative or an imperative sentence.

Use a **question mark (?)** at the end of an interrogative sentence.

Use an **exclamation mark (!)** at the end of an exclamatory sentence.

The earth travels around the sun. (declarative)
How does the sun provide heat? (interrogative)
What a hot place the sun must be! (exclamatory)
Study the notes on the sun. (imperative)

Some of the sentences below do not begin or end properly. Write each sentence so that it begins and ends correctly.

1. hot gas floats near the sun
2. what heat the sun makes
3. how many planets circle the sun
4. a ship near the sun melts
5. can you measure the earth
6. scientists measure the earth

Subject and Predicate Parts pages 10-11

The **subject part** of a sentence names whom or what the sentence is about.

The **predicate part** of a sentence tells what action the subject part does.

The scientists designed a new spaceship.

Write each sentence. Draw one line under the subject part. Draw two lines under the predicate part.

1. The sun makes Mercury hot.
2. The heat boils away the water.
3. Rockets travel to other planets.
4. Scientists search for new facts.

Workbook

Building Sentences pages 12-13

A **complete sentence** must have a **subject part** and a **predicate part**. You can make a sentence give more information by adding words to the subject part or the predicate part.

The rocket flew.   The huge rocket flew upward.

Add words to the subject part of each sentence. Then write each new sentence.

1. Workers put fuel in the rocket.
2. Scientists check equipment.
3. The astronauts arrive.
4. The crowd watches.

Add words to the predicate part of each sentence. Then write each new sentence.

5. Engineers watch the clock.
6. A scientist pushes a button.
7. The rocket climbs.
8. The crowd cheers.

Commas pages 14-15

Use a **comma (,)** to set off words such as *yes, no,* and *well* when they begin a sentence.

Yes, I saw the article about the new rocket.

Use a **comma (,)** to set off the name of a person who is spoken to directly in a sentence.

Did you cut the article out, Juan?

Use a **comma (,)** to separate the date from the year.

An astronaut walked in space on March 18, 1965.

Write each sentence. Use commas where they are necessary.

1. Mona when did the first airplane flight take place?
2. The Wright brothers flew on December 17 1903.
3. John do you know who was the first American to orbit earth?
4. Yes the first American to orbit in space was John H. Glenn.

Workbook

Workbook

Parts of a Book pages 18-19

Many books are divided into parts. The *title page* is the first important page in the book. It tells the title, author, and publisher. The *table of contents* follows the title page. It lists the units or chapters. It tells on what page each unit or chapter begins. The *body* of the book is the main part. It contains all the units or chapters. The *index* is at the back of the book. It is an alphabetical list of all the things in the book. It tells on what page you can find each thing.

Title Page

Beginner's Guide to Space

Ricky Chen

Star Publishers, Inc.
Galway, New York

Table of Contents

Index

Use the sample pages above to answer each question.

1. What is the title of the book?
2. What is the name of the publisher of the book?
3. What is the name of the author?
4. What is the name of chapter 5?
5. On what page does chapter 3 begin?
6. On what page does the index begin?
7. Which pages tell about manned space flights?
8. On what page can information about Pluto be found?
9. Which chapter would you read for information about the sun?
10. On which pages would you find information about Mars?

Direction Paragraphs pages 22-23

Remember the rules for writing a paragraph that gives directions.

1. Begin with a main idea sentence. This sentence tells what the directions are for.
2. Next add detail sentences. Each detail sentence gives one step of the directions. The detail sentences must be in order. They must clearly tell what to do. You can use words such as *first, second, third, next, then,* and *finally.*

Remember to indent the first word of a paragraph.

Read these sentences. First choose the main idea sentence. Then put the detail sentences in order. Write the paragraph. Remember to indent the first word.

A. **1.** First you roll a piece of construction paper into a tube.
2. You can make a model rocket.
3. Second you cut three triangle shaped pieces of paper.
4. Then glue the cone to the top of the tube.
5. Next you roll one triangle into a cone.
6. Finally attach the remaining two triangles to opposite sides of the tube near the bottom.

B. **1.** Finally tack the tied strings to a large cork.
2. First cut a rag into a twelve inch square.
3. Third tie the four strings together.
4. You can make a model rocket parachute.
5. Next tie a foot long piece of string to each corner of the rag.

C. **1.** Then fold the parachute loosely and neatly.
2. Second find a wide open area for your test.
3. Last toss the parachute high.
4. You can test your model rocket parachute.
5. To begin with choose a nice day with a slight breeze.

How to Edit Your Work page 26

Edit means to read carefully and correct any mistakes.
After you write a paragraph, you should edit it.
Make sure it says what you want it to say.
Make sure other people can read it.

Example

¶ making a sponge garden is easy. first you wet a sponge. Next spread gras seed on top. Third you put the sponge on a sauser. Finally water the seeds each day until they sprout.

Editing Symbols

- ≡ capitalize
- ¶ indent
- take out
- ^ add

Correct the mistakes in each of the following. Write each sentence correctly.

1. you can mak a postar about space.
2. first look through old magazines for pixtures of stars, planets, or spaceships.
3. Than carefully cut the pictures out.
4. Next arrange thim on a large piece of construction paper
5. Finally paste them in the construction paper
6. making model of the solar system is fun
7. First find out how larg eache of the planets is
8. Then roll different size balls of cley to represent each planet
9. next attach the clay balls to a piece of cardbord.
10. Last your draw lines on the cardboard to show their orbits

Look at the paragraph below. What mistakes need to be corrected? Write the paragraph correctly.

making a star map is fan. First chose a star group that you like Next you copie the pattern a piece of blue paper. Then you cut out star shaped hols the paper. finaly you paste a piece of white paper behind the blu paper

Workbook

Independent Writing: Writing a Direction Paragraph page 27

Prewriting Imagine that you are helping scientists to plan a journey to an unexplored planet. You have to write a report giving directions to the astronaut who will land on the planet. Think about these questions, and jot down some notes.

What should the astronaut do first?

What would be some other important things that the astronaut should do?

Look at you notes again. Make sure the directions are in the right order.

Writing Write a paragraph giving directions. You will tell an astronaut what to do after landing on a new planet. Start your paragraph with a main idea sentence. Then write detail sentences that tell each step in the directions.

Editing Use the check questions on page 26 and the editing symbols to edit your paragraph.

Learning About Nouns pages 36-37

A **noun** is a word that names a person, a place, or a thing. Notice the underlined nouns in the examples below.

The *birds* build a *nest*.

The *badgers* dig a *hole*.

Write each sentence. Draw a line under each noun.

1. Animals play in the forest.
2. A moose eats leaves from a tree.
3. A fawn drinks water from a stream.
4. A squirrel runs up a tree.
5. Rabbits sniff the air.
6. A storm approaches the forest.
7. Birds build nests in the tree.
8. The animals seek shelter.

Singular and Plural Nouns pages 38-39

A **singular noun** is a noun that names one person, place, or thing.

A **plural noun** is a noun that names more than one person, place, or thing.

You can make many nouns plural by adding **-s** to the end of the singular noun.

bicycle (singular noun) bicycles (plural noun)

Write the plural form of each singular noun.

1. hiker
2. sled
3. swimmer
4. wagon
5. sneaker
6. boat
7. arrow
8. river

Write each sentence. Underline each noun. Write **singular** above each singular noun. Write **plural** above each plural noun.

9. Some campers put up tents on the campground.
10. The boy hammers a peg into the ground.

Spelling Plural Nouns pages 40-41

If a singular noun ends with **s, ss, x, ch, z,** or **sh,** add **-es** to form the plural.

Singular	Plural	Singular	Plural
bus	buses	watch	watches

Some nouns form the plural in different ways.

Singular	Plural	Singular	Plural
child	children	goose	geese

Write each sentence using the plural form of the noun.

1. Two ____ went to the game. (bus)
2. Some ____ fell. (branch)
3. Many ____ clapped. (child)
4. Many ____ enjoyed the game. (fan)
5. Six ____ swam. (goose)
6. Two ____ fell. (box)

Workbook

More About Plural Nouns page 42

If a singular noun ends with a consonant and **y,** change the **y** to **i** and add **-es** to form the plural.

Singular	**Plural**	**Singular**	**Plural**
company	companies	city	cities
party	parties	berry	berries

Write each sentence. Use the plural form of the noun in parentheses.

1. Several ____ went to the park for a picnic. (family)
2. Three ____ enjoyed the fresh air. (baby)
3. Two ____ played in the grass. (puppy)
4. The children ate many ____ for dessert. (cherry)
5. The boys found four ____ on the ground. (penny)
6. The girls picked many wild ____ . (strawberry)

Compound Nouns page 43

A **compound noun** is a noun that is formed from two smaller words.

Sunlight is light from the sun.
Basketball is a game played with a basket and a ball.

Write the meaning of each compound noun.

1. doorknob
2. sailboat
3. snowplow
4. sunburn
5. clothesline
6. airmail
7. roadside
8. stepladder
9. shipwreck
10. tablecloth
11. steamship
12. thunderstorm
13. seaplane
14. fireplace
15. mailbag
16. moonlight
17. ashtray
18. streetcar

Common and Proper Nouns pages 46-47

A **common noun** names any person, place, or thing.
A **proper noun** names a special person, place, or thing.
Begin each important word in a proper noun with a **capital letter.**

A hiker climbed to the top of Thunder Mountain.
common noun proper noun

Write each sentence correctly. Use capital letters where they belong. Then underline each common noun. Circle each proper noun.

1. The class boarded the bus at pennsylvania station.
2. The bus took the class to harriman park.
3. The teacher took juan and richard to the fountain.
4. Some students hiked to welsh lake.

Capitalizing Proper Nouns pages 48-49

You can use the titles **Mr., Dr., Mrs., Miss,** and **Ms.** with last names. Begin a title with a **capital letter**. End most titles with a **period**. You can use some shortened words when you write addresses. Two words are St. (Street) and Ave. (Avenue). Begin each shortened word with a capital letter. End each shortened word with a period.

Dr. Mary Adams 102 Fourth St.

Write each sentence correctly.

1. The racket belongs to mrs Green.
2. mrs Green calls dr Jansen.
3. dr and mrs Martin play tennis.
4. mr. Ramos keeps score.

Write each address correctly.

5. ms Joan Colley
870 Elmhurst ave.
6. dr Jack Roberts
1023 Belford st.
7. mrs Luisa Perez
654 rock ave.

Workbook

Possessive Nouns pages 50-51

A **possessive noun** is a noun that names who or what has something. Add an **apostrophe and s ('s)** to form the possessive of most singular nouns. Add an **apostrophe (')** to form the possessive of plural nouns that end with **s.**

dog**'s** collar (singular) dog**s'** collar (plural)

If a plural noun does not end with **s**, add **'s** to form the possessive.

Singular	Plural	Singular	Plural
child**'s** toy	children**'s** toys	man**'s** coat	men**'s** coats

At the end of each sentence is a singular or plural noun. Write each sentence using the correct possessive form.

1. Two ____ bikes won prizes. (boys)

2. Rita rides to the ____ zoo. (children)

3. One ____ bike is blue. (girl)

4. Ann calls one ____ name. (dog)

Making New Words pages 52-53

A **suffix** is one or more letters added to the end of a word. The suffixes **-er** and **-or** usually mean a person who.

work	worker	a person who works
act	actor	a person who acts

If a word ends with **e**, drop the **e** before you add **-er** or **-or.**

ride	rider	a person who rides

Most words add the suffix **-er**. Only a few add the suffix **-or**.

Visit**or** operat**or** invent**or** sail**or**

Add an **-er** or **-or** suffix to these words to form new words. Write the new words. Then write the meaning of each new word.

1. paint

2. visit

3. help

4. operate

5. bake

6. clean

Alphabetical Order pages 56-57

Alphabetical order is the order of letters in the alphabet. To put words in alphabetical order, look at the first letter of each word. If the first letters are the same, look at the second letter. If the second letters are the same, look at the third.

Write the words in each list in alphabetical order.

1.	2.	3.	4.
butter	chill	stare	tint
button	child	star	tin
bun	chicken	starve	tiny
bunk	chin	stamp	tinder

Learning About the Dictionary pages 58-59

A dictionary is a book that tells the meanings of words. Each word is called an *entry*. The entries are in alphabetical order. If a word has two meanings, they are numbered 1 and 2. An *example sentence* may show how a word is used.

The dictionary gives a pronunciation key which helps you say the word. The words are broken into parts called syllables.

Use the sample dictionary page to answer each question. Write the answer.

kite / knighthood

kite (kīt) *n.* **1.** a lightweight frame flown in the air at the end of a long string. **2.** hawks having a hooked bill, a forked tail, and narrow wings.
kit•ten (kit′ən) *n.* a young cat.
kit•ty (kit′ē) *n. pl.* **kit•ties.** a kitten or cat.
knight•hood (nīt′hood′) *n.* **1.** the rank of a knight. **2.** the behavior or qualities befitting a knight; chivalry.

at; **ā**pe; c**ä**r; **e**nd; m**ē**; **i**t; **ī**ce; h**o**t; **ō**ld; f**ô**rk; w**oo**d; f**o͞o**l; **oi**l; **ou**t; **u**p; t**u**rn; si**ng**; **th**in; **th**is; **hw** in white; **zh** in treasure. The symbol ə stands for the sound of **a** in **a**bout, **e** in tak**e**n, **i** in penc**i**l, **o** in lem**o**n, and **u** in circ**u**s.

1. How do you write the pronunciation for *kite*?
2. How many syllables does the word *kitten* have?
3. Which entries have more than one meaning?
4. Write a sample sentence for the first meaning of kite.

Independent Writing: Writing a Description Paragraph page 67

A *paragraph* can describe a person, a place, or a thing. The *main idea sentence* tells whom or what the paragraph is about. The *detail sentences* use words that describe the person, place, or thing. The words tell how someone or something looks, sounds, tastes, smells, or feels.

Prewriting Think of a team sport you like to play. Suppose you were choosing new uniforms for your team. Jot down some notes about the way you would like the uniforms to look. Describe the color, the design, and other details.

Writing Write a paragraph that describes the new team uniform you have chosen. Start your paragraph with a main idea sentence. Then use the notes you made to write the detail sentences.

Editing Use the check questions on page 67 and the editing symbols to edit your paragraph.

Verbs pages 76-77

An **action verb** is a word that names an action. You can find action verbs in the predicate part of a sentence. The **predicate part** tells what action the subject does.

predicate part
A boat sails to Europe.
verb

Write each sentence. Underline each action verb.

1. A family travels to a palace.
2. The Smiths ride on a tour bus.
3. The driver describes the sights.
4. A guide shows the palace grounds.
5. Two men guard the entrance.
6. The group moves through the palace.

Workbook

Verb Tenses pages 78-79

The **present tense** of a verb names an action that happens now. The **past tense** of a verb names an action that already happened. The **future tense** of a verb names an action that will take place in the future.

Present: The pilot flies the plane.
Past: The plane raced down the runway.
Future: The plane will land at a different airport.

Verbs that show action in the future have a main verb and the helping verb *will* or *shall*.
Has and *have* are action verbs that tell about owning something. They are in the present tense.

Write each sentence. Underline each verb. Then write if the verb is in the **past, present,** or **future** tense.

1. The tour boat arrived at the dock.
2. The crew tied the boat to the dock.
3. People climb off the boat.
4. The ticket seller sells tickets for the next tour.
5. People buy tickets from the ticket seller.
6. Tourists walk to the boat's gangplank.
7. The boat will travel down the river.
8. The people will take pictures of the sights.
9. Some people have lunches with them.
10. The people will eat lunch on the boat.
11. The man has a huge picnic basket.
12. A young girl ate a sandwich.
13. Another girl asks for some milk.
14. The baby will eat the cookies.
15. The mother gets some juice.
16. The boat left the dock early.

Using the Present Tense pages 80-81

A **singular noun** names one person, place, or thing.
A **plural noun** names more than one person, place, or thing.
The verb in a sentence must agree with the noun in the subject part. Most verbs in the present tense end in **-s** when they agree with a singular noun. Most verbs in the present tense do not end in **-s** when they agree with a plural noun. *Has* and *have* are present tense verbs. *Has* agrees with a singular noun. *Have* agrees with a plural noun.

Singular Noun + Verb	**Plural Noun + Verb**
The man sails a boat.	The men sail the boat.
The boy has a rope.	The boys have ropes.

Write each sentence. Use the correct verb for each sentence.

1. The traveler ____ a film about Venice. (show, shows)
2. Students ____ the film on the screen. (watch, watches)
3. The traveler ____ about the city. (tell, tells)
4. One tourist ____ pictures of a famous palace. (has, have)
5. Some students ____ questions about the film. (has, have)
6. Water ____ many streets in Venice. (fill, fills)
7. People ____ boats in the city. (use, uses)
8. Some boats ____ motors on them. (have, has)
9. Water buses ____ people to different parts of the city. (take, takes)
10. The traveler ____ the history of the city. (discuss, discusses)
11. Students ____ after the talk. (clap, claps)
12. The questioners ____ for an hour. (continue, continues)
13. One student ____ more information. (want, wants)
14. Some friends ____ with great interest. (listen, listens)
15. The city ____ a long history. (has, have)
16. A scholar ____ its works of art. (study, studies)
17. Statues ____ every building. (decorate, decorates)

Spelling and the Present Tense page 82

Add **-s** to most verbs in the present tense when they agree with singular nouns.

The train travels to Ohio.

The passenger boards the train .

If a verb ends in **s, ss, x, ch, z,** or **sh,** add **-es** to the verb to make it agree with a singular noun.

A girl watches the train. Tina's dog rushes after it.

Write each sentence with the correct present tense form of the verb.

1. The train ____ through a forest. (pass)

2. A locomotive ____ up a hill. (chug)

3. The train ____ a bridge. (cross)

4. The train ____ out of sight. (rush)

5. A man ____ the train. (miss)

6. A man ____ another ticket. (buy)

Making New Words page 83

A **prefix** is a letter or a group of letters added to the beginning of a word.

Prefix	Meaning	Example
un-	the opposite of	unsnap
re-	again	reread

Replace the underlined words in each sentence with a word with the prefix *un-* or *re-*. Write the sentence with the new word.

1. Mary did the opposite of locked the front door.

2. Father planted again the flowers in the sun.

3. The small girl did the opposite of dressed her doll.

4. The student wrote again the homework.

5. The boys did the opposite of tangled the string.

Verbs in the Past Tense pages 86-87

The **past tense** of a verb names an action that already happened. Add **-ed** to most verbs to form the past tense. If a verb ends in **e**, drop the **e** and add **-ed** to form the past tense.

Mary visited many cities in France.
Mary liked the trip.

Write each sentence using the correct form of the verb.

1. Mary ____ to France. (travel)
2. The plane ____ at the airport (land)
3. A worker ____ the bags in a taxi. (place)
4. Mary ____ the windows. (open)
5. Mary ____ to the woman. (call)
6. The woman ____ back in French. (shout)

The Past with Have and Has pages 88-89

The **main verb** in a sentence shows the action. A **helping verb** is a verb that helps a main verb to name an action. You may use the helping verbs *have* and *has* with the past tense of the main verb. The past with *have* or *has* tells about an action that started in the past but has no real ending time. You may also use the past with *have* or *has* to name an action that continues in the present.

Verb	Past	Past with Have or Has
walk	walked	have or has walked

Write each sentence. Use the correct form of the main verb.

1. Marvin's family has ____ to many different countries. (travel)
2. The family ____ several countries in Europe last year. (visit)
3. Two cousins have ____ in France a long time. (live)
4. Bill ____ Marvin about his favorite country. (ask)
5. Marvin ____ some cities. (describe)

More About the Past pages 90-91

You add **-ed** to most verbs to form the past tense. You also add **-ed** to most verbs to show past action with have or has. Some verbs change to the past tense and to the past with *have* or *has* in different ways.

Verb	Past	Past with Have or Has
bring	brought	have or has brought
come	came	have or has come
draw	drew	have or has drawn
drive	drove	have or has driven
fall	fallen	have or has fallen
fly	flew	have or has flown
go	gone	have or has gone
ride	rode	have or has ridden
run	ran	have or has run
say	said	have or has said
see	saw	have or has seen
speak	spoke	have or has spoken
teach	taught	have or has taught
throw	thrown	have or has thrown
write	wrote	have or has written

Write each sentence. Use the correct form of the main verb.

1. Last month Tonia ____ to Canada with the family. (fly)
2. Tonia has ____ French words. (say)
3. The family has ____ some presents back for us. (bring)
4. Tonia has ____ some pictures of Canadian cities. (draw)
5. Tonia has ____ a story about the travels. (write)
6. Yesterday Tonia ____ to the class about the trip. (speak)
7. The class ____ pictures of many Canadian places. (see)
8. Tonia has ____ so many sights. (see)
9. Tonia has ____ us all a lot about Canada. (teach)
10. The families have ____ to Niagara Falls. (go)
11. Many rocks have ____ into the water. (fall)
12. Another friend ____ along with us. (come)

Spelling Verbs page 92

If a one-syllable verb ends with consonant, vowel, consonant, double the last consonant and add **-ed** to make the past tense.

Verb	**Past**	**Past with Have or Has**
flap	flapped	have or has flapped
dim	dimmed	have or has dimmed

Write each sentence using the past tense of each verb.

1. The teacher has ____ a trip to the zoo. (plan)
2. The entire class ____ with joy. (clap)
3. The teacher ____ the desk with a pencil. (tap)
4. The students ____ the noise. (stop)
5. The class ____ for more details about the trip. (beg)

More About Spelling Verbs page 93

If a verb ends in a consonant and **y**, change the **y** to **i** and add **-es** to form the present tense.
If a verb ends in a consonant and **y**, change the **y** to **i** and add **-ed** to form the past tense.

Verb	**Present**	**Past**
cry	cries	cried
hurry	hurries	hurried

Write each sentence two times. First use the verb in the present tense. Then use the verb in the past tense.

1. The man ____ . (hurry)
2. Jan ____ . (worry)
3. Paco ____ . (try)
4. The boy ____ . (study)
5. The ink ____ . (dry)
6. Ruby ____ it. (spy)
7. The store ____ . (empty)
8. The meat ____ . (fry)

Reading Graphs and Tables pages 96-97

A *graph* shows information in picture form.
A *table* lists information in columns and rows.

Examples

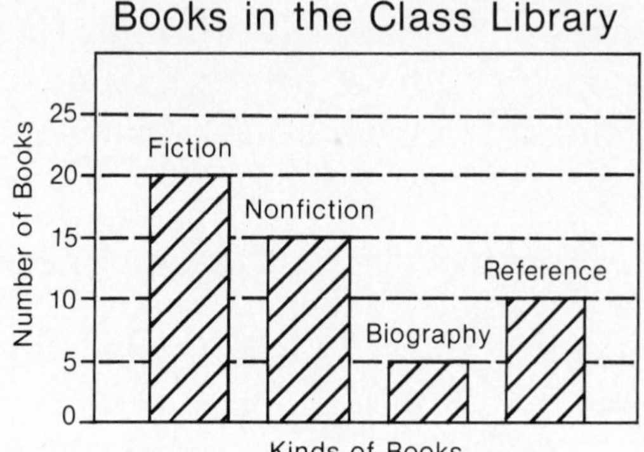

Method of Travel	Number of Students Who Have Traveled by This Method
Car	30
Train	18
Bus	12
Bicycle	29
Plane	6

Write a short answer to each question about the graph.

1. What do the numerals on the left side show?
2. Which kind of book is the most plentiful in the class library?
3. How many reference books are in the library?
4. What are the four kinds of books in the library?

Write a short answer to each question about the table.

5. Which method of travel is used by the most students?
6. Which method of travel is used by the least students?
7. How many children have taken the train?
8. How many children have ridden on bicycles?

Independent Writing: Writing a Factual Paragraph in a Friendly Letter pages 100-105

Remember the five parts of a friendly letter. They are the **date**, **greeting**, **body**, **closing**, and **name**.

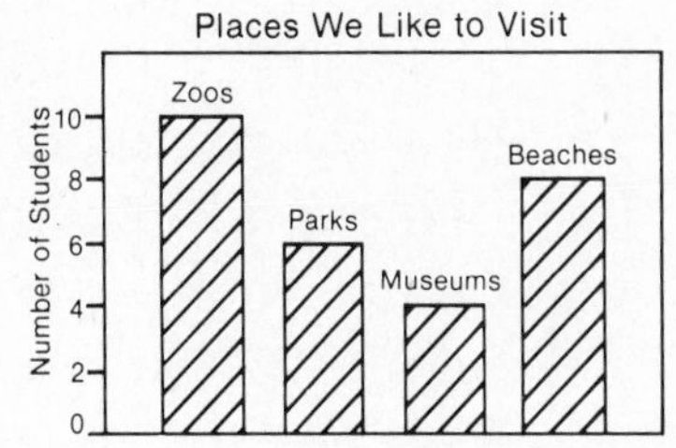

Prewriting Imagine you have taken a survey of your class. The graph shows the information you gathered. Jot down notes that tell the facts you might include in a letter to a friend. You might tell which place was most popular, how many students liked each place, and why students liked them.

Writing Write a letter to a friend describing the results of your survey. Use your notes and the graph to help you. Make sure all the parts of your letter are written correctly.

Editing Read your letter again. Use the check questions on page 105 and the editing symbols to edit your letter.

Pronouns pages 116-117

A **pronoun** is a word that takes the place or one or more nouns. Some pronouns are *I, you, it, she, he, we,* and *they*.

Mary works outdoors. She grows trees.
Tom works inside. He sells the trees.
One tree is dry. It needs more water.

Read each pair of sentences. Write the second sentence of each pair. Underline the pronoun in each sentence.

1. Sandra works in a market. She helps Mr. Jones.
2. Mr. Jones owns the market. He teaches Sandra.
3. Sandra's job is fun. It requires attention.
4. Mrs. Jones helps Sandra pack bags. They work together.
5. The package holds many groceries. It will be heavy.
6. The shopper cannot lift the bag. She needs help.

Using Pronouns pages 118-119

A **pronoun** is a word that takes the place of one or more nouns.
Pronouns must agree with the nouns they replace.

Use *I* to talk about yourself.
Use *we* to talk about one or more persons and yourself.
Use *you* to talk directly to one or more persons.
Use *she* to talk about one female.
Use *he* to talk about one male.
Use *it* to talk about one thing.
Use *they* to talk about two or more persons or things.

Read each pair of sentences. Write the second sentence of each pair. Use the pronoun that takes the place of the underlined word or words.

1. Harold works in a factory. ____ operates a machine.
2. The machine drills holes. ____ works fast.
3. Several workers bring parts. ____ put them down.
4. The parts need holes. ____ hold bolts.
5. Harold likes his job. ____ requires great skill.
6. Harold's sister works at the factory. ____ will take me to the factory.
7. Harold's sister and I will go there. ____ will see Harold.
8. A bus goes to the factory. ____ stops near my house.
9. Father drives past the factory. ____ takes me there.
10. The car is quick. ____ does not make stops.
11. The factory produces auto parts. ____ are used in new cars.
12. The car has a part from the factory. ____ improves the engine.
13. Harold tests the part. ____ fixes the problem.
14. Nora works with Harold. ____ paints the cars.

Pronouns with Verbs pages 120-121

The pronouns *I, you, he, she, it, we,* and *they* are used in the subject part of a sentence. The pronoun and the verb in a sentence must agree.

A verb in the present tense does not change when it agrees with the pronouns *I, you, we,* or *they*.

The pronouns *he, she,* and *it* work with verbs that end in **-s** or **-es**.

If a verb ends in **s, ss, x, ch, z,** or **sh,** add **-es** to make the correct form of the present tense.

Add **-s** to most other verbs to make the correct form of the present tense.

I hammer the nail.
You cut the wood.
We finish the job.
They sand the floor

He fixes the step.
It needs a new edge.
She watches the workers.

Write the second sentence of each pair. Use the form of the verb in the present tense that agrees with the pronoun.

1. Ms. Peters sells hardware. She ____ the customers. (help)
2. Some customers ask questions. They ____ her help. (need)
3. Mr. Sun needs help with a saw. She ____ him how. (show)
4. The saw makes a noise. It ____ loudly. (buzz)
5. Mr. Sun tests the saw. He ____ boards with it. (cut)
6. Mr. Sun uses the boards. They ____ excellent steps. (make)
7. Mr. Sun likes the saw. He ____ it. (buy)
8. Mrs. Gray buys paint. She ____ a bright color. (pick)
9. The woman opens the can. She ____ the paint on the wall. (brush)
10. Mrs. Gray paints the room. It ____ the old color. (match)
11. Mrs. Gray finishes the job. She ____ the brush. (wash)
12. Mrs. Gray's son helps her. He ____ for the can of paint. (reach)

More About Using Pronouns pages 122-123

A pronoun can take the place of a noun only if the meaning is clear.

Clear: Joe puts the nails in a box. They have sharp points.

Unclear: The men saddle the horses. They stand in the sun.

Read each pair of sentences. Write the second sentence of each pair using the correct word.

1. Jeff watches the zookeeper. ____ stands near the cage. (Jeff, He)
2. Jeff and I feed the seals. ____ bought the food. (We, The seals)
3. A seal eats the food. ____ floats on the water. (It, The food)
4. Some boys see an elephant. ____ have peanuts. (They, It)
5. The zookeeper cleans a cage. ____ uses a hose. (It, He)

Possessive Pronouns pages 126-127

Possessive pronouns show who or what has something. *My, your, his, her, its, our,* and *their* are possessive pronouns. A possessive pronoun must agree with the noun or nouns it replaces.

Our uncle sells shoes. His store is large.

Read each pair of sentences. Write the second sentence with the correct possessive pronoun.

1. Uncle Tom owns a shoe store. ____ store opens early. (His, My)
2. Mary goes to the store. ____ shoes need laces. (His, Her)
3. Fred repairs shoes. ____ work takes time. (His, Their)
4. Tina and I visit the store. ____ shoes need taps. (Her, Our)
5. Ted waits in the store. ____ shoes need new heels. (His, Its)

Using Pronouns After Action Verbs pages 128-129

Pronouns can appear in the **predicate part** of a sentence. The pronouns *me, you, him, her, it, us, you,* and *them* come after an action verb. A pronoun in the predicate part must agree with the noun it replaces.

The waiter calls the chef. The waiter calls him.

Read each pair of sentences. In the first sentence, some nouns are underlined. Write the second sentence using the correct pronoun in place of the underlined words.

1. Ms. Diaz owns a card shop. Ms. Diaz owns ____ .
2. Ms. Diaz starts the machine. Ms. Diaz starts ____ .
3. Ms. Diaz called Joan. Ms. Diaz called ____ .
4. She invited Tod and Ed. She invited ____ .
5. A worker paints a sign. Another worker admires ____ .

Words Often Confused pages 130-131

Homonyms sound alike but have different meanings and spellings.

Word	Meaning	Word	Meaning
their	shows what two or more people have	*too*	also or more than is needed
		to	in the direction of
there	in that place	*it's*	short for it is
two	the numeral 2	*its*	shows what one thing has

Write each sentence. Use the correct word for each blank space.

1. The news reporters liked ____ jobs. (there, their)
2. ____ reporters worked together. (To, Two)
3. They went ____ the scene of a big fire. (to, too)
4. The fire burned ____ way through a store. (it's, its)
5. The reporters described the scene ____ . (their, there)

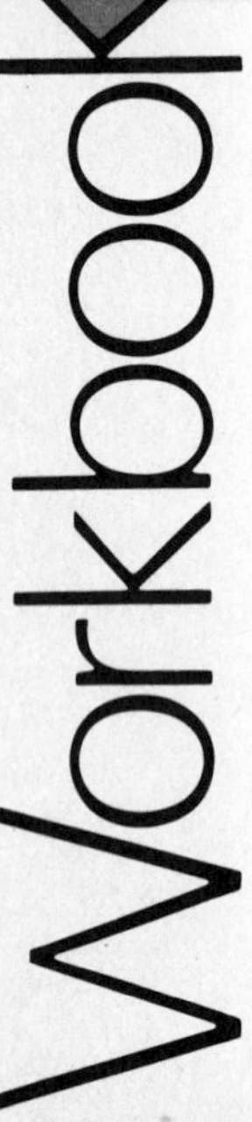

Using the Library pages 134-135

There are three main parts in a library. *Fiction* books are about people and things that are not real. *Nonfiction* books tell facts. *Reference* books give facts about many different subjects.
The *card catalog* lists all the books in the library. There are three kinds of cards in a card catalog. *Title cards* list books by their titles. *Author cards* list books by the author's last name. *Subject cards* list books by the subject of the book.

Write each sentence. Then write **fiction, nonfiction,** or **reference** to show where you would find each book.

1. An atlas
2. A history book
3. A mystery book
4. A book about cats
5. A book about magic tricks
6. An encyclopedia
7. A mathematics book
8. A dictionary
9. A ghost story
10. A book about fishing

Write the card in the card catalog that would help you find each book. Write **title card, author card,** or **subject card**.

11. A book about insects
12. A book by Ed Doty
13. A book called *Mr. Magic*
14. A book about space
15. A book called *Fishing Fun*
16. A book by Richard Scarry
17. A book called *Shipwrecked*
18. A book about mice

Independent Writing: Writing a Story pages 140-141

You can write a two-paragraph story. The first part of a story tells who the characters are. It also tells when and where the action takes place. The second part tells what happens as the action continues. The story ends by telling what happens to the characters.

Prewriting Imagine that on your way home from school a spaceship landed near you. As you watched, a door opened and a strange creature came out of the ship. What would you do? How would you feel? What would you say to the creature? Jot down some notes.

Writing Write a story about your adventure with the spaceship. Use the notes you made. Write your story in two parts. Begin by introducing the characters. Then tell what happened.

Editing Use the check questions on page 141 and the editing symbols to edit your story.

Writing or Presenting Book Report pages 142-143

In *written* or in *oral* book reports, state the book's title and author. Describe the main character in a main idea sentence. Tell more about the character and the story in detail sentences.

Write these notes for a book report in the correct order.

1. Nadia wants to visit Earth, which her friend Kim tells about.
2. This book is *A Girl of the Future,* by Toni Anne Chandler.
3. Nadia and Kim hide together aboard a ship headed for Earth.
4. The main character, adventurous young Nadia, grows up on Venus.

Workbook

Sentence Messages pages 156-157

A **declarative sentence** is a sentence that tells something. A declarative sentence ends with a **period (.)**.

An **interrogative sentence** is a sentence that asks something. An interrogative sentence ends with a **question mark (?)**.

An **exclamatory** sentence is a sentence that shows strong feeling. An exclamatory sentence ends with an **exclamation mark (!)**.

An **imperative sentence** is a sentence that tells or asks someone to do something. An imperative sentence ends with a **period (.)**.

Use a **capital letter** to begin the first word of every sentence.

The **subject part** of a sentence names whom or what the sentence is about. The **predicate part** tells what action the subject does.

Write each sentence so that it begins and ends correctly. Next to each sentence write **declarative, interrogative, exclamatory, or imperative.**

1. who mows the lawn of that big house on the hill
2. my older brother cuts the grass for the owners
3. what an excellent job he did around the trees and bushes
4. tell him about a job
5. do you know whether Mr. Ellis needs any leaves raked
6. my sister rakes leaves for people in the neighborhood

Write each sentence. Draw a line under the subject part of each sentence. Draw two lines under the predicate part.

7. The leaves fall from the trees in the autumn.
8. Meg rakes the leaves on the lawn into large piles.
9. My brother stuffs the leaves into large bags.
10. A truck collects the bags during the week.
11. The town burns the leaves in a large machine.

Simple Subjects pages 158-159

The **subject part** of a sentence names *whom* or *what* the sentence is about.

The **simple subject** is the main word in the subject part.

Cows eat hay in the barn. (*Cows* is the simple subject.)

A young boy feed them. (*Boy* is the simple subject.)

Write each sentence. Draw a line under the subject part. Draw a second line under the simple subject.

1. The farmer plants seeds in the fields.
2. The farm workers operate the tractor.
3. The powerful tractor pulls the plow through the soil.
4. The careful driver drives in straight lines.
5. Two workers fill the tractor's empty gas tank.

Compound Subjects pages 160-161

The **subject part** of a sentence names *whom* or *what* the sentence is about. The **simple subject** is the main word in the subject part of a sentence.

A **compound subject** has two or more simple subjects joined by *and*.

He and I stopped for lunch at noon.
(Pronouns in a compound subject)

Joe and I enjoyed the delicious sandwiches.
(Noun and pronoun in a compound subject)

Write each sentence. Draw a line under the subject part. Draw a second line under the simple subject in each sentence.

1. The baker and her helper bake fresh cakes.
2. Some boys and girls watch the baker through a window.
3. David and I walk into the bakery.
4. He and I smell the delicious odor of fresh bread.
5. A man and a woman buy an apple pie.

Workbook

Subjects and Verbs pages 162-163

A verb must agree with the compound subject in a sentence. When a compound subject is joined by *and*, a verb in the present tense does not add **-s** or **-es**.

A verb in the past tense does not change to agree with a subject.

Margaret and Robert walk together.
Margaret and Robert walked together.

Write each sentence. Use the correct form of the verb.

1. The boys and girls ____ to a show today. (travels, travel)
2. A teacher and a parent ____ on the bus yesterday. (climbed, climbs)
3. Marvin and Neil ____ last week's show. (discusses, discuss)
4. The teacher and the bus driver ____ about the schedule now. (talk, talks)
5. David and I ____ our library books on the bus. (reads, read)

Simple Predicates pages 166-167

The **predicate part** of a sentence tells what action the subject does. In the two sentences below the predicate part is in a box.

The **simple predicate** is the main word or group of words in the predicate part. The simple predicate is underlined.

Ms. Davidson races model cars. She builds them also.

Write each sentence. Draw a line under the predicate part. Draw a second line under the simple predicate.

1. The model race cars speed around the track.
2. One car crashes into another car.
3. The driver squeezes the speed controls.
4. Some model cars race around the corners on two wheels.
5. The fans shout with excitement.

Building Sentences pages 168-169

You can combine the subject parts of two sentences that have the same predicate part to form a sentence with a **compound subject.**

The man painted. The girl painted.

The man and the girl painted.

You can combine the predicate parts of two sentences that have the same subject part to form a sentence with a **compound predicate**.

The dog barked The dog growled.

The dog barked and growled.

Combine the subject parts or the predicate parts of each sentence to form one new sentence. Write the new sentence.

1. Angela rows the boat. Angela steers the boat.
2. Marvin sits carefully. Angela sits carefully.
3. The dock wobbles. The dock sways.
4. Parents wave from the dock. Friends wave from the dock.
5. A large fish jumps. A large fish swims.
6. Small fish swim. The green frogs swim.
7. Butterflies fly in the air. Birds fly in the air.
8. Emily ties a rope. Emily throws an anchor.
9. Marvin dives. Marvin swims.
10. Kim splashes. Kim blows bubbles.
11. The sun shines. The sun heats.
12. A motorboat passed by. A sailboat passed by.
13. The boys ate their lunch. The girls ate their lunch.
14. Nina waved. Nina shouted.
15. Marvin floated on the water. The boat floated on the water.
16. Diana climbed into the boat. Diana dried.
17. Shelly pulled up the anchor. Maria pulled up the anchor.
18. The boat bounced. The boat rocked.

Using Commas pages 170-171

Use a **comma (,)** to separate each noun in a series of three or more nouns.

Terry, Mark, and Jack visited the zoo.

Use a **comma (,)** to separate each verb in a series of three or more verbs.

Mr. James planned, cooked, and served the meal.

Use a **comma (,)** to set off words such as *yes, no,* and *well* when they begin a sentence.

Yes, Leslie hit a home run yesterday.

Use a **comma (,)** to set off the name of a person who is spoken to directly in a sentence.

You do excellent work, Margarita.

Use a **comma (,)** to separate the name of the day from the date and the date from the year.

I won that prize on Thursday, June 12, 1981.

Write each sentence. Use commas where necessary.

1. David Tami and Tommy took a trip to the museum.
2. They looked listened and learned at the museum.
3. Yes the tour guide explained everything to them.
4. They took their trip on Tuesday August 10 1981.
5. School groups families and tourists stop at the museum.
6. No the museum does not open on Monday.
7. A small child ran fell and cried.
8. His father his mother and his brother comforted him.
9. No he did not hurt his hand.
10. Mary what do you know about the building?
11. They finished the building on Monday May 11 1936.
12. The mayor the governor and the museum director celebrated.
13. A news reporter took pictures asked questions and wrote about it.
14. Yes everyone spoke in favor of the new museum.

Using Context Clues pages 172-173

Sometimes you look up the meaning of a new word in the dictionary. At other times, you can learn the meaning of a new word by looking for clues near the new word.

Mary stopped when she reached her destination.
She had finally arrived where she was going.

The second sentence helps you learn that *destination* is the place a person travels to.

Read each pair of sentences. Write the meaning of each underlined word.

1. Mark's strategy won the game. His plan worked well.
2. I could not kindle the wet wood. I needed several matches.
3. Ann's hooded coat is warm. She wears the parka every day.
4. Jim compressed the sponge tightly. The water squeezed out.

Punctuating Conversations pages 174-175

Remember the rules for writing conversations: Put *quotation marks* around each speaker's words. Use *conversation words* to tell how each person speaks. Put a *comma* after each conversation word. Put a *period* before the last quotation mark at the end of the sentence. *Indent* the first word each time the speaker changes. *Capitalize* the first word in each conversation.

Write each sentence. Use correct punctuation and capitalization.

1. Dogs make excellent pets said Bill
2. Angela replied they are warm and friendly animals
3. Joan exclaimed I did not feed my dog today
4. Perhaps you should feed him now suggested Tommy
5. Angela added you should give him water also

Independent Writing: Writing a Persuasive Conversation page 185

Remember the rules for writing conversations: Put **quotation marks** around the exact words that each speaker says. Use **conversation words** to tell how each person speaks. Put a **comma** after each conversation word when the conversation word comes before the speaker's words. Put a **period** before the last quotation mark at the end of the sentence. Put a **comma** before the last quotation mark when a conversation word ends the sentence. **Indent** the first word of each speaker. **Capitalize** the first word in each conversation.

Prewriting Imagine you are having a conversation with a friend. Each of you wants to go to a different place. You must try to persuade your friends to go to the park, the beach, or the museum. Choose which place you would prefer. Jot down notes about what you and a friend might say during the conversation.

Writing Write a conversation between you and your friends discussing how you will spend the day. Use your notes to help you.

Editing Use the check questions and the editing symbols on page 185 to edit your conversation.

Adjectives pages 194-195

A **noun** is a word that names a person, a place, or a thing. An **adjective** is a word that describes a noun.

The blue (Adjective) shirt (Noun) dried in the hot (Adjective) sun (Noun).

Write each sentence. Draw one line under each adjective. Then draw two lines under the noun that the adjective describes.

1. The large truck raced down the straight road.
2. A red flag hung from a long pipe.
3. The tall driver looked through the dirty window.
4. The careful driver slowed the big truck.

Adjectives That Compare pages 196-199

To compare one thing with another, add **-er** to the end of many adjectives. To compare more than two things, add **-est** to the end of these adjectives.

A swift bird flew. A swifter bird flew. The swiftest bird flew.

Some adjectives end with a consonant, vowel, consonant. Double the final consonant and add **-er** or **-est** to make the correct form.

I see a red bird. I see a redder bird. I see the reddest bird.

If an adjective ends with a consonant and **y**, change the **y** to **i** and add **-er** or **-est** to make the correct form of the adjective.

A tiny bird flies. A tinier bird flies. The tiniest bird flies.

Write the correct form of the adjective in parentheses to complete each exercise.

1. A crow eats a big seed. A turkey eats a ____ seed. (big)
2. That eagle has the ____ cage in the zoo. (big)
3. Eagles have ____ sight than humans. (sharp)
4. The peacock has the ____ feathers of all the birds. (pretty)
5. A robin has small wings. A sparrow has ____ wings. (small)
6. Hummingbirds seek nectar. They seek the ____ nectar. (sweet)
7. A raven has a shiny coat. A blackbird has a ____ coat. (shiny)
8. Sea birds fly ____ distances than other birds. (long)
9. Parrots have the ____ feathers of all the birds. (bright)
10. Birds sing pretty songs. One bird sings the ____ songs of all. (pretty)
11. An ostrich lays the ____ egg of all birds. (large)
12. A crow sits on a high branch. A hawk sits on a ____ one. (high)
13. Ostriches are tall. They are ____ than condors. (tall)
14. Owls fly well even on the ____ nights. (dark)

Using Adjectives pages 202-203

Some short words point out nouns in a special way. *A* and *an* refer to any person, place, or thing. Use *a* with singular nouns that begin with a consonant. Use *an* with singular nouns that begin with a vowel.

A tree grows near the lake. An elephant drinks water.

Use *the* with a singular noun to point out a special person, place, or thing. Use *the* with plural nouns, too.

The kite soared up. Children watched the kites.

Number words such as *one, two,* and *three* tell exactly how many people, places, or things you mean.

One kite crashed. Two kites tossed in the wind.

Write each sentence. Complete each sentence by using *a* or *an* with singular nouns. For plural nouns use *the*.

1. William ate ____ apple for dessert after dinner.
2. Margaret squeezed ____ orange for its juice.
3. Robert cooked ____ egg for his breakfast.
4. My brother and I washed ____ pots.
5. That old truck needs ____ engine.
6. The driver checked all ____ tires on the truck.
7. The truck carried ____ elephant to the zoo.
8. The driver watched ____ airplane high in the sky.
9. People caught the elephant in ____ jungle.
10. ____ young boy walked along the side of the road.
11. The small girl ate ____ apricot.
12. He kicked at ____ rocks near the road.
13. The driver talked to the boy for ____ hour.
14. They both watched ____ eagle circle in the sky.
15. They heard ____ cry from the eagle above them.
16. ____ boy waved his arms.

Making New Adjectives pages 204-205

You can add **-y** or **-ful** to many words to make new adjectives.

Ending	Meaning	Example
-y	having or full of	dirty
-ful	full of	helpful

If a word ends with consonant, vowel, consonant, double the last consonant and add **-y** to form the adjective.

If a word ends in **e**, drop the **e** and add **-y** to form the adjective.

If a word ends with a consonant and **y**, change the **y** to **i** and add **-ful** to form the adjective.

fun + n + y - - - - - - - - - -funny
paste + y - - - - - - - - - - - pasty
fancy + ful - - - - - - - - - - fanciful

Write each sentence. Complete the sentence by adding *-ful* to the word at the end of the sentence.

1. The ____ child cleaned the table. (help)
2. That ____ boy never does sloppy work. (care)
3. A ____ student left her umbrella in school. (forget)
4. Those ____ flowers brighten up the whole room. (color)
5. The band played a very ____ song. (sorrow)
6. Mary wrote a ____ poem about the forest. (beauty)
7. They had a ____ experience with a wild bear. (fright)
8. That ____ puppy chewed up my shoe. (play)

Write each sentence. Complete the sentence by adding *-y* to the word at the end.

9. We had a ____ meal last night. (taste)
10. Carla and I play ball on a ____ day. (sun)
11. The ____ boy drank all the water. (thirst)
12. It was a ____ night. (star)
13. The ____ child woke up his parents. (noise)

Workbook

Using Synonyms and Antonyms in Sentences

pages 206-207

A **synonym** is a word that has nearly the same meaning as another word. You choose one synonym over another to make your meaning clearer.

The happy children played.

The cheerful children played.

An **antonym** is a word that means the opposite of another word.

Phyllis carried a light package.

Phyllis carried a heavy package.

You can make antonyms of some words by adding **un-** to the beginning of the words.

A friendly dog sat in the yard.

An unfriendly dog sat in the yard.

Read each sentence. Write the sentence using the synonym for each underlined word.

1. The good student did her work well. (excellent, quiet)
2. The nervous waiter dropped the dishes. (excited, foolish)
3. A crooked pipe carried water around the corner. (rusty, bent)
4. The eager man could hardly wait. (anxious, sad)
5. A weary runner rested in the shade. (tired, dusty)
6. The unhappy child cried. (lonely, sad)

Read each sentence. Write the sentence using the antonym for each underlined word.

7. We saw a giant tree in the forest. (tiny, old)
8. He wiped the car clean with a dry rag. (small, wet)
9. The pilot had a safe trip over the ocean. (unsafe, long)
10. The waiter served a thick soup to us. (hot, thin)
11. A hiker rested on the hard ground. (soft, cold)
12. The young woman carried a large purse. (strong, old)

Dictionary: Words with Two Meanings

pages 212-213

Some words in a dictionary have two meanings. The first meaning has **1.** in front of it. The second meaning has **2.** in front of it. There may also be an example sentence to help you learn a meaning.

play / please

play 1. Something that is done for fun or pleasure; sport. The children spent several hours at *play.* **2.** A move or turn in a game. The catcher made a great play.

please 1. To give pleasure to. The cool swim on such a hot day *pleased* him. **2.** choose. Buy whatever you *please.*

Use the sample dictionary page to write an answer to each question.

1 What is the example sentence for meaning 1. of *play*?

2. Write an example sentence for meaning 2. of *please*.

3. Use the sample to write the meaning of each underlined word.
   a) Joan's fine play kept the other team away from the goal.
   b) That sweater and shirt please your father.

Independent Writing: Writing a Report

pages 214-219

A report tells facts and ideas about a topic. The main idea sentence tells the report's main idea. Detail sentences give facts. Surveys or interviews provide information for a report.

Prewriting You will write a report on the favorite places of fourth-grade students. Survey your class. Ask each person if they most enjoy a zoo, a museum, or other place. Note each answer.

Writing Write a report on the favorite places of fourth-grade students. Write a title and a main idea sentence. Then use your notes in detail sentences.

Editing Use the editing symbols and the check questions on page 219 to edit your report.

Linking Verbs pages 230-231

An **action verb** is a word that names an action.

Ronda packs her books. The boy hammers the nail.

A **linking verb** is a verb that connects the subject part of a sentence with a noun or adjective in the predicate part. It tells what the subject is or is like. The verb *be* is a linking verb. These are some of the forms of *be*: *am, is, are.*

That tomato is fat. My new shoes are black.

Write each sentence and draw a line under the verb. If the verb names an action, write **action verb.** If the verb is a linking verb, write **linking verb.**

1. The class works on the problems.
2. These math problems are difficult.
3. One student erases her answer.
4. Many answers are wrong.
5. Some students raise their hands.
6. The young teacher is helpful.
7. She explains the problem to the students.
8. She writes the correct answer on the board.
9. The other problems are easy now.
10. Some students give their papers to the teacher.
11. Now the teacher is busy.
12. She checks each paper.
13. The teacher is happy with the class.
14. She gives the students a big smile.
15. One boy drops his books on the floor.
16. He is a careless person sometimes.
17. His friend picks up the books.
18. Now the boy is happy.

Nouns and Adjectives After Linking Verbs pages 232-233

A **linking verb** is a verb that connects the subject part of a sentence with a noun or adjective in the predicate part. A **noun** is a word that names a person, a place, or a thing. An **adjective** is a word that describes a noun or pronoun.

Mary is a baker. (noun)
Her breads are delicious. (adjective)

Write each sentence. Draw a line under the word that follows the linking verb. If the verb is a noun, write **noun.** If the word is an adjective, write **adjective.**

1. The man was a hero.
2. His clothes were dirty.
3. The sky is dark.
4. Sue is a scientist.
5. Her job is exciting.
6. We are helpful.
7. The work is hard.
8. Mr. Kim is my teacher.

Using Linking Verbs in the Present Tense pages 234-235

The **linking verbs** *am, is,* and *are* are in the present tense.

I am a student.
She is a student.
He is a student.
It is a dark night.
The moon is small.

You are a student.
We are students.
They are students.
The students are tired.

Write each sentence using the correct form of the linking verb *be*.

1. I ____ a bird watcher. (am, is)
2. My cousin ____ one, too. (is, are)
3. You ____ an artist. (are, is)
4. I ____ happy with my hobby. (am, is)
5. You ____ a builder. (are, am)
6. I ____ proud of you. (is, am)

Workbook

Contractions pages 236-237

A **contraction** is a word made up of two words. The words are joined together to make one word by leaving out one or more letters.

Use an **apostrophe (')** in a contraction to show that one or more letters are missing.

Contraction	**Short for**	**Contraction**	**Short for**
I'm	I am	it's	it is
you're	you are	we're	we are
he's	he is	they're	they are
she's	she is		

Some contractions sound like other words.

you're	You're lonely
your	Your work is good.
it's	It's a long trip.
its	Its tail wagged.
they're	They're on a trip.
their	Their bags are packed.
there	There is the plane.

Write each sentence. Use the contraction that can take the place of the underlined words.

1. We are the best dancers in the entire class.
2. We are not afraid of hard work.
3. I am practicing for a part in a play.
4. You are my partner in two of the dances.
5. They are trying out for other parts in the show.
6. He is one of the writers of the play.
7. She is wearing the costume for the show.
8. It is not time yet for a rest.
9. They are graceful on the stage.
10. We are late for the practice.
11. You are tired after all that exercise.
12. I am thirsty.

Workbook

Linking Verbs in the Past Tense pages 240-241

Action verbs in the **past tense** name an action that already happened.

I wrote a letter. She called me last night.

A **linking verb** connects the subject part of the sentence with a noun or adjective in the predicate part. The verbs *was* and *were* tell what a subject was or was like in the past.

The game was fun. We were dancers.

Write each sentence. Draw a line under the verb. If the verb names an action, write **action verb**. If the verb is a linking verb, write **linking verb.**

1. They were baseball players.
2. One boy carried a heavy bag full of equipment.
3. Tom was the star of the game.
4. He hit more runs that anyone else in the game.
5. Willona was the pitcher.
6. Her pitch flew over the plate.
7. On that day she was excellent.
8. The fans in the stands cheered wildly.
9. They were excited about the game.
10. My friend missed the ball three times in the game.
11. He was upset about that.
12. The coach called him from the bench.
13. The coach was worried about him.
14. She talked to my friend about the game.
15. My friend hit the ball over the fence.
16. The coach was pleased with him.
17. The players on the team were glad.
18. Two other players touched home plate.
19. Our team won this very important game.
20. The prize was a large silver cup.

Using Linking Verbs in the Past Tense pages 242-243

The **linking verb** in a sentence must agree with the subject part. Linking verbs in the present tense are *am, is,* and *are.* Linking verbs in the past tense are *was* and *were.*

Past Tense

I was happy.	You were happy.
She was happy.	We were happy.
He was happy.	They were happy.
It was happy.	The men were happy.
The baby was happy.	

Write each sentence. Use the correct form of the linking verb.

1. They ____ the children with the masks on. (was, were)
2. We ____ happy about our score. (were, was)
3. He ____ an excellent catcher. (were, was)
4. She ____ the reporter for the school paper. (was, were)
5. You ____ the best player this season. (were, was)
6. I ____ grateful for the reward. (was, were)
7. The game ____ the most important one of the season. (was, were)
8. We ____ the winners of many games this season. (were, was)
9. It ____ important to the team. (was, were)
10. He ____ the judge for the games. (was, were)
11. They ____ tired after the long game. (was, were)
12. The fans ____ excited about the results of the game. (were, was)
13. I ____ sad that the season ended. (was, were)
14. He ____ nervous at the beginning of the game. (was, were)
15. It ____ cold on the playing field this morning. (was, were)
16. After the game, the field ____ empty. (was, were)

Adverbs pages 244-247

You use **verbs** to name an action. You use **adverbs** to describe these actions. Some adverbs tell *how* an action is done.

The snow *fell fast*. The cat *calmly sat* in the window.
verb adverb adverb verb

Other adverbs tell *when* an action is done.

Later the class *began*. Her day *started early*.
adverb verb verb adverb

Write each sentence. Underline the adverb in each sentence once. Underline the verb it describes twice. Then write whether the adverb tells *how* or *when* the action is done.

1. The runners ran quickly.
2. The coach yelled loudly.
3. One athlete suddenly ran faster.
4. The runners' parents cheered wildly.
5. Soon the coach blew on her whistle.
6. Other students exercised slowly.
7. Another coach counted silently.
8. A player jumped high.
9. Next she ran a race.
10. Another girl rested lazily.
11. Today the wind blew.
12. Now rain fell.
13. Workers carefully covered the sand pit.
14. People ran immediately.
15. Some people unselfishly shared their umbrellas.
16. Other people cleverly held newspapers.
17. Later the players left.
18. The driver drove carefully.

Reference Materials pages 250-251

One part of a library has reference books. You have learned about the dictionary. An *encyclopedia* is a set of books with information about many things. An *atlas* is a book of maps. An *almanac* is a book with facts, numbers, and records.

Write each topic. Write the name of the best reference material you would use to find out about each. Write **encyclopedia, atlas, almanac,** or **dictionary.**

1. A map of South America
2. The results of the 1968 Summer Olympics
3. How to pronounce the word *decisive*
4. The history of baseball
5. The mayor of Dallas
6. Facts about Martin Luther King.
7. Whether the word *talk* can be used as a noun
8. Award winning songs

Independent Writing: Writing a Report page 261

Some reports on a main subject have two paragraphs. Each paragraph tells about a different part of the subject. Each paragraph has a main idea sentence and detail sentences.

Prewriting Suppose you are writing a report about the ways people travel and why they like to travel that way. Ask people how they like to travel. Do they like to travel by plane, by train, by bus, by boat, or by car? Make notes on the ways people like to travel. Also make notes on why they like to travel that way.

Writing Use your notes to write a report about three ways people travel. Describe the ways in one paragraph. Then describe why they like each way in the other paragraph.

Editing Use the check questions on page 261 and editing symbols to edit your report.

Reviewing Sentences pages 270-271

A **sentence** is a group of words that state a complete idea. The **subject part** names whom or what the sentence is about. The **predicate part** tells what action the subject does.

A **declarative** sentence is a sentence that tells something.

An **interrogative** sentence is a sentence that asks something.

An **exclamatory sentence** is a sentence that shows strong feeling.

An **imperative sentence** is a sentence that tells or asks someone to do something.

Begin all sentences with a **capital letter.** Use a **period (.)** at the end of a declarative sentence or an imperative sentence. Use a **question mark (?)** at the end of an interrogative sentence. Use an **exclamation mark (!)** at the end of an exclamatory sentence.

Write each sentence. Decide what kind of sentence each one is. Write **declarative, interrogative, exclamatory,** or **imperative** next to each.

1. Look at that clown's large shoes and green nose.
2. Where are the rest of the workers?
3. I can see a group of clowns on a tall ladder.
4. How loudly the crowd cheers!
5. What does that small clown in the red suit carry?
6. He has a large bottle of water in his hands.

Write each sentence so that it begins and ends correctly.

7. are the elephants going to be in this show
8. they will soon enter the tent with their trainers
9. please hand me that small container of milk from the bag
10. how excited those girls in the front row are
11. I think they have waited a long time for this show.
12. do you see any of those famous dancing bears

Workbook

Reviewing Subject Parts pages 272-273

The **subject part** of a sentence names whom or what the sentence is about.
The **simple subject** is the main word in the subject part.

The careful workers hammered nails into the wood.

Write each sentence. Draw a line under the subject part. Draw a second line under the simple subject.

1. A large truck brings cement to the workers.
2. Several workers walk up to the cement truck.
3. The driver talks to some workers about the next delivery.
4. Three other workers pour cement into pails.
5. Another truck arrives with a load of wood and nails.
6. More workers unload the wood from the truck.
7. Seth checks off each item on a piece of paper.
8. A big brown dog barks loudly at the noisy trucks.

Reviewing Predicate Parts pages 274-275

The **predicate part** of a sentence tells what action the subject does. The **simple predicate** is the main word in the predicate part.

The driver stopped her car.

Write each sentence. Draw one line under the predicate part. Draw a second line under the simple predicate.

1. The auto repair person fixed the broken car.
2. People from the town took cars to the shop.
3. A truck towed some damaged cars to the shop.
4. One car needed two new tires.
5. The repair person checked each car for problems.
6. Some cars leaked oil from their motors.

Compound Subjects pages 276-277

A **compound subject** has two or more simple subjects that have the same predicate. The simple subjects are joined by *and.* The verb in the sentence must agree with the compound subject.

The boys and the girls discuss the party.

Write each sentence. Draw one line under the subject part. Draw a second line under the simple subject.

1. Jose and Angelo fold napkins for the tables.
2. The teachers and the parents unfold chairs for the guests.
3. Ms. Weaver and Mr. Santos hang paper from the lights.
4. Charles and a friend carry the tables to the gym.
5. Mike and I place the chairs around the many tables.
6. The principal and a teacher carry bags of food into the gym.
7. A parent and her daughter unpack the bags.
8. A worker and his helper sweep the floor of the gym.

Compound Sentences pages 282-283

A **compound sentence** contains two sentences joined by *and.*
Use a **comma (,)** before *and* when it joins two sentences.

We put on our skis, and our bindings fit perfectly.
The snow was deep, and the mountain was beautiful.

Write each sentence. Write **compound** if the sentence is compound. Write **not compound** if the sentence is not compound.

1. The wind blew strongly, and the snow flew.
2. The bright sun shined on the mountain.
3. My boots fit well, and my poles were the right size.
4. The snow was fresh, and the mountain was steep.
5. My ski poles fell in the snow.

Building Compound Sentences pages 284-285

If two sentences go together, you can join them to make a compound sentence. Use a **comma (,)** before *and* when it joins two sentences.

Jack has many tools. Greg uses them for projects.

Jack has many tools, and Greg uses them for projects.

Make each pair of sentences into one compound sentence. Write the compound sentence.

1. Greg goes to a craft class. His teacher teaches him about woodworking.
2. Greg picks up a saw. He cuts a piece of wood.
3. The teacher looks at the wood. She says it was cut well.
4. Another student takes a hammer. He uses it on his project.

Parts of Speech pages 286-287

Each kind of word does a special job in a sentence. A **noun** is a word that names a person, a place, or a thing. A **pronoun** is a word that takes the place of one or more nouns. An **action verb** is a word that names an action. A **linking verb** is a verb that connects the subject part with a noun or adjective in the predicate part. It tells what the subject is or is like. An **adjective** is a word that describes a noun or pronoun. An **adverb** is a word that decribes an action.

Read each sentence. Write whether each underlined word is a **noun**, a **pronoun**, a **verb**, an **adjective**, or an **adverb**.

1. Mary visited a large farm.
2. She saw many animals.
3. A beautiful horse ran quickly.
4. It had a white star on its head.
5. A colt ran after the horse.
6. A dog barked loudly.

Workbook

Using Commas pages 288-289

Use a **comma (,)** to separate each noun in a series of three or more nouns.

Dave, Tom, and Martin put on a show.

Use a **comma (,)** to separate each verb in a series of three or more verbs.

Dave's mother designed, cut, and sewed the costumes.

Use a **comma (,)** to set off words such as *yes, no,* and *well* when they begin a sentence.

Yes, everyone liked the show.

Use a **comma (,)** to set off the name of a person who is spoken to directly in a sentence.

Tom, did you put on any other shows this year?

Use a **comma (,)** to separate the day of the month from the year.

We had another show on May 7, 1981.

Use a **comma (,)** after conversation words that come before a speaker's exact words.

Elliot said, "I hope I can see the next show."

Use a **comma (,)** before the last quotation mark when the conversation word comes after a speaker's exact words.

"Bring your friend with you," replied Martin.

Write each sentence. Use commas where they are necessary.

1. "I took a trip to Canada on April 23 1981" said Mark.
2. "Well did you enjoy the trip?" asked Harold.
3. Yes it was a very enjoyable trip for me and my family.
4. Mark what things did you like about Canada?
5. I liked the small towns the nice people and the mountains.
6. We talked laughed and sang on the bus trip.
7. Mark said "Once my family and I went to Niagara Falls."
8. Yes that is right on the border of Canada.
9. We rested dressed and ate at our hotel.
10. We wanted to visit a museum a battlefield and a fort.

Fact and Opinion pages 292-293

Facts state information that is true. Facts can be checked.
Opinions tell what someone thinks or feels.
Fact: This book contains poems and stories.
Opinion: This is the best book in the world.

Write each sentence. Write **fact** if it is a statement of fact. Write **opinion** if it gives an opinion.

1. The library stores books and valuable papers.
2. The library is the nicest building in town.
3. Each library shelf receives a number which readers use.
4. The librarian is always the most helpful person.
5. Books of fiction stand on a separate set of shelves.
6. Reference books should be loaned to students.
7. Some libraries contain collections of pictures and records.
8. Records provide more facts to people than pictures do.
9. Libraries keep fiction and nonfiction separate.
10. An atlas shows the many countries of the world.
11. Encyclopedias are the most interesting reference books.
12. Every library needs a better way to keep track of its books.
13. A library card allows a person to borrow most materials.
14. Scholars spend many hours at work in the world's libraries.
15. Everybody should be familiar with their local library.
16. Some libraries record conversations with people of the town.
17. These are fascinating recordings about the town's history.
18. Pictures and recordings may help one understand the past.
19. Books on the sciences provide information to many people.
20. Alexandria's ancient library was the world's greatest.
21. The loss of that library is very regrettable.
22. New York's Public Library has several branches in the city.
23. People learn more at that library than anywhere else.

A Persuasive Paragraph of Reasons pages 294-295

A *persuasive paragraph* has a main idea sentence and detail sentences. The main idea sentence tells your opinion about something. The detail sentences give good reasons for your opinion. Sometimes the final sentence emphasizes your opinion.

The sentences below are from a persuasive paragraph. Change the order of the sentences so that the paragraph begins with the main idea sentence. Then write the detail sentences in an order that makes sense. Write the whole paragraph on your paper. Add a final sentence that emphasizes the main idea of the paragraph.

1. Quite a few students have few or no records of their own.
2. We could have fund raising activities to help buy equipment.
3. Students could help keep the department in good order.
4. A record department for our school library is a good idea.
5. Other students are willing to give some of their records.

Independent Writing: A Persuasive Paragraph pages 296-299

Prewriting Think of a subject you would like to learn more about. It should be one not already taught at your school. Write a persuasive paragraph to the school board. Think of good reasons why your school should offer a course on the subject. Make notes on the reasons.

Writing Write a persuasive paragraph telling why your school should offer a new course of your choice. Name the subject of the course in your main idea sentence. Give good reasons for the new course in detail sentences. Add a final sentence for emphasis.

Editing Use the check questions on page 299 and the editing symbols to edit your persuasive paragraph.

Index